EXPERT DINGHY AND KEELBOAT RACING

EXPERT DINGHY AND KEELBOAT RACING

by Paul Elvström

QUADRANGLE BOOKS
ONE-DESIGN & OFFSHORE YACHTSMAN MAGAZINE
Chicago

First published by Creagh-Osborne and Partners, 6/7 Station Street, Lymington, Hampshire, England, in a British edition in June 1967.

Library of Congress Catalog Card Number: 67-25632

CONTENTS

EDITOR'S NOTE

In assembling this book for Paul Elvström I have used transcripts of tape-recordings as well as many photographs and notes supplied by him. I have also obtained at his request a fair amount of material from many sources, notably photographs. The photographers are credited where applicable and I would like to take this opportunity of thanking these people and others, such as class associations, who have given valuable assistance.

Paul Elvström's earlier book, 'Joller og Kapsejladstaktik', known in Britain as 'Expert Dinghy Racing', has been out of print for some time, and was left deliberately so for two reasons. Firstly, parts of it were becoming out of date, and secondly Paul Elvström felt that his thoughts were now sufficiently established, not only with regard to dinghy racing, but also in the field of racing keelboats, to assemble a much more permanent and widely useful volume.

Here then we have compiled a thought-provoking but, we hope, easily assimilated text book with a very great deal of new material as well as a smaller amount of revised and redesigned matter from the earlier work. We think that this book can be read and re-read and the pictures studied again and again without exhausting its possibilities for the teaching of successful yacht racing.

We hope that you will agree.

RICHARD CREAGH-OSBORNE

FOREWORD

I hope that the situations described in this book in the chapters on techniques, racing rules and tactics, both in words and in pictures, will impress themselves on your mind so that when you meet such situations in actual races you will not have to think but will take the right action automatically. This will happen because you will have been able here to think the situation out in detail at your leisure and will be clear about all the problems.

Learning how to make a boat go fast is easier ashore than it is afloat because there is no time to stop and think when you are racing. I intend, therefore, that this book will help you to become automatic in many details.

Tuning the boat and sailing techniques are the foundations of good racing because they lead to boat speed, and without boat speed it is difficult to get a good result. In this book I also want to help you to make a normal non-racing day interesting so that you can go out and try the various things that I am going to discuss and describe for you here.

The tuning and sailing technique in keelboats is based on my experiences in the Star, the Dragon and the Five-point-Five. These experiences can of course be used with benefit in other keelboat classes. In this book I have left out almost entirely ocean racing and this is not because I am lacking in ideas on this subject but it is just that I have not yet proved that my ideas are right.

Paul Elvström

We are starting this book with two very old pictures of racing boats. Compare these with the highly developed boats shown in some of the other illustrations in the book. Above is one of the world's first Stars with the original gaff rig. The class was started in 1911 and has now the strongest organisation of any. The boat has developed enormously during 56 years but can still be improved. Fibreglass hulls are just coming in, whilst a trapeze would make it far easier to sail in strong winds.

Photo: Beken

In the 1920's the International Fourteen was almost the only racing dinghy class in the world. The only people who could be called 'expert' at racing in dinghies sailed these boats. Mrs. Richardson sailed this boat into sixth place in the class championships. It seems that ladies even wore skirts when racing, whilst hanging-out, toestraps, kicking straps, wooden centreboards and tiller extensions had not been heard of. The boats which are raced in all parts of the world have improved out of all recognition as a result of developments in this and later classes. But the technique of the expert dinghy racing helmsman has improved even more.

THE RACING

CLASSES

FINN

Length overall 4,500 mm. (14 ft. 9 3/16 in.)
Beam . . 1,510 mm. (4 ft. 11 1/2 in.)
Hull weight . . 105 kilos (231 lb.)
Sail area . . 10 sq. m. (107·6 sq. ft.)

In 1949 Finland held a designing competition for a boat for the Scandinavian Single-handed Championship, and this boat was also to be the new Olympic single-handed dinghy. The dinghies that finished first, second and third in these trials were not eventually chosen; instead of that they preferred the design submitted by the Uppsala hairdresser Rickard Sarby.

Sarby, who is a very good dinghy sailor with an intense interest in sailing, gave the best of his great experience to the design, and thus enabled thousands of people to get a great deal of fun and interest out of his Finn dinghy.

As it is very hard to learn how to sail a Finn properly, and difficult to tune the mast and sail, I would advise only those who are really interested in the hardest competition to take up Finn racing. If you take the trouble to learn how to handle this boat you will find

A FINN being sailed by Bruce McCurrach of South Africa.

Beauvais-Nautisme

its sailing qualities are so good that you will get more fun out of this boat than racing almost any other class.

In recent years the sailing technique for the Finn dinghy has advanced to such an extent that now even light crews can compete on level terms with the heavy ones, because it is now well understood how to allow for different flexibility in the mast to match the weight of different helmsmen.

The Finn has become the standard top class single-handed dinghy and there are fully recognised Finn associations in 35 countries with a total of over 7,000 boats. The boat has been used now for four successive Olympic Games and will be used in Mexico in 1968 and almost certainly in Germany in 1972. In fact it seems very likely that the Finn will be gradually developed and become the Olympic single-hander for many Olympiads yet.

There is a World Championship held in a different country each year and, in theory,

11

anyone can enter. In practice, each country is allowed a quota of about 15 boats who have to qualify because the event is so popular that there could easily be 500 entries some years.

Secretary: Dr. F. Auer, La Nuschpigna, St. Moritz, Switzerland.

FINN CHAMPIONS

1956 Burnham-on-Crouch, England: Andre Nelis, Belgium

1957 Karlstad, Sweden: Jurgen Vogler, East Germany

1958 Zeebrugge, Belgium: Paul Elvström, Denmark

1959 Copenhagen, Denmark: Paul Elvström, Denmark

1960 Torquay, England: Vernon Stratton, England

1961 Travemunde, West Germany: Andre Nelis, Belgium

1962 Tonsberg, Norway: Arne Aakerson, Sweden

1963 Medemblik, Holland: Willy Kuhweide, West Germany

1964 Torquay, England: Hubert Raudaschl, Austria

1965 Gydnia, Poland: J. Mier, East Germany

1966 La Baule, France: Willy Kuhweide, West Germany

Olympic Champions in Finns:

1952 Helsinki, Finland: Paul Elvström, Denmark

1956 Melbourne, Australia: Paul Elvström, Denmark

1960 Naples, Italy: Paul Elvström, Denmark

1964 Tokyo, Japan: Willy Kuhweide, West Germany

FLYING DUTCHMAN

Length overall 6,050 mm. (19 ft. 10 $\frac{3}{16}$ in.)	*Mainsail area* . 10 sq. m. (107·6 sq. ft.)
Beam . . 1,800 mm. (5 ft. 10$\frac{7}{8}$ in.)	*Genoa area* . . 8·4 sq. m. (90·5 sq. ft.)
Hull weight . . 125 kilos (276 lb.)	*Spinnaker area* . 18·0 sq. m. (194 sq. ft.)

Holland wanted to make a fast modern two-man racing boat with the crew on a trapeze. The result was the world's fastest single-hull dinghy. It gained international status and was selected for the Olympic Games in 1960, when Peder Lunde of Norway gained the Gold Medal and Denmark's Hans Fogh and Ole Petersen won the Silver Medal in Naples Bay, and it has been used for each Games since then.

The sailor who really wants speed should choose a Flying Dutchman, but must know that it is a costly sport, even though it may be cheaper than a keelboat. You need to have two people to own this excellent dinghy and

work together as a team in order to gain the maximum enjoyment from racing it. Finding the right and steady crew should not be too difficult. I myself have been the crew on a Flying Dutchman for a season and I can assure you that being the trapeze hand is much more amusing than being the helmsman.

Until 1960 there was a world championship every year, but from 1960 this was changed to a European and world championship on alternate years, with only one competitor from each nation.

Secretary: I.F.D.C.A., 69 G.W. de Oude-laan, Naarden, Holland.

European Champions:

1960 Marstrand, Sweden: Hans Fogh, Ole
Petersen, Denmark

1961 Bendor, France: The brothers Kraan,
Holland

1962 Muiden, Holland: Johnson Wooderson,
Chris Davies, England

1964 Whitstable, England: K. Musto,
A. Morgan, England

1966 Hortens, Norway: J. Oakeley, D. Hunt,
England

World Champions:

1956 Starneberg, Germany: Rolf Mulka
Ingo von Bredow, Germany

1957 Rimini, Italy: Rolf Mulka, Ingo von
Bredow, Germany

1958 Attersee, Austria: Rolly Tasker,
Ian Palmer, Australia

1959 Whitstable, England: Mario Capio,
Tullio Pizzorno, Italy

1960 (Olympic Games) Naples, Italy: Peder
Lunde, Norway

1962 St. Petersburg, Florida: H. Fogh,
P. Elvström, Denmark

1963 Starneberg, West Germany: Jean-Pierre
Renevier, Serge Graz, Switzerland

1964 (Olympic Games) Tokyo, Japan:
H. Pedersen, E. Wells, New Zealand

1965 Rimini, Italy: R. Pitcher,
I. McCormack, England

STAR

Length overall		6,909 mm. (22 ft. 8 in.)
Beam	.	1,727 mm. (5 ft. 8 in.)
Draught .	.	1,016 mm. (3 ft. 4 in.)
Sail area .	.	26·5 sq. m. (285 sq. ft.)

The International Star was introduced in America in 1911 as a light keelboat which could be built by amateurs or small boat yards very cheaply. Originally it was gaff rigged but it was very soon modified and has been brought up to date several times. It is now highly refined and uses flexible spars.

For a keelboat the Star has tremendous speed in light and medium winds and also down wind in strong winds but its big disadvantage is that it was not designed for very strong winds. If you have a little bad luck in big seas you can easily sink when running in these conditions. There is another disadvantage in hard weather, which is that you are never sure that you are going to be able to get back home with the boat intact. It is because of this that the boat is not popular in centres such as England and Scandinavia.

If anyone today wanted to design a two-man keelboat of similar size you could not find a better result for use in light winds. Because they have such a large sail area Stars have problems beating to windward in strong winds. In my opinion this difficulty could be avoided simply by having one man on a trapeze. When the time comes that trapezes are allowed on Stars – as surely they will be – the young people who will then be sailing them will laugh when they look back at the time when crews were hanging over the sides of the boats as they do now.

But the difficulty that one has in getting to windward in strong winds can largely be forgotten because of the excitement in sailing down wind after one has learnt how to stop the rig from collapsing. The Star is the boat which teaches one more about tuning sails than any other, chiefly on account of the large sail area and the very light gear.

We have seen that most new ideas concerning sails and rigs and the tuning and adjusting of them have come from the Star Class and it has also been the Olympic two-man keelboat class since 1932. In the 1966 world championships 19 different countries were represented by 83 boats which all had to compete for the chance of a place by becoming top of their own respective fleets.

I would say that the Star Class organisation is certainly the strongest that you can find in yacht racing today. It is also the most active and the one which works best.

The first world championship winner who was not an American was W. von Huetschler in 1938 and he was also competing in the 1966 world championship. Durward Knowles of the Bahamas made his first attempt at an Olympic Gold Medal in 1948 when, but for two broken masts, he could easily have won. It was not until 16 years later that he finally won at Tokyo, having competed in each Games since the war.

OLYMPIC GAMES

1932 Los Angeles, U.S.A.: G. Gray, A. Libano, U.S.A.

1936 Kiel, West Germany: Dr. Bischoff and Weise, Germany

1948 Torquay, England: H. and P. Smart, U.S.A.

1952 Helsinki, Finland: A. Straulino and N. Rode, Italy

1956 Melbourne, Australia: H. P. Williams, U.S.A.

1960 Naples, Italy: Timir Pinegin, U.S.S.R.

1964 Tokyo, Japan: Durward Knowles, Bahamas

A STAR start in Tokyo.

Hashimoto

WORLD CHAMPIONS

1922 Inslee, U.S.A.	1938 W. von Huetschler,	1950 Lippincott, U.S.A.
1923 Inslee, U.S.A.	Argentine	1951 Etchells, U.S.A.
1924 Robinson, U.S.A.	(Hamburg fleet)	1952 A. Straulino, Italy
1925 Iselin, U.S.A.	1939 W. von Huetschler,	1953 A. Straulino, Italy
1926 Comstock, U.S.A.	Argentine	1954 de Cardenas, Cuba
1927 Hubbard, U.S.A.	(Hamburg fleet)	1955 C. de Cardenas, Cuba
1928 Edrington, U.S.A.	1940 Cowie, U.S.A.	1956 A. Straulino, Italy
1929 Johnson, U.S.A.	1941 Fleitz, U.S.A.	1957 L. North, U.S.A.
1930 Knapp, U.S.A.	1942 Nye, U.S.A.	1958 Ficker, U.S.A.
1931 McHugh, U.S.A.	1943 Deacon, U.S.A.	1959 L. North, U.S.A.
1932 Fink, U.S.A.	1944 Driscoll, U.S.A.	1960 L. North, U.S.A.
1933 Waterhouse, U.S.A.	1945 Burnham, U.S.A.	1961 Buchan, U.S.A.
1934 Beardslee, U.S.A.	1946 Fleitz, U.S.A.	1962 R. Stearns, U.S.A.
1935 Beardslee, U.S.A.	1947 D. Knowles, Bahamas	1963 J. Duplin, U.S.A.
1936 Iselin, U.S.A.	1948 Pirie, U.S.A.	1964 Edler, U.S.A.
1937 Wegeforth, U.S.A.	1949 Nye. U.S.A.	1965 D. Bever, U.S.A.
	1966 P. Elvström, Denmark	

DRAGON

Length overall　　*8,891 mm. (29 ft. 2 in.)*
Beam　.　.　*1,931 mm. (6 ft. 4 in.)*
Draught .　.　*1,194 mm. (3 ft. 11 in.)*
Sail area .　.　*21·87 sq. m. (235 sq. ft.)*
Plus spinnaker

The Dragon was designed in 1928 by the Norwegian Johan Anker and was intended to be a cheap Scandinavian family racing class. But after a few years it became a specialist racing class for top Scandinavians and in 1948 it was selected as an Olympic class. In 1945 the rig had been modified so that the fore triangle was higher, enabling a genoa to be carried and at the same time the boat was given a spinnaker.

15

When the Dragon became an Olympic class it was also adopted by the I.Y.R.U. and today the class organisation has redrawn the building rules and made the boats into true one-designs.

In the 1966 Gold Cup nearly 100 boats competed, coming from all over the world. Every alternate year there are world championships and each year there is also a Dragon Gold Cup regatta and a European and North American championship.

The Dragon is really a hard weather boat and is quite difficult to sail fast in light winds. The hull shape is very flat under the bow and it is thus easily stopped by waves, and therefore the exact trim for the genoa is really critical.

Today the Dragon can only be built in wood by the carvel method and so it is rather expensive to buy.

Secretary: I.Y.R.U., 171 Victoria Street, London, S.W.1.

DRAGON GOLD CUP
1937 Clyde: Rolf Billner, Sweden
1938 Travemunde: Herbert Dobler, Germany
1939 Gotenborg: Pella Gedda, Sweden
1947 Clyde: Eric Strain, Northern Ireland
1948 Arendal: Thor Thorvaldsen, Norway
1949 Marstrand: Ole Berntsen, Denmark
1950 Vejle: Thor Thorvaldsen, Norway
1951 Clyde: Thorkild Warrer, Denmark
1952 Hanko: Ovind Christensen, Norway
1953 Marstrand: Theodor Thomsen, Germany
1954 Copenhagen: Ole Berntsen, Denmark
1955 Muiden: Theodor Thomsen, Germany
1956 Clyde: Thorkild Warrer, Denmark
1957 Hanko: Ole Berntsen, Denmark
1958 Marstrand: Sergio Sorrentino, Italy
1959 Copenhagen: Walter Windeyer, Canada
1960 Muiden: Ole Berntsen, Denmark
1961 Clyde: Sir Gordon Smith, England
1962 Hanko: Ole Berntsen, Denmark
1963 Marstrand: Aage Birch, Denmark
1964 Travemunde: Aage Birch, Denmark
1965 Medemblik: Henning Jensen, Denmark
1966 Copenhagen: Aage Birch, Denmark

OLYMPIC GAMES
1948 Torquay, England: Thor Thorvaldsen, Norway
1952 Helsinki, Finland: Thor Thorvaldsen, Norway
1956 Melbourne, Australia: F. Bohlin, Sweden
1960 Naples, Italy: Crown Prince Constantine, Greece
1964 Tokyo, Japan: Ole Berntsen, Denmark

WORLD CHAMPIONSHIP
(Held every two years)
1965 Sandhamn, Sweden: Ole Berntsen, Denmark
1967 Toronto, Canada:

The DRAGON is at its best in fresh winds.

5·5 METRE

Length overall . 9,754 mm. (32 ft.)
Beam . . 1,900 mm. (6 ft. 3 in.)
Draught . . 1,350 mm. (4 ft. 5 in.)
Sail area . 28 sq. m. (300 sq. ft.)
Plus spinnaker
(Specifications are approximate)

When the six-metre boats became too expensive the I.Y.R.U. chose the 5.5-metre Class to replace them. The first time the class appeared in the Olympic Games was in 1952 at Helsinki. The idea of having this class in the Olympic Games is so that new ideas can be developed. The special thing about the 5.5 is that it has a very big spinnaker which makes the crewing very much more important than it is in a Dragon for example. From that point of view it is, in my opinion, much more of a real three-man keelboat than is the Dragon.

It seems to me that the tuning and the sail shape on these boats is much more important than the small differences which you find today in hull shapes. You can see in a true one-design class like the Dragon the big difference in speed between a well tuned and a poorly tuned boat. The same thing happens in the 5.5 Class but very often people think that these differences are caused by hull design and generally this is not so but of course you cannot be absolutely sure.

Secretary: I.Y.R.U., 171 Victoria Street, London, S.W.1.

OLYMPIC GAMES
1952 Helsinki, Finland: Dr. B. Chance, U.S.A.
1956 Melbourne, Australia: L. Thorn, Sweden
1960 Naples, Italy: George O'Day, U.S.A.
1964 Tokyo, Japan: W. Northam, Australia

WORLD CHAMPIONS
1961 Helsinki, Finland: Louis Noverraz, Switzerland
1962 Poole Bay, England: Dr. B. Chance, Snr., U.S.A.
1963 Oyster Bay, U.S.A.: Ray Hunt, U.S.A.
1965 Naples, Italy: Agostino Straulino, Italy
1966 Copenhagen, Denmark: Paul Elvstrom, Denmark

This is Web, *winner of the World Championship in 1966 when 46 boats were entered.*

OPTIMIST

Length overall	.	2,310 mm. (7 ft. 7 in.)
Beam	.	1,130 mm. (3 ft. 8½ in.)
Hull weight	.	29·5 kilos (65 lb.)
Sail area	.	3·5 sq. m. (37·7 sq. ft.)

For more than twenty years North Americans have played about in tiny sailing dinghies, less than nine feet long, all the year round except when the water was covered in ice. Over there they call these little boats 'Frost-bite Dinghies.' In 1954 the so-called Optimist dinghy, or rather, pram, was designed. It became a great success all over the world through the famous international sailing magazines and the following year it came to Denmark.

Danish sailing sport owes a great debt to the yachting architect Axel Damgaard, of Vordingborg, who now lives in the United States. He was the first man who foresaw the many good points about the Optimist dinghy, wrote to New York for the building rules, built a couple of them, tested them in all sorts of conditions, and then took great pains to see that they became well known, because he was absolutely sure of the boat's value. Just like setting fire to dry grass, this little coloured object spread along our shores. A long time ago the class passed 2,000 boats in Denmark, and it is now easily the largest class in Scandinavia with over 5,000 all together. In Norway they are called 'A-Dinghies', because the Oslo newspaper *Aftenposten* sponsored them.

Racing in the little Optimist pram dinghy is just as exciting as it is in any other class and the boys and girls work at their tuning and technique just as much as their fathers do.

I would recommend this little boat as being the best sort of training boat for children until they get so heavy that they become too slow and cannot keep up with their lighter friends.

I have mentioned here the name of the architect Axel Damgaard who looked into the future and saw the value of this little boat and introduced it into Scandinavia and Germany. Axel Damgaard was also the man behind the idea of the O.K. Dinghy which has had an even greater success than the Optimist.

Clark Mills designed this splendid little boat, which is so cheap and which can be built by amateurs extremely easily. The Optimist also makes an ideal yacht's tender and is easy to rig and stow away, since all the spars fit within the hull length. It is also very simple to carry the boat on a car roof.

The latest development in this class is a World Championship regatta, the first of which was held in 1966 in Florida, U.S.A.

Secretary: J. Flaherty, 472 E. Shore Drive, Clearwater, Florida, U.S.A.

Racing in Optimist prams is just as sensitive, and you have to be just as accurate and precise, as in any other class.

MOTH

Length overall   .   3,350 mm. (11 ft.)
Beam   .   .   1,350 mm. (4 ft. 5 in.)
Sail area .   .   6·7 sq. m. (72 sq. ft.)
Hull weight   .   .   36 kilos (80 lb.)
(Apart from sail area and length overall
the specifications are approximate)

The International Moth is a splendid single-handed boat which can be extremely easy and cheap to build. The boats are very light in weight, enabling young school boys and girls to get them in and out of the water without help. The boat makes the ideal next step up from the Optimist for budding racing helmsmen.

The Moth is a free development class. There are very few rules and hulls can be made almost any shape so long as they are not more than 11 ft. long. The leading dimensions of the sail are also fixed, though in Australia a taller and narrower sail plan is used in National races. However, the normal sail plan is very effective and the average schoolboy will have no difficulty in keeping the boat upright.

A large number of widely differing hull shapes have evolved for the Moth, though all the modern ones are very similar in overall performance. Some have advantages in certain conditions.

The hull of the American 'Florida' Moth is made from two sheets of ply only, and the bottom is a nearly constant vee all through. It is very wide and shallow and will not float level if left unattended, flopping over on to one bottom panel or the other, and taking up an angle of about twenty degrees to the horizontal. However, it is surprisingly easy to sail and goes well to windward in light airs.

The Australian 'Torpedo' Moth is a complete contrast. Scow shaped with a wide flat bow and a very flat bottom it has to be sailed well heeled in lighter winds, to reduce the wetted surface area. It comes into its own in strong winds and planes extremely fast. Owing to the very light hull weight of around 80 lb. it can keep up with the very much larger International Finn in some conditions. This boat is cold moulded from two layers of veneer.

Half way in between these is the latest development called the 'Europa' Moth. It looks rather like a small but very beamy Finn and is made from two sheets of ply cunningly slit and wrapped to form a round bilged hull shape. The fastest versions use a similar cantilever mast to the Finn and the boat is a splendid performer in all conditions, and is particularly suitable for rough water.

Recently the New Zealand 'Shelley' design and variations of this have been showing great promise in Europe but the Europa and similar boats have still been the choice of recent world champions.

In Australia and New Zealand a taller, non-standard rig is used which should produce higher speeds.

So you can see that in this class the keen young racing helmsman can learn a great deal about boats and boat design without spending much money. The boats can easily be built in school workshops and take little room to store. At least three can be carried on one small car and trailer. If you want to experiment with different hulls, then the same rig and gear can often be used on each.

The International Secretary for the class is Mrs. David Tufts, 83 Shore Road, Old Greenwich, Conn., U.S.A.

WORLD CHAMPIONSHIPS

1963 Larchmont, U.S.A.: Bill Schill, U.S.A.

1964 Bandol, France: J-P. Roggo, Switzerland

1965 U.S.A.: J-P. Roggo, Switzerland

1966 Lausanne, Switzerland: J-P. Roggo, Switzerland

Right:
An Australian scow MOTH beating to windward in Sydney Harbour with a special bendy boom.

———————————

Below:
Henning Schachtshabel, World Champion in 1964 in Roskilde, Denmark in O.K. Dinghies.

OK DINGHY

Length overall   4,000 mm. (13 ft. 1½ in.)
Beam   .   .   1,420 mm. (4 ft. 8 in.)
Weight of hull   .   72 kilos (158½ lb.)
Sail area (actual) 8·25 sq. m. (88·8 sq. ft.)

The O.K. Dinghy came into existence because of the desire of the Pirat helmsman Axel Damgaard to introduce a cheap single-handed dinghy which was able to plane. He asked the boatbuilder and yacht designer Knud Olsen to make the drawings. In the first year about sixty dinghies were built.

The moving spirit behind the class was Axel Damgaard, whose great work enabled it to be spread all over Denmark and overseas. He carried the dinghy on the roof of his car and showed it in Oslo, Hamburg and other centres. I myself distributed the drawings farther abroad to countries such as France, where series production immediately started. Also in Norway, Sweden, Germany and England, this attractive and lively dinghy started to spread quickly.

The rapid development of the class showed clearly the Danish sailors' desire for such a cheap and fast sailing dinghy, but at the same time it also showed that Denmark was a young and developing dinghy nation.

Most of the O.K. Dinghy sailors were at first Junior-boat helmsmen (a small Danish training keel boat) and thus were really keelboat sailors, and therefore quite unused to balancing a dinghy. The fixed keel had slowed down their reactions and it took time to remove this inbred characteristic. Time after time they capsized the dinghies. Certain racing clubs refused to start the O.K. Dinghy Class in their regattas, giving the strange reason that the design of the boat must be at fault. Some of us who knew about dinghy sailing were able to see after only one trial sail that the boat itself was excellent, and it was only the failings of technique of the new helmsmen which caused the trouble, and this was proved after only one season's experience.

From Hvidovre and Vordingborg they tried to get the Dansk Sejlunion to adopt the class, which would mean that the Union would administer the class. Here the Dansk Sejlunion showed their lack of experience in the small dinghy field by setting up a committee consisting of six people of whom only one was a dinghy sailor who knew anything about light racing dinghies, such as the O.K.; but luckily the dinghy was finally adopted.

The O.K. Dinghy is very light on the helm and easy to handle for a trained dinghy sailor, who is soon able to become familiar with its feel.

In the beginning you think that the dinghy is going to take charge of you, but after some hard work and thought you realise that you are able to control the boat. The O.K. Dinghy is a real racing boat which needs to have a quick reacting helmsman who will take advantage of the qualities of a light and lively planing dinghy.

There are now (1967) 6,000 boats and you can race an O.K. Dinghy in nearly all countries. There is a World Championship which is held in a different country each year. The boat can be built in either fibre glass or plywood, except the masts and the boom which have to be made in wood.

The O.K. Dinghy is the best example that the I.Y.R.U. could have as to how a class can grow on its own internationally without their assistance. This class has only grown to the extent it has because it is cheap and the youngsters like the boat.

O.K. Dinghies can also be built by the composite plywood/fibreglass tape system introduced by the Norwegian sailor, designer and plastics expert Ole With.

Full details of this method, and also leaflets and information on every aspect of building, fitting out and sailing O.K. Dinghies is obtainable from:-

Secretary: A. B. Crosby, Lion Works, West Street, Farnham, Surrey, England.

CADET

Length overall	3,200 mm. (10 ft. 6½ in.)
Beam . .	1,270 mm. (4 ft. 2 in.)
Hull weight . .	54 kilos (120 lb.)
Mainsail area .	. 4·0 sq. m. (43 sq. ft.)
Jin area . .	. 1·2 sq. m. (13 sq. ft.)
Spinnaker area	. 3·5 sq. m. (38 sq. ft.)

The editor of *Yachting World*, one of the world's best yachting magazines, Group Captain Haylock, was the instigator of the excellent junior racing class, the Cadet. His father was the owner of a 70-ton yacht and was a keen sailor, and thus his many children learned sailing and boat handling from their earliest days. None of the children can remember the time when they first started to sail in dinghies.

For many years Haylock had been thinking about a really light and lively dinghy for the young. Straight after the war the building prices and the cost of all materials rose steeply and he realised that if only the labour costs could be cut, leaving only the cost of timber, the cutting, the sail and the fittings, then it would be possible for people to build boats themselves at a very reasonable price.

Everything should be made as simple as possible; that is the reason for the snub pram bow which is much easier to construct than any other type of stem and does not affect the sailing qualities of the boat. The dinghy was to have a foredeck and sufficient side decks for it not to fill with water when it capsized. The dinghy also was to have a sail plan which was interesting enough to keep everyone amused; therefore a jib, mainsail and spinnaker were provided so that the young helmsman would realise that he had a proper racing boat, and so that he would not get bored with it after only one season. He wanted to have a spinnaker for light weather, because Haylock realised that far too few helmsmen regarded this sail as being part of the normal equipment of a racing boat. The small total sail area ought not to be too large even for an eight-year-old to handle.

Haylock went to the well-known boat designer Jack Holt with all these very definite ideas. And in 1947 the result appeared as the first-class little dinghy for a crew of two, the Cadet. The construction drawings were made with the greatest of care. All the sections were drawn full size, and any part with the slightest difficulty was illustrated. Thousands of parents and children with only a sketchy knowledge of boatbuilding and short practice in the use of tools have been able to construct this little boat all over the world.

Very soon an international class organisation was needed and the following rules were decided upon, and these have to be observed if owners want to race within the class:

1. All boats must be built exactly as on the drawings.
2. All competitors must be able to swim at lease 50 yards in normal clothes which consist of shorts, shirt, sweater and shoes.
3. Every competitor must be able to swim for at least 20 seconds under water dressed in these clothes.
4. Everyone must wear an authorised life jacket whilst racing.
5. Each Cadet dinghy must carry two people when racing.
6. No person may race in a Cadet dinghy after their 18th birthday.
7. Every dinghy which races must have surplus buoyancy material sufficient to hold up the boat with mast and sail and 506 lb. (230 kilos) of additional ballast.

The Cadet Dinghy Class spread very quickly over the whole world. In France from 1952 it became a National Junior Class; New Zealand and Australia followed in the same year. The first British National Regatta in 1950 had 25 starters, and the next in 1951 had 44.

The following year saw the first overseas competitors, and in 1951 the first Danish sailor, the 12-year-old Ib Andersen, competed and finished seventh out of 132 competitors.

Haylock and Holt have reason to be proud of their Cadet dinghy, which is safe and fast and easy to handle. The Cadet dinghy is also the first international junior class to be recognised by the International Yacht Racing Union, because it is so suitable in every way.

In every issue of the yachting magazine *Yachting World* there is at least one page of news on this class, not only from England, but also from other lands where the Cadet dinghy flourishes.

Secretary: c/o 19 Farrington Street, London. E.C.4.

Though a very small boat, the CADET carries everything found on thoroughbred two-man racing boats including a spinnaker. Young crews are thus able to learn from the start the working of this sail.

CLASS CHAMPIONS

1950 D. C. Thorpe, R. S. Pratt, England.
1951 R. Ellis, B. Ellis, England
1952 B. W. Appleton, R. S. Vines, England
1953 B. Ellis, R. Walsh, England
1954 B. Ellis, R. Walsh, England
1955 B. Ellis, R. Walsh, England
1956 J. Prosser, P. Assheton, England
1957 B. Steel, R. Steel, England
1958 P. V. Godtsenhoven, J. P. Lefevre, Belgium
1959 J. Rogge, P. Rogge, Belgium
1960 R. Pattisson, J. Pattisson, England
1961 P. Bateman, T. Jenkins, England
1962 G. Wackens, A. Verhaegen, Belgium
     S. Clifford, A. Harden, England
     (equal first)
1963 I. Gray, K. Gray, England
1964 M. Harrisson, A. Tucker, England
1965 N Boult, D. Long, England
1966 B. Wyskowski, A. Nowicki, Poland

SNIPE

Length overall   4,720 mm. (15 ft. 6 in.)
Beam   .   . 1,520 mm. (4 ft. 11½ in.)
Weight (complete) . 193·2 kilos (425 lb.)
Mainsail area .   . 7·0 sq. m. (75 sq. ft.)
Jib area   .   .   . 3·5 sq. m. (38 sq. ft.)

William F. Crosby, the well-known editor of the great New York yachting magazine *The Rudder*, designed in 1931 the Snipe two-man dinghy. This has now become the largest two-man class in the world, with 17,000 boats, mainly because of the extremely effective organisation which sends out every month a bulletin with news and reports on the activities of this class throughout the world.

For anyone who is interested in international two-man racing the Snipe is easily the best class to obtain top competition not only in Scandinavia but also in most other European countries, except Germany and Austria.

The Snipe, like most other dinghy classes, can be constructed by amateur builders and many of them are in fact built this way. Most new boats, however, are built today in reinforced plastics but the original design was for amateur construction in timber.

A metal mast is allowed, which is a great advantage because metal is uniformly elastic, and the sails can easily be made to match the mast flexibility.

The biggest disadvantage that this boat has is its high weight which makes it very difficult to transport and also to get in and out of the water. Therefore if you have to carry your boat over a beach into the water I would not advise you to sail a Snipe.

In spite of the heavy weight a Snipe sails very well to windward but off the wind it is rather slow, compared with the lighter classes.

Every alternate year there are world championships and in the intervening years there are European championships. At national championships it is usual for all club dinghies to be able to enter, whereas at many area championships only three may enter, whilst some continental and all world championships accept only one entry from each country.

Secretary: 655 Weber Avenue, Akron 3, Ohio, U.S.A.

WORLD CHAMPIONS

1934 New Rochdale, U.S.A.: W. E. Bracey, U.S.A.
1935 Dallas, U.S.A.: Perry Bass, U.S.A.
1936 Oshkosh, U.S.A.: Philip Benson, U.S.A.
1937 Sea Cliff, U.S.A.: A. M. Deacon, U.S.A.
1938 Lake Wawasee, U.S.A.: Charles Gabor, U.S.A.
1939 Los Angeles, U.S.A.: Walter Hall, U.S.A.
1940 Canandaigna, U.S.A.: Darby Metcalf, U.S.A.
1941 Fort Worth, U.S.A.: Darby Metcalf, U.S.A.
1942 Lake St. Clair, U.S.A.: Heinzerling brothers, U.S.A.
1945 Chicago, U.S.A.: Bob and Betty White, U.S.A.
1946 Lake Chautauqua, U.S.A.: Bob Davis, U.S.A.
1947 Geneva, Switzerland: Ted Wells, U.S.A.
1948 Palma de Mallorca, Spain: Carlos Vilar Castex, Argentina
1949 Larchmont, U.S.A.: Ted Wells, U.S.A.
1951 Havana, Cuba: Jorge Vilar Castex, Argentina
1953 Monaco: Conde Martins, Portugal
1955 Santander, Spain: Mario Capio, Italy
1957 Cascais, Portugal: J. Alonso Allende, Spain

1959 Porto Allegre, Brazil: Paul Elvstrom, Denmark

1961 Rye, U.S.A.: Axel Schmidt, Brazil

1963 Bendor, France: Axel Schmidt, Brazil

1965 Las Palmas, Canary Islands: Axel and Eric Schmidt, Brazil

The SNIPE has the world's largest membership and one of the very best class organisations.

HORNET

Length overall	4,876 mm. (16 ft.)
Beam	1,400 mm. (4ft. 7½in.)
Hull weight	104·3 kilos (230 lb.)
Mainsail area	8·5 sq. m. (91·5 sq. ft)
Jib area	3·0 sq. m. (32·3 sq. ft.)
Spinnaker area	7·5 sq. m. (80·7 sq. ft.)

The Hornet was designed by Jack Holt of Britain in 1951.

The dinghy is fast under all conditions, and Jack Holt has made, in the Hornet, a boat which is light, cheap, and very easy to plane – it can even plane with the wind forward of the beam – and it can also be amateur built. In England many firms sell construction kits and frequently you find even middle-aged couples performing very well during races. They have a lot of fun and would never think of sailing another type of dinghy. The Hornet is very easy to capsize in hard weather but it is also easy to right and get sailing again without taking in much water. The design of the interior is fairly free and the boat is also fantastically fast for its size. On the normal Olympic course off Copenhagen some of the fastest British Hornet sailors were able to beat the best Finn sailors by up to six minutes.

The sliding seat which can be extended 4 feet outboard from the side is the reason for its great speed. The crew balances on the end of the seat with his feet on the outside of the gunwale and in this way a light crew of only about 11 stone is not handicapped against a heavier one.

The Hornet has a spinnaker, which means that the work of the crew is interesting, and in fact is at least of the same value as that of the helmsman, and this is really the way that a two-man dinghy should be arranged. The sliding seat means that sitting out is comfortable and the helmsman does not need to hang out, but it also means that quicker reactions are needed than for boats having no such crewing aids.

Secretary: 19-21 Farringdon Street, Ludgate Circus, London, E.C.4

WORLD CHAMPIONS

1952 R. Pitcher, M. Rubens
1953 Beecher Moore, Barbara Moore
1954 Beecher Moore, Barbara Moore, equal
     Oliver Lee, Brian Fisher, equal
1955 M. Corbin, Ted Harper
1956 T. Greenslade, Roy Coombs
1957 T. Greenslade, Roy Coombs
1958 L. Partridge, R. Fisher
1959 Beecher Moore, Barbara Moore
1960 T. M. Wheeler, A. Morgan
1961 A. Clifford, P. Goodfellow
1962 C. C. Hobday, J. Oddie
1963 C. C. Hobday, J. Oddie
1964 Loch Earn, Scotland: R. White, J. Osborne, England
1965 Hayling Island, England: M. Derry, B. Barnes, England
1966 Warsaw, Poland: T. Wade, R. Fisher, England

FOURTEEN

Length overall (maximum) . 4,267 mm. *(14 ft.)*
Beam 1,422–1,676 mm. (4 ft. 8 in.–5 ft. 6 in.)
Hull weight . . 102·3 kilos *(225 lb.)*
Sail area (actual) approx. 14·9 sq. m. (160 sq. ft.)
Spinnaker area approx. 14·9 sq. m. (160 sq. ft.)

The Fourteen Foot Class has always allowed a designer considerable latitude both in hull shape and sail plan, though development after about sixty years is confined more nowadays to the use and exploitation of new materials and methods of construction than radical improvements in hull or rig, which are now rather severely restricted.

The class is the forerunner of all modern racing dinghies, and most of the worthwhile developments in all dinghy racing stem from the efforts of such notable designers as Uffa Fox, Morgan Giles, Charles Bourke and others. In fact, over seventy designers have had a hand in the progress of this class, and thus have been directly responsible for the remarkably able racing dinghies of many types which the world sails today.

The Fourteens alone have remained as an open undecked boat, and give a severe test of skill to the tough two-man crew, who are allowed no trapeze aids since the now I.Y.R.U. President, Peter Scott, won the Prince of Wales Cup in 1938, using this 'revolutionary' device, which was immediately banned.

The class evolved out of the West of England Conference Class of the early years of this century. It became International in 1927. The first proper planing dinghy appeared in 1928 – the famous *Avenger* designed and sailed by Uffa Fox, which won 53 races in 57 starts that season.

The class has been raced continuously in Canada, U.S.A., Bermuda, New Zealand and Britain, and has never been more live

FOURTEENS carry about 160 sq. ft. of sail and have no aids to keeping the boat upright, other than two strong men. They also carry a large spinnaker, and are completely open. Only very small bailers are allowed, and thus there is great advantage in being able to sail the boat is such a manner that it stays dry.

than today, 95 boats appearing for the British Championships in 1963. No one has done more to promote the health of this class since 1930 than Olympic Gold Medallist Stewart Morris. He has now won the Prince of Wales Cup twelve times, and is still more than a match for all except the very cream of the international helmsmen, and he usually beats even them. But the records are strewn with names which have become famous in many waters in many other classes, and this class is still the best of its type in the world, even though it may seem a little old-fashioned since it does not have a trapeze.

Secretary: R. M. Burley, Hockley Cottage, East Meon, Hants, England.

PRINCE OF WALES CUP WINNERS

1927 Cecil Atkey (41 entries)	1939 Colin Ratsey (33)	1956 David Thorpe (53)
1928 Uffa Fox (40)	1946 Peter Scott and	1957 Stewart Morris (41)
1929 Uffa Fox (35)	John Winter (59)	1958 Geoff Smale (50)
1930 Tom Thornycroft (32)	1947 Stewart Morris (48)	1959 Charles Currey (44)
1931 Morgan Giles (31)	1948 Stewart Morris (44)	1960 Stewart Morris (63)
1932 Stewart Morris (34)	1949 Stewart Morris (52)	1961 Stewart Morris (73)
1933 Stewart Morris (35)	1950 Bruce Banks (54)	1962 Stewart Morris (84)
1934 John Winter (39)	1951 Bruce Banks (57)	1963 Mike Peacock (96)
1935 Stewart Morris (37)	1952 Mick Martin (33)	1964 Stuart Walker (95)
1936 Stewart Morris (40)	1953 Bruce Banks (41)	1965 Stewart Morris (83)
1937 Peter Scott (42)	1954 de Forest Trimmingham	1966 Mike Peacock (85)
1938 Peter Scott and nd	(51)	
John Winter (55)	1955 Bruce Banks (43)	

FIVE-O-FIVE

Length overall . *5,050 mm. (16 ft. 6 in.)*
Beam   .   . *1,910 mm. (6 ft. 3 3/16 in.)*
Hull weight   .   . *100 kilos (220 lb.)*
Mainsail area . *10 sq m. (107·6 sq. ft.)*
Jib area   .   *4·5 sq. m. (48·4 sq. ft.)*
Spinnaker area . *20 sq. m. (215·2 sq. ft.)*

There are over 3,000 of these boats in the world, though the greatest number is in France. The Five-O-Five is fast and only one dinghy is faster, namely, the much larger Flying Dutchman, and yet the difference in speed between them is very small.

The Five-O-Five is a difficult boat to sail properly and only keen helmsmen with quick reactions should choose it. The type originated in England, but the first prototype, which was called 'Coronet,' was about the size of a Flying Dutchman. The French liked the design but they built it a little smaller and lighter, so that it could fit within the French 'Caneton' rules. France and England tried in vain to get it accepted as an Olympic Class in 1960, but the Flying Dutchman was accepted instead. The supporters of the Five-O-Five insisted that it ought to be chosen because it was much quicker to tack than the Flying Dutchman and this meant that in a shifting wind during a race it was better able to make use of the whole course.

The Five-O-Five does not have so large a genoa as the Flying Dutchman and this does not slow it down so much when tacking. Also, because the crew can work faster with a jib than a genoa the Five-O-Five is in some ways more interesting to race. The Five-O-Five is a true thoroughbred racing boat, and people will always be trying to make it an Olympic Class.

The Five-O-Five is really my favourite class because the boat is so lively and responsive in all types of wind and sea conditions. It is also easy to handle out of the water and is light and strong. This is an example of a really first-class boat which has become popular by its own efforts and virtues without being an Olympic class. In fact many people said that the Five-O-Five was finished after it lost the original battle with the Flying Dutchman for Olympic selection. How wrong they were!

After having sailed all types of dinghy and all types of keelboat I would like to tell you that no other boat is able to give me so much pleasure as this one.

The class is growing faster than any other international trapeze class, and it must be for the reason that it is reasonably priced and also because it gives the greatest pleasure to its owners.

The class has a very good organisation and arranges a world championship in various parts of the world each year and also a European championship.

Secretary: Jean Cettier, 165 Boulevard Haussmann, Paris 8e, France.

The Five-O-Five is the liveliest of all boats when planing. In really strong winds you might think that it could be too lively but with experience it is always possible to control it.

1956 La Baule, France: J. Lebrun,
P. Harinkouck, France

1957 La Baule, France: P. Elvstrom,
P. Poullain, Denmark

1958 La Baule, France: P. Elvstrom,
P. Poullain, Denmark.

1959 Cork, Ireland: M. Buffet, P. Wolff,
France

1960 La Baule, France: M. Buffet, P. Wolff,
France

1961 Weymouth, England: A. Cornu,
M. Pellmelle, France

1962 La Baule, France: Keith Paul,
R. Noakes, England

1963 Larchmont, U.S.A.: B. Farren-Price,
Chris Hough, Australia

1964 Cork, Ireland: J. B. Parrington, Chris
Hough, Australia

1965 Tangier, Morocco: D. and F. Farrant,
England

1966 Adelaide, Australia: Jim Hardy,
Australia

LIGHTNING

Length overall	.	. *5,792 mm. (19 ft.)*
Length waterline	.	*4,648 mm. (15 ft. 3 in.)*
Beam	.	. *1,988 mm. (6 ft. 6¼ in.)*
Draught	.	. *1,510 mm. (4 ft. 11½ in.)*
Sailing weight	.	. *318·2 kilos (700 lb.)*
Area, mainsail and jib		*16·45 sq. m. (177 sq. ft.)*

The Lightning was designed in 1938 by the famous firm of Sparkman & Stephens in America to fill the need for a really efficient, but simple, family racing boat for a crew of three, which could also be hauled out and taken home between regattas.

The original design was for hard chine construction in planked wood, but the boats can now be built in fibreglass.

Besides having an efficient modern sail plan and rig, there is a really worthwhile spinnaker. Racing has developed at a considerable pace, and there are now eleven thousand of these large and robust centre-boarders sailing, not only in America but also in parts of Europe and Australia. The I.Y.R.U. has recently granted International status to this class and thus its development is further encouraged.

This boat should suit older racing helmsmen and also those people who wish to race in a really keen class and yet want to bring their families along too. All-girl crews can compete with the top male crews and one frequently sees a husband and wife amongst the prizewinners.

The boat can also double up for camping and day sailing and even fishing, when used with an outboard, though these activities do not directly concern this book. I only say this to show that you can race in this class and also use the boat for many other purposes, which will save a great deal of money for some families who would otherwise have to own two boats.

The Lightning Class Association put out a great deal of information and a splendid Year Book. They also issue a booklet called 'How to Build a Lightning' with every set of plans.

Secretary: Lightning Class Association,
808 High Street, Worthington, Ohio 43085

CLASS CHAMPIONS

1939 Barnegat Bay: John S. Barnes in No. 35

1940 Long Island Sound: John S. Barnes in No. 35

1941 Skaneateles, N.Y.: John M. Stern in No. 680

1942 South Haven, Michigan: David G. cluett

1943 Bay Head, N.J.: Karl Smither

1944 Lake Eirie, Canada: Theodore Maher

1945 Long Island Sound: George R. Barnes in *Westerly*

1946 Skaneateles, N.Y.: Walt E. Swindeman, Jnr., in No. 800

1947 Toledo, Ohio: Walt E. Swindeman, Jnr. in No. 800

1948 Point Abino, Ontario: Richard H. Bertram in No. 2891

1949 Miami, Florida: Richard H. Bertram in No. 2891

1950 Point Abino, Ontario: H. R. Krauss in No. 447

1951 Toledo, Ohio: John Teigland in No. 4571

1952 Spray Beach, N.J.: Robert W. Graf in No. 467

1953 Point Abino, Ontario, Hank Cawthra in No. 4924

1954 Detroit, Michigan: Tom Allen in No. 4811

1955 New Orleans, La.: Tom Allen in No. 4811

1956 Point Abino, Ontario: William Cox in No. 5841

1957 Milford, Conn.: William Cox in No. 5841

1958 Beach Haven, N.J.: Henry Cawthra in No. 6066

1959 Detroit, Michigan: Herman Nickels in No. 7207

1960 East Tawas, Michigan: Carl Eichenlaub in No. 7420

1961 San Diego, California: Thomas Allen III in No. 7811

1962 Point Abino, Ontario: Thomas Allen III in No. 7811

WORLD CHAMPIONS

1961 Thomas Allen III in No. 7811; runner-up Jorge Salas-Chavez, Argentina, in No. 7721

1963 Lima, Peru: Tom Allen, U.S.A.

1965 Naples, Italy: Tom Allen, U.S.A.

Sailing a Japanese FINN in Tokyo.   *Hashimoto*

For record purposes I give below the last results of the I.Y.R.U. European Championships up to 1962 when they were discontinued:

ONE-MAN DINGHIES

1954 Berlin, Germany, in Olympiajollen: Andre Nelis, Belgium.

1955 Holland, in Finns: J. Vogler, East Germany.

1956 Naples, Italy, in Finns: Andre Nelis, Belgium.

1957 Cascais, Portugal, in Finns: A. Pelaschiar, Italy.

1958 Gemunde, Austria, in Olympiajollen: W. Erndl, Austria.

1959 St. Moritz, Switzerland, in Finns: Koos de Jongh, Holland.

1960 Ostend, Belgium, in Finns: P. Elvstrom, Denmark.

1961 Warnemunde, East Germany, in Finns: W. Kuhweide, West Germany.

1962 Kiel, West Germany, in Finns: B. Jacobson, Sweden.

TWO-MAN DINGHIES

1954 Rimini, Italy, in F.D.: P. Elvstrom and Aage Birch, Denmark.

1955 Oslo, Norway, in Snipes: C. H. Illies and P. Schaermach, Germany.

1956 Zadar, Yugoslavia, in Snipes: B. Mach and E. Patry, Switzerland.

1957 Chiemsee, Switzerland, in F.D.: P. Siegenthaler and M. Buzzi, Switzerland.

1958 La Baule, France, in Five-O-Fives: P. Elvstrom and O. G. Petersen, Denmark.

1959 Juelsminde, Denmark, in F.D.: D. Kriedel and J. Moeller, Germany.

1960 Turku, Finland, in Snipes: U. Libor and R. Bartnig, West Germany.

1961 Attersee, Austria, in F.D.: P. Siegenthaler and M. Buzzi, Switzerland.

1962 Ostend, Belgium, in F.D.: H. Samuel and J. Samuel, France.

DINGHY

FD
D4

TECHNIQUES

Above:

In this case the wetted-surface area is obviously too great. By heeling the dinghy a little to leeward you will be able to reduce this and at the same time you should obtain a reduction of the turbulence at the stern.

I mean to discuss here the techniques for making the dinghy go at its maximum speed in any conditions of wind, sea and wave. I do not only mean normal physical training but also the feel of the boat. The more delicate the feel that you can develop the quicker will you be able to learn how to get top speed.

In the following pages I set out the problems so that you can discover your own weaknesses and by intensive study can train yourself so that you can improve your speed.

Going to Windward in Smooth Water

The resistance of the water depends on the wetted-surface area of the hull, that is to say that part of the dinghy which, when sailing, is under the water. Therefore this has to be reduced as much as possible by giving the dinghy a small angle of heel to leeward. By this means the lee side of the dinghy will go deeper in the water, but the increased area will be small compared with that on the weather side which you have lifted out. You must also sit far enough forward so that the stern of the dinghy is raised in order to reduce the disturbance to the water caused by the passage of the boat, and this can be seen by the wake smoothing out.

On the previous page:

This Five-O-Five dinghy is going to windward and the wetted-surface area has been reduced by giving the boat a slight angle of heel to leeward. Here you can also see that I am steering the boat from the trapeze, and I will discuss this later on.

Left:

In this case the wetted-surface area is as small as possible, but the boat is heeled so much that it is out of balance and this puts on the brakes. Before he gets into this position the helmsman should push the tiller away from him so that the boat always remains in the correct balance. The excessive heel shown in the picture will then be avoided.

Going to Windward in Waves

When sailing in waves the reduction of wetted-surface area is not so important because it is impossible to control this accurately in a dinghy. The turbulence at the stern is also not as important as it is in smooth water and the position of the crew in the dinghy is normally farther aft in order to allow the stem to lift up and over the waves, rather than go straight through them.

In smooth water you can sail very close to the wind, or point very high, because there are no waves to stop the dinghy. In order to maintain speed in waves, it is quite wrong to pinch the dinghy as the waves are normally at right angles to the wind and you would merely slam into them. By freeing off a little the wave resistance decreases and you will go faster. If you see a big wave coming which you would normally hit very hard, you must point closer to the wind to slow down and ride easily over the wave, and then you must bear away in order to gain speed again, and you will then get past it much quicker than if you had gone straight into it.

Accurate steering depends on a good speed through the water; the higher the speed the quicker can you adjust the course to follow the wind. Therefore never let the dinghy slow down.

In between the bigger waves you will find smoother water. If you see, for instance, that the sea is smoother ahead and to leeward, it is an advantage to free off and go through that area. If the sea is smoother on the windward side you must point up closer to the wind. The amount that it will pay to pinch the dinghy or to sail free depends on the characteristics of particular classes. It depends a great deal on the weight of the dinghy.

If you bear away slightly and at the same time ease the sheets in a Flying Dutchman you will increase the speed greatly. The Pirat

This is a clear example of the jib being sheeted too hard. The dinghy is heeling and is not going fast. It seems to be 'dead.'

Mainsail and foresail are here adjusted in sympathy with each other. You can almost feel that the dinghy is sailing freely and is in balance, and has the minimum wetted surface.

Mainsail and foresail are here adjusted in sympathy with each other. You can almost feel that this Lightning is sailing freely and in balance, and also has the minimum of wetted surface area.

Look how precisely this young helmsman is handling his boat sailing to windward.

dinghy, which is heavy compared with its sail area, will shoot head to wind for quite a distance but, on the other hand, it will not accelerate very much if it is freed off. Therefore in heavier dinghies it is much better to pinch rather than free off.

Sail Sheeting when going to Windward

The amount to sheet-in the sails is and always will be a matter of feel; but I can give you some indication of what to do. In light winds the main-sheet traveller has to be nearer the centre of the boat but, of course, the sheets are left quite slack. The harder the wind the more you should move the traveller outboard, especially if you find it difficult to hold the boat upright. In two-man boats the jib must not be sheeted in so hard that it backwinds the mainsail and stops it drawing. On the other hand, you must make sure that the main sheet is not eased too far so that it is still being backwinded by the jib, even though the latter is sheeted correctly.

How do you find the Right Relationship between the Angle of Sheeting of the Foresail and the Mainsail?

First sheet the sails in to the normal position. Then if the jib is backwinding the mainsail too much and yet you can still easily hold the dinghy upright, then you must sheet in the mainsail by bringing the boom inboard. If the dinghy does not sail any faster after this alteration, then you must find another solution. Try freeing off the jib and resetting the mainsail outboard again. Now you should be able to feel the difference in speed which results from the jib drawing better even though you may only have slacked the sheet a tiny amount. If the jib is fluttering on the leach, then you must move the fairlead forward so that it takes up a fair curve from foot to head. All this, of course, depends on the sails having been made correctly in the first place.

In very hard winds when you are unable to hold the boat upright and in balance you must move the mainsheet traveller to leeward and ease the jib slightly but not so that the leach flutters. If you cannot move the traveller then you must ease the mainsheet in order to free off the top of the mainsail. If the dinghy is slamming into waves without there being much wind you must have the boom nearer the centreline but ease the sheets off in order to gain speed after each wave.

Sailing on a Reach

In light winds the same rules apply as for going to windward; however, you can with advantage reduce the resistance of the keel against the water by raising the centreboard and pointing a little closer to the wind. It is easier to sheet the sails correctly if you use the lightest rope possible.

This boat is out of balance because the genoa has been pulled in too hard. The mainsail is already being back-winded and so the helmsman will be unable to regain balance until the genoa is eased.

In this case the wetted surface has been reduced by heeling the boat slightly to windward and this also gives a very good balance on the tiller. The chine tends to turn the boat to leeward and this counteracts the opposite turning moment from the sail pressure. This gives a better result in these conditions than trying to steer solely with the rudder. The tiller is thus used to correct minor errors only.

This picture of a Snipe shows that the longer you make the horse rope the more near the centreline can you sheet the boom without increasing the leach tension.

Look at these two pictures. The Flying Dutchman mainsail can be set on the mast in three different positions corresponding to three different sets of black bands. D10 has the sail set in the highest position and US600 is using the middle set of marks. Note that the latter does not have to use so much tension on the sheet in order to get the sail sheeted to the same position because the boom is lower and closer to the traveller.

The trimming of a genoa on a Flying Dutchman is almost the most important factor is sailing this type of dinghy. If the leach is too tight it will throw too much back wind into the mainsail. If the leach is too slack only the bottom of the sail will be drawing, the dinghy will feel very light on the helm, but will not be travelling fast. In order to tack a trapeze dinghy the crew must come into the cockpit, unhook the trapeze wire, only slack off the genoa when it is taken aback by the wind, move over to the other side under the boom, haul in the genoa on the new tack, hook on the trapeze wire to the trapeze belt, and then push out and hang horizontal again.

Balancing the Boat in Strong Winds with the Wind Aft

If the dinghy is heeling to windward you must pull in the mainsheet. If the boat is heeling to leeward then you must slack off the sheets.

In boats under spinnaker if you are heeling to windward pull in the sheet; if heeling to leeward pull in the guy.

Try to follow the movements of the sea and do not keep altering the sails if the waves are the cause of heeling; for example, if there is a swell at right angles to the waves and this is making you heel.

Left and below:
There are several reasons here for this capsize but the most important one is that the mainsheet is let out too far. The moment that a skipper feels that the boat is beginning to get out of balance and is lurching to windward he must get the mainsheet in fast to restore equilibrium. In this case you can see that, because the kicking strap is too loose, the sail has twisted and the top part of the sail is pulling the mast over to windward. There is yet another cause for this capsize – the centreboard is right down and the boat is 'tripping over' it. One-third down is enough.

Above:
In very strong winds you must always play your mainsheet soon enough so that the boat does not lose its balance, otherwise the end of the boom will hit the water and will not allow you to free off. This helmsman wanted to free off the mainsheet but because the end of the boom touched the water the boom could not be freed and he could not then avoid capsizing. The boat is a Moth.

This incident in very strong gusty winds resulted in at least three capsizes, all because 2353 lost the balance of his boat. His rudder was too small to correct the trouble. (See the left-hand boat in the bottom picture.)

In the second picture he has let his mainsheet out too far and is capsizing to windward as a consequence. The skipper of 2610 is looking at the capsize and forgets to pull his mainsheet in . . .

. . . and so he capsizes at just the same moment as a gust strikes the group. Look at 313 and 2612 nearly out of control with the ends of their booms in the water.

No. 2352 manages to stay afloat but look at 2512 who is the only skipper doing the right thing. He looks straight ahead and keeps his boat in perfect balance.

Below:
In this case the dinghy has run into a big wave. The skipper ought to have leaned right aft with his body quite horizontal in order to lift the bow, and if this was not enough he ought to have luffed slightly in order to get the bow to lift over the wave.

Above:
When you are running, if it is the waves that are causing your boat to heel to windward, then you should not pull in your mainsheet to correct the trim because when you come off the wave the heel will be corrected of its own accord.

Above:

Remember that the genoa must be slowly drawn in exactly at the same time and speed as the mainsail. And the speed of hauling in the mainsail governs the minimum time that the complete manoeuvre can take.

Below:

Here we have an example of a skipper who has pulled his mainsheet in too rapidly as he rounds this mark.

Tacking

When going to windward it is very hard to tack a dinghy without losing speed. To get the dinghy to continue immediately on the new tack with the same speed as it had before is a difficult art. Wait until you are sure the dinghy will not strike a wave at the beginning of the new tack, wait until you feel that the dinghy wants to tack – until it is trying to luff. Let it go round on its own with just a little help from the rudder and you should then find that it will continue on the new tack with the same speed as it had before. On the other hand, if you decide that you want to tack without taking any regard to the feel of the boat, and you push the rudder hard down, the dinghy will stop dead on the new tack, and you will have a good chance of losing two, three, four or even up to ten boat lengths.

In light winds and smooth water you can make the dinghy tack on its own by allowing it to heel a little to leeward. Merely follow up with the rudder sufficiently to adjust the dinghy on to its new tack. Because a tack starts with a luff with consequent increase in wind pressure on the sails, and thus increasing speed, you must not ease the mainsail or jib sheets until the sails actually start to lift. When the dinghy is head to wind slack off the sheets a little and when the sails fill on the new tack start hauling them in again gently as the dinghy gradually increases speed.

As we have said before, in strong winds and sea do not tack before you feel the dinghy is ready to go about. Particularly in the Flying Dutchman, which has a large genoa, the jib sheet must not be eased before the sail starts to lift.

Most people think wrongly that the jib sheet should be eased before tacking in order to avoid hindering the boat in going about. It is more important to keep up the speed and then to catch the wind on the new tack as soon

At this moment the crew should already be on his way over to the other side of the boat.

as possible. Let the jib remain sheeted in until it starts to lift, and then immediately ease off and haul in on the new tack. Remember to alter the sheet smoothly. Do not first slacken the jib sheet then shift over to the other side and finally pull in the new sheet with a jerk.

In the case of a swell which is running at right angles to the wind, it is quite natural that the boat should roll. Do not try to stop it.

Hornet No. 520 is losing after tacking because the jib is still lifting long afterwards. Remember the very important golden rule – whenever it is possible for a sail to draw, then it must be made to draw immediately. In Hornet No. 530 the helmsman is not paying attention to the course or the other competitor. This may be caused by the fact that he is using the normal English system of having the mainsheet led to his hand from the stern. It is not a great help for the crew to have his head so far downwards. The English method of sheeting where the rope comes from a block on the transom to the helmsman's hand is wrong for use when racing. You are forced to turn your head away from the course and at the same time it is harder to pull the sheet in and it is also more difficult to balance the boat properly.

Beauvais Nautisme

This skipper is using the English method of sheeting the mainsail which makes tacking difficult because you have to face aft when you cross the boat and so for a short time you are sailing like a blind man.

Gybing

Gybing in hard winds is the most difficult manoeuvre in a dinghy. I will try to explain the best way to gybe without capsizing. Most gybes end with a capsize particularly because the helmsman and crew are not sure what points to watch out for, and at exactly what moment the boom should go over. In hard winds it is easiest to gybe in the calmer periods, but gybing normally has to take place when you are level with a mark, and you will be very lucky if the wind eases at this particular moment. You must only gybe when the dinghy is going at maximum speed and not when it is accelerating. It is obvious when the dinghy is accelerating that the wind is pressing very hard on the sail, and this makes it very difficult to pull the boom across. But when you are travelling at maximum speed

the wind pressure on the sails will be less because the difference between the wind speed and the boat speed will be at a minimum.

In many cases you become nervous when the boat is travelling very fast, which is why most people do not like to gybe at this point. But you must force yourself to do it then. By practising you will discover why it is so much easier to gybe when the boat is travelling at maximum speed and not when it is accelerating. You will frequently see people trying to gybe when the dinghy is slowing on the face of a wave. Then the speed is very low and the wind pressure is very high. Most people say to themselves 'This is the point when the speed is not high and I ought to gybe' – and so they capsize. Once more, I say, gybe when the speed is greatest, or alternatively, when

the wind has dropped. If the wind is abaft the beam or dead aft you can luff a little to windward, then take the first chance when the wind eases, gybe, and aim straight for the mark.

When gybing in hard winds under planing conditions you must do the following: Start by pulling in the mainsheet as far as you can without causing the boat to heel. When you have reached maximum speed, heel the dinghy a little to windward, put the helm over and at the same time throw the boom across firmly with one hand.

Just at the moment when the boom crosses the centreline you must put the helm back so that the dinghy points dead down wind and in this way it is easier to maintain balance. If you do not reverse the helm in this way there is a danger that the centrifugal force will pull the mast over and you will capsize. Before you start the gybe you must remember to raise the centreboard to halfway or a little more to avoid the danger of the boat 'tripping over the keel.'

Here I am trying to gybe by grabbing hold of all the parts of the sheet but at this moment there is a very hard puff which means that I have not got the strength to be able to pull the boom across.

The puff was so heavy that the dinghy got out of control and the boom hit the water. I had no other option but to let go both the sheet and the tiller . . .

. . . and throw myself out to windward.

As the centreboard is completely raised the dinghy is able to slide sideways . . .

. . . and is therefore easily got under control again.

The reason why this gybe failed was because firstly, the dinghy was not going at maximum speed, and also It did not realise that there was a hard puff coming up astern.

The dinghy is heeling enough to windward and at this moment the boom should be pulled firmly over on to the new gybe, but the helmsman has allowed the mainsheet to slack off too far and the crew has not enough strength to pull the boom across by means of the kicking strap.

Because the keel was right down, and the gybe was miscalculated, this dinghy capsized over the keel. This probably would not have happened had the centreboard been only 8 inches higher.

Hornet No. 576 shows the correct way to gybe. The crew has grabbed hold of the kicking strap and slammed the boom over to the other side. The helmsman and the crew of Hornet No. 550 are falling out of the dinghy and this will make it much more difficult to pull upright.

In Very Hard Squalls

You must raise the centreboard when you are out in a thunderstorm or in very bad weather and you are nervous of capsizing. In very hard squalls pull the centreboard half up and keep the boat sailing on a reach. As long as you keep a good speed on the dinghy it is then quite difficult to capsize. Even a very hard puff should not capsize the dinghy because it will be able to slide sideways.

Of course it can blow so hard that you will be unable to pull the boom across at all. In this case there is nothing else you can do but to sail far enough by the lee so that the wind gets behind the sail and blows the boom across on its own. Before this happens you should haul in on the mainsheet as much as possible. And here I should also point out that you should never have the centreboard down more than about eight or nine inches.

Watch out that the boom does not hit you as it goes across.

When you are not sure that you can gybe successfully during the actual rounding of the mark, you can luff up to gain maximum speed, then gybe, bear away and steer straight for the mark.

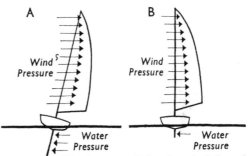

Dinghy A will heel a great deal and not be balanced, whereas dinghy B will merely slide sideways.

An O.K. Dinghy in very hard weather in New Zealand.

Planing

By planing we mean that the dinghy is lifted up on top of the water and travels at high speed, making the surface area in contact with the water as small as possible and the resistance at a minimum. The technique of making a boat plane is very easy. Again, balancing is the most important part. If this is correct then there should be no weight on the helm and it is only the strength of the wind which governs the speed of planing. When sailing to windward it is almost impossible to plane; the dinghy is heeling too much and the water resistance is too great. If you free off the sheets a little, harden down on the kicking strap as much as possible, and raise the centreboard, then you will immediately start planing. Whilst you are planing you must be careful to avoid hitting waves when you are hanging out. You should place the boat on the waves in such a way that they will help you to maintain maximum speed.

If you put the stem into the face of a wave you will not be able to go any faster than the wave itself is travelling. If you are planing in a good wind in which you are going faster than the waves, then you must luff up so that you stay on the same wave and you must avoid allowing your stem to be stopped by running into any waves. Steer so that you are always sailing on the downward face of the waves. It can be quite difficult to do this because you are continually being hit by waves in the face, but after some practice you will be able to get the feel so that you can sail correctly automatically. Sooner or later you will not be able to continue planing on the face of the same wave any longer. When this happens you can bear away into the proper direction for the next mark but this is not quite so important as attempting to get planing.

The difference between planing speed and normal sailing speed is enormous, and there-fore you should always concentrate on planing at every opportunity, because in this way you will have a chance of gaining anything up to 100 metres at a time. On the other hand, when sailing to windward it is only possible to gain on other competitors very slowly. Therefore always think how you can get the boat planing. This is the best way of getting to the head of the fleet.

The area inside the solid line is the waterline of the boat in still water. The hatched area is that which should be in the water when you are planing at maximum speed.

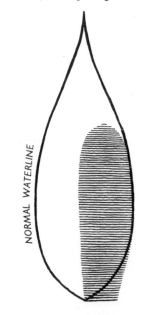

NORMAL WATERLINE

A Finn dinghy in perfect balance.

This planing Pirat dinghy could have had its centreboard a little higher and taken on a little more heel, whereupon it would have been able to travel quite a bit faster.

This British O.K. Dinghy is planing at top speed with the correct amount of heel, and the helmsman is sitting far aft in the boat.

In this case the helmsman should have moved farther aft in order to raise the stem more.

D496 would travel faster and be easier to control if the boom wedge had been pushed in a little harder.

D288 has a very tight boom wedge and will be the fastest when planing as long as he is quick enough at playing the mainsheet so as to avoid the boom end hitting the water.

In very strong winds it can be dangerous to set the kicking strap or boom wedge too tight. In this case the boom end can become so low that it will be very easy to let it hit the water if you are not quick enough in easing the sheet. This almost certainly will result in a capsize.

Before D376 had hit this sea and become stopped he ought to have luffed up in order to get the dinghy to lift and pass more easily over this wave.

When you are racing you can gain great distances by using the spinnaker, but, on the other hand, you can also lose many lengths by faulty spinnaker work. When the wind is aft and of moderate strength you must always use the spinnaker. In winds above 30 knots carrying the spinnaker can be dangerous except in a Flying Dutchman, which has a very stable hull shape. When the wind is dead aft you can in all classes have the spinnaker to windward and carry both the sheets on the windward side also. If the wind is more on a reach you must carry the spinnaker sheet round the forestay and to leeward of the jib, and sheet it as far aft in the boat as possible; in this way you will be able to keep the spinnaker well away from the jib, even if the wind comes more ahead. You will then have to sheet the mainsail in, as it would otherwise be backwinded.

Spinnaker setting needs a lot of practice and very close teamwork between helmsman and crew. There are two main methods of setting spinnakers. You can let the crew hoist the spinnaker and give the helmsman the sheets whilst he is fixing the spinnaker boom, and after this the crew can take over the sheets again. The other method is for the helmsman to hoist the spinnaker, but in this case you must lead the spinnaker halyard from the foot of the mast along the centreboard case, back to the helmsman's hand. Whilst the helmsman is hoisting, the crew is fitting the spinnaker boom and then the helmsman gets hold of the sheets and hands them to the crew. The second method is much to be preferred and has the great advantage that when the time comes to lower it the helmsman has control and can also have a good view of the spinnaker, and can see if it has got hung up anywhere and will not come down.

In a Flying Dutchman you can either have the spinnaker under the deck or you can have it in a bag fixed into holes in the deck so that it does not get sodden in the bilge water.

When the time comes for the spinnaker to be lowered you must steer the dinghy so that it is pointing in such a direction that the genoa or the jib will be drawing properly. If the wind is dead aft and you are coming to a mark after which you will be going to windward, it is essential to take the spinnaker down by the time you are ready to round. If you are going too directly towards the mark with the wind dead aft, then you will have to sail for several boat lengths without any wind filling the genoa. Therefore you should arrange matters so that when you lower the spinnaker you are able to luff up enough so that the genoa will fill immediately.

You must practise hoisting and lowering the spinnaker rapidly, because in close quarters sailing there will be many situations where you will be forced into a luffing match one moment and then immediately have the wind right aft again; for example, as you are approaching the finishing line. You can of course hold out the genoa with your hands, but when you are racing it is much more effective to use the spinnaker properly. If you are pushed up to weather of the mark before rounding, you may have to fall off on to a dead run for a short time. Then the first crew who is able to set his spinnaker will go the fastest and round the mark first.

In a Five-O-Five you can leave the spinnaker boom connected to the spinnaker when you take it down. You can also leave the halyard connected. You always lower the spinnaker to windward and you can take it in either above the jib sheets or below just as you wish. The only difference is that when you sheet in the jib on the same side as you took down the spinnaker you will either have the halyard or the sheet round the outside of the jib sheet. You cannot avoid one or the other.

If you then have to hoist the spinnaker again from the other side of the boat the only thing you can do is to disconnect the pole from the spinnaker first.

In the Flying Dutchman you can have the spinnaker bag in the middle of the boat near the genoa fairlead and then you can do it in the same way but the more normal method is to have a loose ring round the halyard with a thin nylon line connected to it and leading round a fairlead in the stemhead and passing under the deck to a long piece of elastic. Thus when the spinnaker is hoisted the ring is right up by the halyard sheave and the elastic under the deck is stretched tight. When you lower the spinnaker the nylon line pulls the halyard down forward of the forestay. When it gets to the bottom you can still pull the head of the spinnaker back along the foredeck and into the cockpit and the halyard will slide through the ring. By this method

you can only take the spinnaker down underneath the genoa sheets. (See drawing on page 61.)

In practice the way to do it is to pass the genoa sheets aft of the crew before you take the spinnaker down.

How close you should be able to carry the spinnaker on a reach is a matter of feel, but of one thing you can be quite sure: when you are sailing with the wind dead aft you must try to spread the spinnaker so that it presents the greatest possible area to the wind. If the wind is coming over the quarter then you must have the spinnaker a little over on the lee side. Between a broad reach and a

Above:
This spinnaker bag built into the foredeck will catch a lot of water but it will only do this if there is a great deal of wind. There will then be no problem with a wet spinnaker since there will be enough wind to blow it out to its right shape.

Left:
In this case the spinnaker sheets are set on opposite sides of the mast. The genoa is rolled up by a special roller fitting and the luff wire alone holds the mast, and the forestay is kept clear of the genoa by an elastic from the stemhead. The genoa halyard has a swivel on it, whilst under the deck there is a roller reel, and by pulling a line on this you can furl the genoa round its own luff wire. When the genoa jib is rolled up and out of the way, gybing is made much easier.

When gybing in light winds you first disconnect the spinnaker boom at the mast end and reconnect to the lee spinnaker clew. When you have done this you gybe the main boom and at the same time disconnect the spinnaker boom from the old weather clew and connect this end to the mast. Whilst gybing the helmsman holds both the sheets.

In strong winds gybe the main boom first and then disconnect the pole.

beam reach the spinnaker should be even farther to leeward, but it should always be kept full so that it is drawing properly. On a beam reach you should think of the spinnaker as if it was a genoa and set it accordingly. You must never allow the spinnaker boom to get closer to the forestay than about six inches. If you slack off the guy so that the spinnaker boom touches the forestay, and if you then sheet the spinnaker in so that it is full of wind, you will merely pull the whole spinnaker aft and it will hold the boat back instead of drawing it forward.

It is particularly exciting to race with the spinnaker in planing breezes. In these conditions the crew can help the boat to get planing by jerking the spinnaker sheets. When the boat starts to plane on the face of a wave the helmsman must bear away a little when the crest reaches the transom. In this way he will be able to keep on the face of the wave and plane with it, and at this moment the crew must take both the sheet and the guy and pull them sharply in. If more help is needed then he can go on jerking both sheets. Though, be careful, because 'pumping' the sheets is not now allowed under the racing rules. (See page 223 for the definition.)

If it blows so hard that you can only use a spinnaker on a dead run you should lead both the spinnaker sheet and the guy through fairleads much farther forward than you were using in lighter winds. It will then be much easier to stop the spinnaker from swaying from side to side which causes the boat to roll. Then you also will not have trouble when you gybe with the spinnaker flying upwards and also swinging out of control. The worst thing that can happen is that the spinnaker goes upwards and forwards because it is then so difficult to get it back again.

If you get a very hard gust and want to reduce power let the windward sheet (guy) go

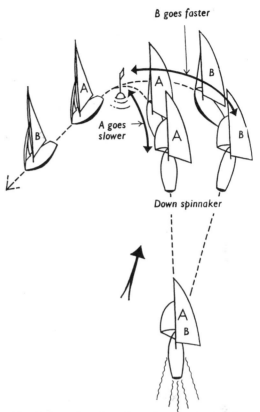

After B has taken down her spinnaker she is able to luff up towards the mark and thus go faster than A.

and haul in on the lee sheet. The spinnaker will then collapse behind the mainsail.

Using the Genoa with the Spinnaker

If you are going to use a genoa at the same time as a spinnaker you must have a cleat for the genoa sheet so that you can set the genoa easily according to the direction of the wind.

With the wind dead aft you can let the genoa nearly hang, but if the wind is on the quarter or on the beam then you must try to make it draw. It does not often pay to carry the spinnaker on a beam reach, because in this condition you can raise the centreboard a little more and by pointing higher carry the genoa full of wind whilst sliding sideways, which you could not do if the centreboard was farther down. If you had the centreboard lower you would be forced to point farther off the wind and thus you would not be able to keep the genoa properly full.

These German and Swedish crews show light weather spinnaker techniques. The German boat is travelling fast with everything set to perfection. The spinnaker is flying high and the crew has both the guy and the sheet under instant control.

The Swedes are too slow and the crew is only now reaching for the topping lift so that the boom can be raised up. In these boats it is usually best to furl up the genoa when the spinnaker is set.

This picture shows a situation where the helmsman has moved over to the lee side in order to balance the crew so that he can remain on the trapeze.

Left:
The text on page 58 refers.

Right:
Here the boat has regained a perfect trim and every sail is drawing perfectly.

62

. . . and when things go wrong . . .

. . . what a tangle!

Sheeting

A rule for all classes of boat: if you find it difficult to hold the boat level, then you should move the sheet position more to leeward, and this is particularly important in one-man dinghies, such as the Moth, O.K. Dinghy and Finn, where in hard weather the traveller is right out to the edge of the cockpit. If you do not do this the leach will 'close' and the sail will be ineffective. If you sheet the

This is an excellent position for the traveller in these conditions and the leach is nicely open and the wind is leaving the sail freely.

Beauvais-Nautisme

sails too close the dinghy will heel too much and will point too close to the wind, whereupon it will tend to hit the waves head on and slam. With the sails sheeted farther to leeward the dinghy will not point so high but will travel much faster.

The mainsail is sheeted here in such a way that the lowest batten is exactly parallel to the centreline of the boat. The jib also is sheeted far enough aft so that it does not give any backwind to the mainsail. In this jib there is too little flow in the lower part because we have had to sheet it so far aft. This jib should have been made so that it had a freer leach in the upper half so that we could have sheeted it further forward without back-winding the mainsail.

The Sailing Weight

In all classes the weight of the boat is extremely important for racing purposes. About twenty years ago in heavier classes they did not think that the weight had much effect on the speed because frequently heavy boats beat light ones. Later people started to build dinghies right down to the minimum weight and found that they could plane, and this was especially effective in wind strengths when the lighter boats could plane and the heavy ones were unable to. In the lighter classes of dinghies it is even more important to keep the weight low, because they are able to plane more often. In practice this means that light dinghies should not be more than 5 kilos over the minimum. This is especially important today because the competition is much harder now than it was a few years ago.

It can be a big advantage to concentrate the weights as much as possible just aft of the middle of the boat and thus make the bow and the stern of the dinghy light. This has a significant effect when sailing in waves. On smooth water it makes almost no difference.

In sea conditions like this it would have been more effective if the helmsman and the crew had been closer together. This is in order to concentrate the weights more amidships and to make the bow and the stern lighter.

Hanging Technique

Hanging – hiking – stacking – sitting-out. Call it what you like, but balancing the boat when sailing to windward in a strong wind is and always will be the most difficult part for a beginner and especially one who is twenty years old or more. At this age it will take a long time for a man to get used to the hanging technique. It took me about five years before I was able to relax in this position. It is most important to be able to relax so that full concentration can be given to the tactics during the race.

During my first Olympic Regatta I realised that the weakest point of all my competitors was in their hanging- and sitting-out technique, and therefore when I returned home I made myself a practising bench. I thought at that time that I could train myself to be able to sit out with my knees outside the boat, but I had to give up after a year and a half of practice. It was not possible to hold this position for more than six minutes of racing. At the same time it was so tiring that it upset the sailing and destroyed one's concentration on tactics. Therefore I started to move farther inboard and placed my knees over the middle of the sidedeck. This made it much easier physically to hold the position but a new problem arose as the sharp edges of the deck tended to stop the blood flowing. It helped a great deal to use shin protectors on the legs.

After a year of training I was able to train myself not to need any padding, but now that I am getting older I may have to start using it again. Foam rubber inside the trousers is very comfortable to use as padding.

If you train on a practice bench you must not just hang there. Do some gymnastics, swing the arms up and over the head, and lean forward and back just as if you were in the dinghy. Training on a bench is harder than really sailing.

To start with you will get very sore in the leg muscles. Then you should stop for a couple of days until the soreness disappears. Every time the rest periods will get shorter until eventually you will be able to train every day. To start off with you will find it very hard to do this but you must always think ahead that one day it will merely be a routine. You must always keep your speed and fitness and therefore you must keep doing gymnastics outside the season, which will help a great deal. See also the section on fitness at the end of the book.

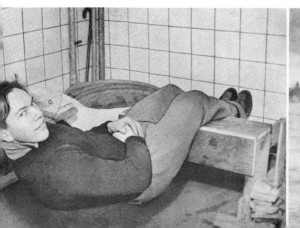

The practice bench which I used for four years.

This is the most relaxed position where the knees are over the centre of the sidedeck and the body is bent.

G. L. W. Oppenheim

Above:
This man will injure his back if he hangs out in the position for too long a time.
This boat is the 1936 Olympic Monotype designed by the famous South African Finn and F.D. skipper, Helmut Stauch. It is bigger and heavier than a Finn.

Below:
This skipper is hanging outboard in a very relaxed position with a bent back and is able to steer the boat very precisely.

Here, hiking with the aid of a trapeze on my single-hander, Trapez, I have adjusted wire and harmess so that my body is on a plane parallel to the water.

Trapezing Technique

The beginner's problem when first starting to trapeze is how to get out there. The picture shows the first stages of this manoeuvre. In this picture it is the helmsman who is going out but the principle is exactly the same if it is the crew.

The forward foot comes out on to the gunwale first and when coming in exactly the reverse happens and the forward foot comes in off the gunwale last.

When moving in and out on the trapeze a good rule is always to relax on the wire and let your weight be entirely taken by the harness. Do not try to lift yourself with your hand.

The balancing of a trapeze dinghy is an art which has to be performed by feel. The man on the trapeze must at all times be placed in the best position for the boat to go fastest and the whole time he must make sure of having his body at the most effective angle to the boat.

The most common mistake is that when the wind drops the man on the trapeze immediately goes back into the boat and this causes the stern of the dinghy to be depressed which slows the boat still more.

When the wind dies you ought to move your weight further forward if possible but this is not so essential as the technique of bending both knees together and also your back at the same time so that you go straight in at right angles to the boat's centreline. Avoid simply bending your aftermost knee which would have the effect of moving your weight aft as you moved inboard.

When planing the weight of the man on the trapeze must be moved aft and in order to get his weight as far out as possible it is recommended that you fit a foot-strap on the

This is the correct way to get out on to a trapeze. You can see that the wire is exactly the right length so that when he is sitting on the gunwale he can hook on to the ring easily. Then he lies back and relaxes with the wire taking his weight. The next move is to put the forward foot out on the gunwale. He is now waiting for a little more wind and he will then simply release his aftermost foot from the toestrap and straighten his forward leg. Coming in is exactly the reverse.

The boat is the prototype of my Trapez class under test.

gunwale for the aftermost foot. Then you will find that the trapeze man can stand so that he is at right angles to the centreline even though he may be well aft.

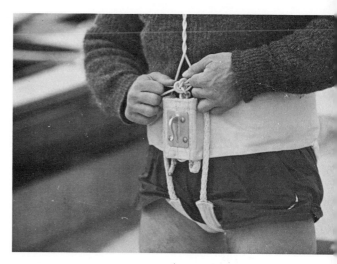

In this case the crew has two hooks connected to his body, the top one connected to a shock cord at the top of his harness. There is also a fitting like a figure of eight with two rings at the bottom end of the trapeze wire. There is in addition a handle a little further up which the crew can grab to help lift him over the gunwale when in the low trapeze position.

A good general rule is to have the higher trapeze position arranged at such a height that you can just comfortably hook yourself on when sitting on the side deck. The low position is about 5 inches lower.

The position the crew has here is mainly intended for close-reach planing. However, in this case, because of the very strong wind, he has stayed in that position for the windward beat.

In this picture you can see that the crew's weight has the maximum effect.

This shows a very good type of hook and harness but in this case the belt has been set too high up.

Right:
This is the best thing that the trapeze man can do to keep the boat upright when his trapeze wire is too short as it is here. You can see that the boat is in balance since there is no pressure on the rudder.

Below:
If your crew is very light the helmsman can take the trapeze himself but in this case you must have an extra hook on your body 5 inches higher than the normal one so that you can get low enough when you are fully out. This technique also has the advantage of keeping the forestay tighter. However, on planing, you must pass the trapeze back to the crew because it is too difficult to steer accurately enough from the trapeze, especially in shifty winds and big waves.

This technique of sailing to windward with the helmsman on the trapeze, as well as being extremely comfortable, has another advantage, which is that he has a better view not only of the sails but also of the race course, enabling him to plan the tactics more easily.

Before an important race you should inspect absolutely everything.

Some Dinghy fittings and gear -

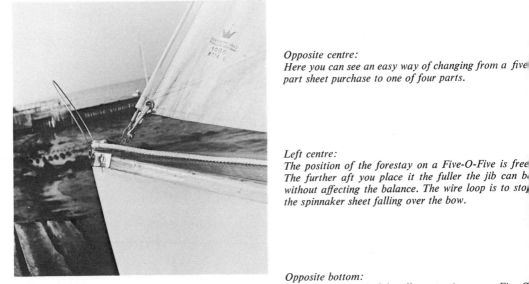

Opposite top:
On the Five-O-Five I adjust the sail at the tack . . .

Far right:
. . . and keep it fixed at the clew.

Left top:
This shows a pair of diamond struts and also a set o,
limited-swing swept-spreaders fitted to an alloy mast

Opposite centre:
Here you can see an easy way of changing from a five
part sheet purchase to one of four parts.

Left centre:
The position of the forestay on a Five-O-Five is free
The further aft you place it the fuller the jib can b,
without affecting the balance. The wire loop is to sto,
the spinnaker sheet falling over the bow.

Opposite bottom:
This shows the end of the tiller extension on my Five-O
Five with a rope hand-grip. To make the extensio,
longer when I am steering it from the trapeze, I fit a
extension tube on to the end and it is held in place b
the elastic.

Left bottom:
This shows a neat type of Highfield lever made i
stainless steel which can be fixed on to the mast or an)
where else on the boat.

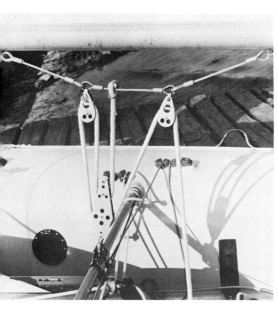

This was the spreader arrangement I used on my Five-O-Five in 1966. The side bracing and the jumper bracing is adjustable at all times.

The wires are led round sheaves at the foot of the mast. They then pass along the floor aft to the transom where they are fixed.

The adjustment is finally made by pulling the wire more or less sideways as shown in this photograph.

Right top:
It is easy to open or close the transom flaps with this lever. Note also the adjustable toestrap fittings.

Right centre:
There is a rope uphaul and downhaul for lifting rudder. Elastic is not strong enough to stop the rudder blade moving. There must be a universal swivel on the extension also.

Right bottom:
This shows a way of adjusting the jib fairlead position.

CENTREBOARD CASE
FROM ABOVE

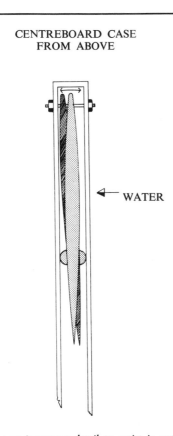

← WATER

Above:
This is a very important detail to assist in getting a short centreboard boat such as a Five-O-Five to go to windward properly. It is an arrangement to get the centreboard to angle itself automatically two or three degrees to windward of the centreline of the boat. This helps to make the hull travel straight through the water rather than crabbing slightly sideways as it does normally.

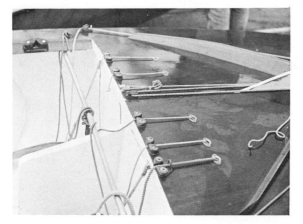

A very good arrangement for easing the lee shroud when reaching. A jib fairlead can also be seen which is adjustable in two directions.

On an O.K. Dinghy the control lines can be led to the fore side of the cockpit but the cleats must be clearly marked or coloured ropes used to avoid confustion.

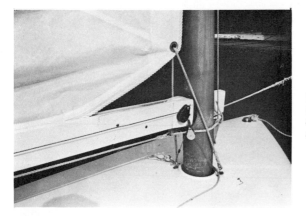

This is the simplest and best way of adjusting the luff tension. You can also see the wire from the clew outhaul control which is led to the cockpit by passing under the deck.

This shows a neat jib roller winch fitted under the foredeck on an International Fourteen.

Right top:
This shows a way of adjusting the tension on the leach of a genoa by using one or other or both of the clew rings.

Below:
This is a type of trapeze belt which is easy and quick to put on and which can be adjusted rapidly to fit anyone.

Right centre:
Here the traveller pipe has been curved so that the tension on the hauling part is evened out. The traveller is then free at all times to move out or in however hard the sail is sheeted in.

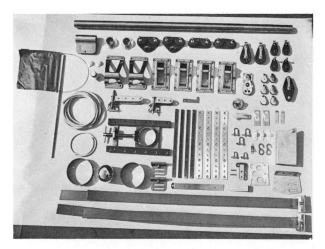

Right bottom:
This shows a complete set of fittings for a Finn. As you can see, the total cost is quite high and yet some types of boat have many more fittings than this.

KEELBOAT

TECHNIQUES

Going to Windward in Waves

Sailing to windward in waves is quite different from one class to another. As an example let us look at the difference between a 5·5-metre and a Dragon.

In a 5·5-metre you can pull in your mainsheet and thus tighten the mainsail leach very hard, and this also applies to the jib (see photo on page 122). You would find that if you tried to do the same thing in a Dragon the boat would completely stop. This is because a 5·5-metre has hull lines which are very sharp and veed and it is not stopped by the waves in the same way as a Dragon which is very flat under the bow. Dragons are very easily stopped by waves and have to be 'coaxed' along. A tight leach is the worst possible thing when a boat is trying to accelerate after having been stopped.

The crew weight in a 5·5-metre and a Dragon is approximately 220 kilos and it is not very difficult to see what a difference it could make to move a weight of 220 kilos from place to place in a boat. Therefore when it is really blowing hard you must try to have all three members of the crew outside the boat on the windward side. The Star, which is the lightest of the Olympic classes, would hardly move at all in these conditions if the crew were not lying out over the side.

World Champion in 5·5-metres in 1966. This shows the correct way of getting the crew weight outboard when sailing to windward in rough water. The helmsman has a perfect view of the sea and the wind and the sails. He is steering with a tiller extension.

Politikens Presse Foto

81

Beauvais-Nautisme

Steering the Boat through Waves

When steering through waves you must abandon your ideas on the old principle of letting the boat go the way it wants for fear of stopping the boat if you alter the helm. The mistake in allowing the boat to follow its own course is that part of the time the sails are at the wrong angle to the wind. I want to impress on everyone that it is, I believe, the most important rule to keep the sails at the most effective angle to the wind all the time. Therefore you must keep a firm hand on the tiller and concentrate on keeping the boat pointing so that the sails are at the same angle to the wind always. This is a main guiding rule but various types of wave conditions may modify this rule, and here

Gold Cup winner, 1966. Chok, Aage Birch, Denmark. The crew in this instance should be hanging further overboard.

you have to use your experience.

You can gain when going windward in big waves by watching to see where the sea is less rough. This is especially important in big waves which are short and steep. Let us take the example where you are steering absolutely straight and only taking notice of the wind direction. Your boat leaps up over a wave and crashes down into the face of the next big wave and is stopped completely by it. Let us assume that the waves are the same height on either side of your course so that whatever course you take you will hit the waves just as hard.

The technique is to luff slightly before you come to the first wave. In this way you will gain say one metre to windward but you will also slow down. You will then go over the first wave more slowly and over the second wave slowly without being stopped so badly. The result will be that you will pass the second wave at about the same speed as you would have done had you been steering straight but you will be one metre further to windward and so you will gain.

You can use the same technique in a short rough sea where the waves are nearly all the same height by pinching because the waves will not allow you to go fast. Sail at the maximum speed the waves will allow and if necessary pinch. But remember that I am not talking about sheeting your sails in harder when you follow this technique. Keep them exactly the same. In any case be careful in these conditions not to sheet the sails in too hard. One of the worst things that can happen in a strong wind is for your boat to start pitching and it will not stop. It starts this pitching motion if you do not take off the speed at the right time. If you have the chance bear away or luff in order to avoid the type of wave which starts you pitching. If you start pitching you can easily lose 10 boat-lengths whereas you might have borne away just before the offending waves appeared and, whilst avoiding the pitching, only lose one boat·length or so to leeward.

In these conditions it is very important for you to go out and practise on your own so that you become absolutely familiar with the sort of waves which will stop the boat and

the sort of waves which can be ignored. Only in this way can you improve and learn to sail automatically at the fastest speed during a race. When racing you may be afraid to free off because there are other boats near you but if you have confidence so that you know that to free off will be fastest in these waves then you must do so. If you had practised on your own you would have known instinctively whether you should have sailed free or carried on pointing high.

Going to Windward in Smooth Water

Going to windward in smooth water occurs in light winds or on small lakes or when the wind is blowing away from the shore. Here you have to adjust your sails so that they are not too full. Because there are no waves to stop the boat you will be able to point very high and this will be helped by setting the sails flatter.

You must continually adjust the genoa and mainsheet to follow the variations in wind strength. The worst thing that can happen is for you to tighten the mainsheet so that the leach becomes too tight and then the boat will seem to stop. Also remember you can tighten the leach of the genoa too much so

Because tiller extensions are not allowed in Dragons the helmsman cannot sit out properly nor lie out on the side. The crew are not much help when it comes to working out tactics since they have their heads down and cannot see well. Therefore the Dragon in the picture is being sailed in the best possible way considering the circumstances.

Beauvais-Nautisme

that it spoils the shape of the mainsail by its backwind. Therefore, when you want to adjust the sails you must alter both the mainsail and the headsail at the same time.

You also must find out the best position for the crew so that the boat is trimmed and can reach its best speed. Another often forgotten weight in the boat is the anchor. Do not forget also the angle of heel of the boat.

Sailing to Windward in Light Winds

You ought never to sit on the leeside when sailing to windward. You must always sit on the weather side as far outboard as possible so that you can see the waves and steer the correct course. If you sit on the leeside you are sailing like a blind man.

Here you can see what a good view the helmsman has of everything around him and also of the sails. You can also see here how loosely both his sails are sheeted and this paid off because he was able to keep up a very good speed and thus take advantage of any freeing of the wind by pointing up quickly.

Get your crew continually to adjust the two sails together. Try to learn to feel that the boat is going at its best speed rather than rely on the sails telling you. If you watch the sails all the time you will not enjoy yourself so much because the main pleasure in racing is the tactics. After you have learned how to handle the boat automatically by constant practice you will find that you will enjoy your sailing much more.

Sail Sheeting when going to Windward

The sheeting of the mainsail and foresail depends on the shape of the sails, the flexibility of the mast and the wind and wave conditions. The whole matter is a question of feel, but there are certain obvious things that you can correct, for example, if the headsail is spoiling the shape of the mainsail by excessive back-winding.

A question always being asked is where to have the mainsheet traveller in strong winds, but I say that you can only experiment by trying various positions and also different tensions for the mainsheet. The simple principle is that you have the traveller further out in harder winds. But you must adjust this principle in certain conditions. For example, if you are sailing a Dragon where you are allowed to have the mainsheet on the end of the boom or in the centre you can try to have your mainsheet at the end of the boom instead of the usual system and thus you can try setting your boom further inboard and hence with less tension on the mainsheet and via this on the leach also. This means that you can have the lowest part of your mainsail further away from the genoa without having the leach tight.

But my experience is that to obtain maximum speed your mainsail must not be too baggy along the boom if you are using this technique. Therefore if your mainsail is very baggy along the boom you would probably gain more by sheeting from the centre of the boom and in this way the boom will be a little further outboard and because of the extra tension on the sheet you will be able to bend the boom a little in the centre to reduce some of the bagginess. This has one further advantage, which is that as the wind varies in strength the end of the boom will automatically move outboard and inboard slightly.

When using this latter technique you may find you have to move your genoa fairlead further aft in order to free off the genoa leach more so that it is further away from the mainsail.

Another rule is that you should move the genoa fairlead further and further aft the

Below left:
In this Star the helmsman has positioned himself so that he has quite a good view of the waves ahead and he also has a good view for assessing the race tactics.

Below right:
This is the normal way of sailing a Star to windward in a fresh wind but the disadvantage is that you are not able to get a very good view of the course and the waves, and all the other things that you have to consider in order to decide on your course and your tactics.

This jib is exactly opposite in shape to the way it should be cut. It is too full in the higher part and it is too flat in the lower part.

This jib is made especially so that it can be sheeted vertically downwards. The leach is cut so that it is especially free and there is still plenty of flow in the foot.

harder the wind blows and never be afraid of pulling the foot of the genoa too hard as long as you do not also pull the leach too

In this case I would have moved the genoa fairlead further aft in order to obtain a freer leach, and then it would have been possible to have eased the mainsheet also.

tight. Remember that pulling the foot tight makes the middle of the genoa flatter. I would point out that this must only be considered as a temporary solution for a sail which is cut too full.

Sailing on a Reach

On this point of sailing you should never cleat your sheets but should always keep them in hand and continually adjust them so that they are at any moment exactly at the right angle to the wind. The helmsman should steer straight for the mark and not follow the wind changes. Instead, the crew should adjust the sails to variations in the wind direction.

On a close reach never try to hoist the spinnaker if you are not absolutely certain that you will gain. When you are not certain you can do so it will only be possible for you to gain a very small amount or even only keep the same position you have, whereas you might lose a great deal of distance if you have trouble in setting it or in keeping it drawing.

On a close reach you should set your traveller further outboard or as far outboard as it will go. You must also experiment with the tightness of your kicking strap or boom vang on a reach because you must realise that by having the kicking strap too hard you can tighten the leach so much that you lose flexibility in the rig and this will slow down your boat.

Off-wind Techniques in Keelboats

When the wind is strong enough and the waves are big enough for a keelboat to have the possibility of surfing you can never pull the kicking strap or boom vang too tight. The tighter you have your kicking strap the sooner you will be able to start surfing. When there is a possibility of surfing the boat must be perfectly balanced because if the boat is heeling a little too much it will not be possible to surf. In order to get the boat into balance so that it can start to surf, you must bear away exactly at the moment when the wave starts to lift your stern and push you forward. Once you have started surfing you can luff a little to keep on the face of the wave but never luff too much so that the boat loses its balance.

The best of the present international keelboats for surfing is the International Star, though we are not speaking of the new Tempest Class at the moment which is half way in between a keelboat proper and a dinghy. When you start to surf you must be very quick and pull in the main and jib sheets slightly in order to enable you to continue surfing. This is necessary because the increase in speed brings the apparent wind further forward. Equally, when you fall off the wave and the speed drops, you must remember to ease out the sheets again.

In most keelboats except the Stars you are only able to surf properly under spinnaker. The most difficult boat to keep surfing whilst close reaching is the 5·5-metre, therefore it is

I think that this boat should not be holding back on the face of this wave as it is in this picture. The boat is not heeled at all and the helmsman could easily luff up with the boat still in balance and pass more easily over the wave.

very important to choose the correct spinnaker for the prevailing wind strength and for the course which you have to sail.

If unfortunately you find that you have hoisted too big a spinnaker and you decide that you are going to keep it hoisted, then the only thing that you can do is to bear away in order to keep the boat in balance and so continue surfing. If the resulting course is too far away from the mark then you must lower your spinnaker and put up a smaller one so that you can point higher and still keep surfing. If, however, it is only a comparatively short distance to the next mark it might pay to keep sailing on the wrong course with the big spinnaker and then to lower it and to sail the rest of the way much higher with no spinnaker at all.

This picture shows exactly just about the limits of conditions when a 5·5-metre can carry the big spinnaker. US31 has chosen the right spinnaker and she is keeping it down tight and flat. And this is the only boat here which is in perfect balance.

When you are close reaching it often pays to carry the genoa as well as the spinnaker and in this picture you can see how much extra area you can obtain by carrying both the sails. When sailing under spinnaker one member of the crew should sit on the foredeck so that he can watch the spinnaker luff and make sure that it is trimmed precisely to keep the boat in balance.

Above:

S40 has chosen too large a spinnaker and this can be very dangerous. In these conditions you are likely to lose far more with too large a spinnaker than you would lose by having too small a spinnaker.

Below:

A short footed spinnaker has to be sheeted near the centre of the boat as if it was a jib. Look at US31's spinnaker sheets compared with those on the other boat.

Beauvais-Nautisme

Planing in a Star Boat

The Star is the only Olympic keelboat which really planes. The same rules apply for planing in a Star as for reaching in a normal keelboat. But in a Star, when the waves reach a certain height, it can be very dangerous to dive off the face of a wave into the back of the wave in front. But you can avoid doing this by moving the crew right aft until he is level with the tiller, but if this is not enough you have to be prepared to luff up and continue on your present wave and then try to find a hole to dive through amongst the waves ahead. If you have tuned your Star-boat rig so that the mast bends sideways at the top then you will find that planing will be much easier because the leach will be free and the tiller will be light.

This picture really shows well the correct teamwork in a Dragon. The helmsman is concentrating solely on keeping up the speed. One man is adjusting the sails, before he returns up on to the weather side, whilst the third man is hanging out to keep the boat balanced.

Changing Tacks in a Keelboat

When tacking in smooth water and light winds you have to make the manoeuvre as smooth as possible and so do not put your tiller over quickly. I mean that you must not put your tiller over firmly to the maximum position and hold it there until you get on to your new tack and then bring it equally firmly back again. You should gradually move your tiller over towards the maximum position and then gradually bring it back again so that at the moment when it becomes central again you are exactly on course on your new tack.

On smooth waters there is no need to ease your mainsheet when tacking. You should never ease your headsail sheet before the moment when the sail starts to come aback. On the other hand you should never have your jib actually aback. You should therefore ease the jib sheet at the moment when the sail begins to start coming aback. The reason why you should not ease your headsail before this point is that when you are luffing you get an increase in wind speed which helps to keep the boat speed up while you are tacking.

Remember, from the point of view of tactics, never turn your face away from the direction you are sailing. Never face aft when you are changing sides in the boat either when tacking or gybing. If you face aft it is the same as if you had closed your eyes for three seconds at one of the most critical moments in the race.

It is much more difficult to make a perfect tack when there are waves and the bigger the waves the more difficult it becomes. You should never start to luff to make your tack until you have gained maximum speed and you should also never luff when you can see

Here is a very good example of how important it is to train so that you are absolutely precise and accurate. 4969 has rounded the lee mark just inside 4593. 4969 is only one length past the mark but already the crew has almost finished sheeting in the jib and the boat is in the correct balance. 4593 is out of balance and will be overtaken in a few seconds.

Werner Goldbach

that your bow will hit a big wave whilst you are tacking. When tacking in waves you will also be stopped more than when tacking in smooth water and so, in order to be able to gather speed again after tacking, you must ease your mainsheet slightly and then haul it in again as you gather speed on your new tack.

It is the same with the headsail when tacking in waves. Never pull the headsail sheet in as tight as you would have it when you are travelling at maximum speed until you have actually gained this speed.

Especially in a rough sea I would like to repeat that you must face forward when you tack so that you can watch the waves and thus be able to calculate how fast you should turn so as to avoid hitting a wave head-on with your bow.

I would recommend that you go out alone and practise tacking so that you become more and more perfect at it and are able to point the boat on to the new course more

Below:
They were too slow. The spinnaker filled with wind before they could get it hoisted right up. The guy is correctly led through the ring in the end of the pole and back into the cockpit.
This could easily break the mast!

precisely each time. You will then lose as little distance as possible to leeward after each tack. By practising I mean that you should try tacking 30 to 50 times on one beat instead of perhaps 10 times. Practise also tacking when you really do not want to tack. This situation often occurs during a real race.

The headsail should never flap during tacking. The sheet should be home at the exact moment when the wind is able to fill it.

Hoisting and Lowering a Spinnaker

In light winds there are never any problems.

In strong winds on a reach you first fix one end of the spinnaker pole in the right place on the mast. You will have led the weather sheet (guy) through the eye on the end of the spinnaker pole and right back into the cockpit and have clipped it on to the spinnaker. The lee spinnaker sheet you pass round the forestay and clip on to the other corner of the spinnaker. You also now clip on the halyard. Then you simply hoist away but you must not let it fill until it is fully up. This is how we hoist a spinnaker on a 5·5-metre.

You clip the spinnaker bag on to the leeward shroud when you are hoisting the

spinnaker on a dead run and therefore it goes up on the lee side of the mainsail. Remember not to tighten the weather sheet (guy) until the spinnaker is completely hoisted up to the top otherwise it will fill with wind and it will then be quite impossible to get it fully hoisted. The man on the halyard has to be very quick and accurate.

The biggest problem in strong winds is to get the spinnaker down when on a close reach. The worst thing that can happen is shown in the picture below, left.

The best method is for the foredeck man to go up and unclip the guy. At the same moment the midship crewman in the cockpit hauls in the lee sheet as fast as he can. We have now arrived at the point where the luff is tight and the leach is flapping free down to leeward. It is only now that we can start easing off on the halyard and the crew gathers in the sail by the foot. This is the only safe way of doing this manoeuvre.

Gybing a Keelboat

When gybing under a spinnaker in light winds you first get hold of the lee sheet and then catch the lee corner of the spinnaker.

Then you unclip the spinnaker pole from the mast and clip it on to the lee spinnaker corner. So you then have both corners of the spinnaker connected by the spinnaker pole and the pole is still held by the uphaul and the downhaul to the mast. The helmsman now bears away until the boat is slightly by the lee, and then the crew gybes the mainboom as fast as possible not by hauling the mainsheet in via the blocks but by grabbing hold of all the parts of the mainsheet and heaving. If you have not got a central mainsheet then you must grab hold of the boom itself and pull it across.

At the moment that the boom is going across, the foredeck hand, who is standing on the foredeck with both hands round the pole, pushes the old lee-end of the spinnaker pole forward. Then he quickly pulls the whole spinnaker pole towards the windward side at right angles to the wind so that the spinnaker does not collapse.

After you are sure that the spinnaker will not collapse the crew unclips the new lee corner of the sail from the boom and clips that end of the boom to the mast. In that

Continued on page 96

This shows clearly how to set the spinnaker as one rounds the weather mark. The pole is already fixed in position and held by the uphaul and downhaul. The guy is led through the end of the pole. The spinnaker is hoisted in lee and must not be allowed to fill till right up. Then you quickly pull in the guy until the tack comes to the end of the pole.

Hashimoto

Hashimoto

You can learn a lot from these photographs from the Tokyo Olympics. A34 is preparing to gybe and the crew is on the foredeck ready to unhook the pole but there is no sign that the lee sheet has been caught hold of. In the lower picture the helmsman of US219 has got hold of the spinnaker sheet and is just about to gybe the mainboom. The foredeck hand is trying to clip the sheet to the boom but is too late. The genoa is not furled, which makes it difficult for the helmsman to see what is happening to the spinnaker.

Here KC101 is gybing much better. The foredeck hand has the pole unhooked from the mast just in time but he has also unclipped it from the sail and has still not connected it to the new tack at the moment of gybing. The sail has remained full of wind so far but he will be lucky to keep it full until the pole is connected, but by adjusting the sheets carefully the cockpit hand may be able to do so. The foredeck hand is in exactly the right attitude to pull the spinnaker across as explained in the text but he has nothing connected to his pole at all!

95

This is a very good example. The boat has gybed and is now on a close reach. You can see that the cockpit hand can easily keep the spinnaker drawing with the tack of the sail resting on the forestay. It is then easy for the foredeck hand to clip on the spinnaker pole.

Here is a case where the spinnaker is not drawing effectively on a close reach. This skipper ought to change to a smaller sail which should have the same curve on the luffs (i.e. the same 'ears') but which is shorter on the foot.

way the spinnaker should not collapse even though during this manoeuvre the mainsail is blanketing the spinnaker for a short period. This is because, by drawing the spinnaker from one side to the other forcibly by hand you are creating your own wind to keep the spinnaker full.

Gybing in very strong winds can be best accomplished by shifting the spinnaker pole before you gybe the mainsail. In order to do this you first grab hold of the lee spinnaker sheet and unhook the spinnaker pole on the mast. Then you clip on that end of the spinnaker pole to the lee corner of the spinnaker, unclip the windward corner of the spinnaker from the pole and then clip that end of the pole on to the mast.

The harder that it is blowing the further you should take the spinnaker over to the lee side behind the mainsail in order to be able to unhook it. And also in strong winds you must lead the sheet and guy further forward in the boat to avoid it lifting and yawing. At the moment that you clip on the spinnaker pole to the mast you should pull in the mainsheet enough so that you do not lose balance and then you should bear away immediately and continue pulling in the mainsheet until the boom slams across on its own.

When you bear away you must be absolutely certain that you go far enough so that you do not miss gybing the first time. You must also avoid gybing slowly because in this way you may lose speed and because of this the wind pressure on the sails will be greatly increased and you may be unable to gybe altogether. The moment that the sails fill on the new gybe you must bear away back again absolutely at once in order to keep the boat in balance and avoid broaching.

Gybing a 5·5-metre or other boats with big spinnakers when the new course will be a close reach under spinnaker, the helmsman

When you have to gybe from a close reach to another close reach under spinnaker it is very important that you free the tack of the spinnaker early in order to be able to gybe rapidly. The second boat has already freed the tack of his spinnaker and so he is absolutely sure to be able to gybe fast without stopping the boat. He also has a chance of gybing without collapsing the spinnaker at all. After this stage the whole thing depends on the handling of the spinnaker from the cockpit. The lee sheet should be eased so that the clew of the spinnaker can reach as far as the forestay and the weather sheet should be hauled aft enough so that the crew is sure the spinnaker will not collapse. In this way the crew on deck has enough time to clip on the spinnaker pole to the new windward corner and then on to the mast without losing anything.

must not luff from a broad reach or a dead run until the crew on the deck has got the pole fixed on to the mast.

Gybing a Star in very strong winds is the most exciting manoeuvre in sail-boat racing. In fact it is exactly the same technique as is used in planing dinghies which use a long boom.

The best method is to change over the whisker pole on the jib to the other side before gybing the mainsail. This is because, before gybing, it will be much quicker to get the whisker pole into position as there is then no wind pressure on the jib since it is behind the mainsail. You will lose less by shifting the jib over before gybing.

The best time to gybe is when you are going at maximum speed and you should never gybe when you are either accelerating or when the boat is ploughing into the back of a wave. Of course the best time to gybe is when the wind drops momentarily but you are almost never able to do this since you usually have to gybe when you are level with a mark. When you obtain maximum speed is at the moment when you are planing.

Just before you gybe the crew loosens the kicking strap a little and you pull the boom in until it is approximately 30 degrees from the centre line. You can easily do this when you are planing and still maintain balance because of the speed and also because you are bearing away in order to start gybing. Then you let the crew release the kicking strap

completely and at the same time you gybe before the speed drops. You have to bear away very quickly far enough so that you are absolutely certain that you will gybe first time because if you bear away too slowly the Star will stop absolutely and there is a very big chance that you will miss the gybe altogether. The helmsman grabs the boom with both hands and swings it across. When the boom crosses the centre line he frees the runner. The crew only concentrates on pulling back the new runner and hooking on the kicking strap again. You will find that you have retained your speed and then you will

This shows a system of arranging the spinnaker pole with a rigid topping lift, the end of which is fastened to the same slide as the pole. You do not need a down-haul and when you are not using the spinnaker the whole pole and topping lift slides down so that the pole lies flat on the deck. When you gybe the operation is exactly as normal and is described in the text, but the disadvantage with this system is that it is rather difficult to gybe smoothly keeping the spinnaker full of wind the whole time because the rigid topping lift controls the movement of the boom with too much restriction.

be able to bear away rapidly again on to your new course and the fact that the jib is already out fixed into its whisker pole will help you to get there.

Luffing Round Marks

When you luff round marks in light winds you gain in wind speed as you turn and therefore you must also gain in boat speed but the only way you can gain maximum acceleration is to draw in the mainsail and the headsail exactly together as you are rounding.

The main rule is that the man on the mainsheet controls the whole operation and draws in the mainsail at the right speed and the headsail sheet must then follow this exactly

and never backwind the mainsail during the manoeuvre. The worst thing that can happen is that the headsail comes in too quickly and this stops the bow from coming up into the wind. At the same time the helmsman tries to bring the bow back to the wind by putting the helm hard down and so the two together stop the boat. Therefore the helmsman has to push the helm hard down in order to continue bringing the boat up in the wind and this completely stops the boat.

Some Keelboat Fittings -

5·5-metre. We adjust the tension on the jib luff this way. Note also the roller for the spinnaker sheets.

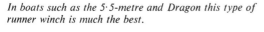

In boats such as the 5·5-metre and Dragon this type of runner winch is much the best.

There must be a tiller extension on a universal joint if the class rules will allow it.

Star boats. This is the special boom outhaul fitting. Note that the top sheave is in front of the clew.

5·5-metre. There is no tack-pin. The luff tension is adjusted this way. The wire is the clew outhaul.

This type of mainsheet cleat makes rounding marks child's play because it is so easy for the helmsman to haul in the mainsheet whilst the crew can concentrate on lowering the spinnaker and adjusting the jib.

Star boats. This is a close-up of the mainsheet system and shows how the traveller control wire is rigged.

Star boats. The runner slide can be released with a sharp blow on the lever. It automatically catches again when pulled aft to set up tension again. The lower shrouds can be adjusted instantly with the self-locking tackle so that the mast can be bent the right amount.

Stars have to have a rather special kicking strap because of the low boom. The fitting on the block slots into keyhole plates in the deck and the wire is tightened after fixing. Note also the way of tensioning the luff and the fact that the tack is fixed to a slide on the mast.

SAILS

DESIGN AND ADJUSTMENT

The shape of a sail for racing is a combination of the basic shape that is cut into the sail and the effect of the flexibility or otherwise of the mast and boom. The basic sail shape is also modified by a combination of the elasticity of the cloth, the tension of the luff and foot ropes and also the tension on the sheets.

The way I try to get the highest speed is to take the fastest boat at the present time in the class, and then to take another boat and try to change the mast and boom and rig and sails and hope to make it faster than the 'control' boat.

I am not going to talk about theory. I am going to advise you on the various things which you must experiment with, because there is one rule only and that is: Whatever is the fastest must be right and anything that is slow must be wrong.

Theory is not important at all. It does not interest us here. It really only concerns people who are working with new ideas. In this book we are only talking about existing classes and in these we are already so close to the potentially fastest speed that we are discussing only very very small differences and variations.

Because you can obtain today stiff or flexible cloth just as you want it, it is possible to reproduce any sail shape which you may care to design exactly. So the problem is to decide which shape is the fastest, and this shape will vary from class to class and from design to design.

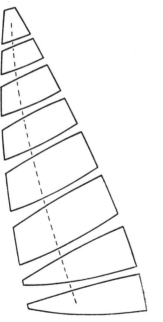

Opposite:

A jib cut in the fashion shown in the picture holds the shape flatter in strong winds than if it had been made in the normal manner. In this photograph you can see that the mainsail around the two lowest battens is too tight and is 'closing' too much.

How a Sail is Made

The drawing shows how the panels are curved in order to build in the shape in the finished sail. The cloth used for a sail designed like this has to be very stable. You cannot build in the shape by this method if you are using a very soft cloth because it will become far too baggy in only a little extra wind. From this drawing you can see how you can alter the curves on the seams so that you can make the sail fuller or flatter in any part of the sail that you wish. It is very easy to tell you this but I think that if you had to start at the beginning to try to decide exactly what curves to put on the edge of each seam in varying types of cloth it would take you a very long time. So I am only able to tell you the principles but nevertheless you will have a chance of being able to alter the sail you have.

The curve on the luff of the sail is intended to create flow which should stay near the mast and does so in the case of a stable cloth,

Continued on page **107**

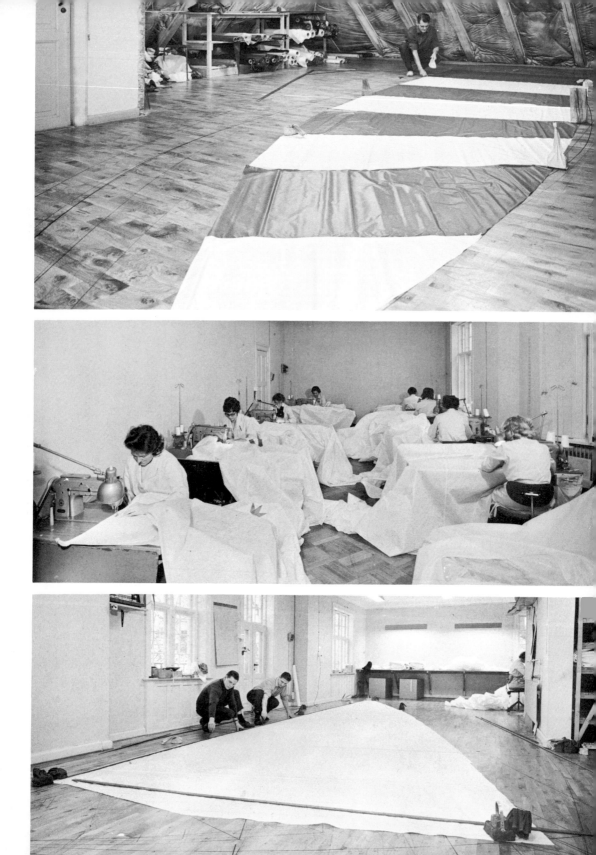

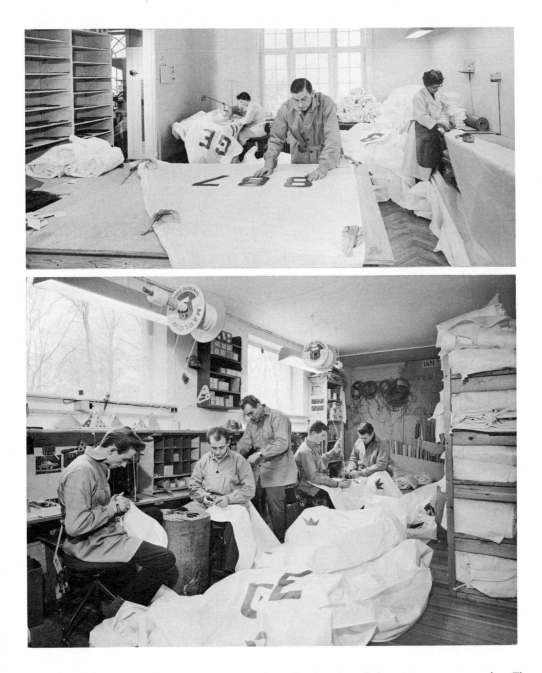

The story of making a sail. When making all types of sails the cloths are laid on the floor after the outline of the sail has been drawn on the floor. Depending on the shape and camber that the sail is to have each of the seams is tapered. One cloth is put on the floor and then a seam is tapered. The second cloth is put next to it and then that seam is tapered and so on until the end of the sail. After that all the seams are sewn together. The sail is then put back again on to the floor and the luff foot and leach curves are drawn on it. In the first picture is a spinnaker. Then the sail goes to be finished in the sewing shop. And after this the numbers are put on. This completes the machine work and then the sails come to the hand-work shop.

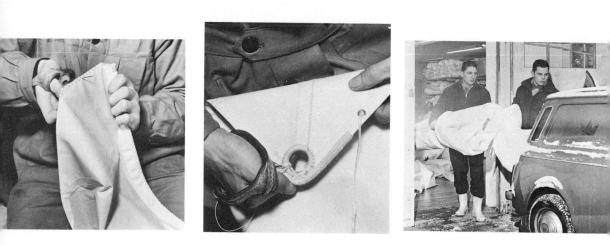

Above and below:

In the next picture you can see how the headboard is being sewn in by hand, and following that the clew ring is being sewn into a headsail. When the sails have been finished they are taken to the test rig to be hoisted and then they come back and are adjusted if necessary. When everything is perfect the sails are packed and stored.

Opposite:

By folding the sail in this way the creases will not be at right angles to the wind direction, and the sail will also last longer because the fibres will not become broken.

Continued from page **103**

and you can remove this flow by bending the mast. The curve on the foot of the sail behaves similarly. The more elastic the cloth the more the flow introduced by the curve on the luff moves aft in the sail. In the old days of cotton sails 100 per cent. of the sail shape was made by cutting the curve on the mast and boom correctly. And all the seams except the one which comes out at the tack were cut absolutely straight.

With cotton the material used was quite different. Some bolts shrunk more than others, and some of the panels shrunk or stretched quite differently to each other. So you could not tell before you made the sail whether it would be too long or too short on the leach or whether the cross measurement would be small enough so that it would still be the right length after the owner had used the sail for a while. Therefore at that time it appeared that every sailmaker had put into every yachtsman's head the idea that if there was anything wrong with the sail later on it was because of the way the yachtsman had stretched it. But I made cotton sails for many years and I never had a problem with any of my customers being able to spoil a cotton sail which had been made correctly in the first place. So without saying anything against sail-makers today, because no one makes cotton sails any more, I can say that it was probably a bad excuse for making a bad sail, either with wrong measurements or with unsuitable cloth.

With cotton sails the tension on the luff and the foot ropes and the luff and foot curves and the type of cloth used were what made the final sail shape together with correctly estimated pre-stretched measurements.

Mainsails

Let us start with the mainsail and let us first talk about sails for light winds. There we find that the amount of flow in a sail should be approximately as shown by the line 'b' in the drawing, all over. This means that it should be a similar curve near the boom and also at the top of the sail.

But we have found that in very light winds it is difficult to see if the sail is set at exactly the right angle to the wind if the cloth is stiff. Therefore if we make the sail in a cloth in which it is easy to see where the wind pressure is, it means that we have to use a soft cloth in these light winds.

Supposing we continue using this sail and the wind increases. This is where the problems begin. To start with the boat begins to heel and this results in an increase in weather helm. To avoid this weather helm it is more important to free off the leach of the sail than to move the mast, which is a subject we will return to later on. But it is only necessary to free off the leach in the shaded area marked 'X' which is the part furthest away from the centre of effort of the sail. If the cloth is too soft, however, as the wind increases the sail will get too baggy in the middle and this will 'tighten' the leach.

If the sail, like in the Star or the International Fourteen, has a very large roach area, you will find that with a flexible cloth the leach will fall away to leeward as is shown by the pecked line on section 'b' in the drawing, and you will have no control over it at all. In other words the leach will free off too much, or will be too 'slack'.

At section 'c' in the drawing we have to find a combination where the shape will be effective enough in light winds and yet flat enough so that additional weather helm is avoided when the wind increases. So already you will see that we have to make com-

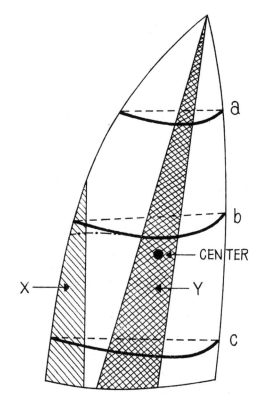

promises and use a cloth which is stable enough for medium to strong winds and soft enough so that you can see the wind acting on it in light winds. For example I can think of some types of cloth which are like metal foil on which you are quite unable to detect any wind pressures in the lighter winds.

When the wind increases so that the sail becomes more baggy in the centre part, you can move this deepness forward by stretching the luff of the sail. However, the sail may then be too full in the forward part so that it starts lifting too early and you can then remove some of this by bending the mast. You can control the amount you take out by controlling the bend in the mast if the rig is arranged so that you can accomplish this.

You can also make the sail flatter in the central chord area, shaded 'Y' in the drawing, by stretching more on the foot rope. This means that the whole of the curve of the sections is made less deep, but this is the only change that this adjustment makes. This stretching of the foot rope makes a small change in sections around 'a' and much bigger changes in sections around 'c'.

Let us consider a rig which is so stiff that you cannot adjust the bend in the mast at all – for example, in a masthead rig in ocean racers. Here you have to compromise and use a very stable cloth because then with this type of material the increase in deepness of the sail as the wind increases will be at a minimum. Therefore you also reduce the need to have further adjustments, such as mast bending, to a minimum. But this means that you will have to change the sails when, for example, your light wind sail becomes, nevertheless, too deep in the middle as the wind increases. However, with a masthead rig, if the cloth is well stabilised, you will probably get away without having to do too much sail changing because, in my experience, the right sail shape for light winds and smooth water is not far off the same that one would use in stronger winds and a bigger sea. You need a sail with the deepest built-in flow, in my experience, when you have medium winds and a short sea. This is because, in a short sea, the boat is being continually stopped and is slower than when sailing in a longer sea. Because the boat is travelling more slowly you need more acceleration and cannot point so high and thus a baggier sail will be fastest. A very stable cloth will hold the shape cut into the sail quite well from very light to fairly fresh winds without the need to bend the mast. But, of course, if you did not have to use a masthead rig and thus be compelled to have a stiff mast, you could use a

The main reason for the crease in this mainsail is that the cloth is too soft.

much more powerful mainsail in some conditions and flatten it when needed.

So now you will begin to realise that sails must be made according to the capabilities of mast tuning on the particular boat you are using. Therefore a boat with a mast which can take away all the flow you need to take away near the mast can use a softer cloth than a boat with a stiffer mast. As I said before, a soft cloth becomes baggier more quickly as the wind increases.

A sail made of soft cloth could be blown out by the wind until it reaches a shape where you will find it is extremely fast for that wind and sea combination. It has stretched to the perfect shape for the prevailing conditions.

If the wind increases or decreases, or the sea changes, the sail will become slower than the optimum because it will become too baggy or too flat. Therefore it can be too unsatisfactory for racing purposes to use too soft a cloth. Remember what happened with the old cotton sails which were comparable with very elastic nylon cloth for example.

Instead of making a sail out of soft cloth which might stretch to its optimum shape in a wind speed of say 4 metres per second (8 knots), it is better to use a more stable cloth and to build in the shape which the first sail would have attained at 4 metres per second so that it retains this shape when the wind drops. And the same stable cloth will keep that optimum shape fairly well as the wind increases also. And yet when the wind increases so much that this shape is too full for maximum speed you can more easily take away the extra flow from a sail made in stable cloth, by stretching on the luff, than from one made in soft cloth. And still again you can take away the extra flow which appears along the luff by bending the mast.

As far as the best combination between sail cloth, shape, and mast and boom stiffness goes I can only tell you approximately what

Compared to sails made with the normal cross-cut cloths the fan-cut sail has no elasticity from the clew to any point on the mast and particularly to the centre of the mast. Thus this sail is very good with a stiff mast but is quite useless with a flexible mast.

is best. I can never tell you exactly the fastest combination. No one can tell you. What I want to do in this book is to tell you the various ways you can experiment with your rig to obtain the fastest combination for yourself.

Genoas and Foresails

In the case of a genoa it is even more important to use a stable cloth because you have no mast which can be used to control the extra flow. In fact, on the contrary, the harder the wind blows, the more flow you get in the headsail because the forestay sags. And also, the straighter you can keep your forestay, the bigger will be the area of your headsail. In the case of classes where you always have trouble with excessive backwinding of the mainsail, the only possible thing you can do is to keep your forestay as

straight as you can so that the line 'A' on the drawing is as near as possible to the pecked line. In this way you will get least backwind in the mainsail.

The principle of building shape into a headsail is exactly the same as for a mainsail, but adjusting the shape in a headsail is quite different. By stretching the luff you can draw the flow forward but you cannot take excessive flow near the luff away because you cannot curve the forestay as you can a mast.

If you find that the headsail is giving too

much backwind to the mainsail, and let us assume that the mainsail is set perfectly, then the reason can be firstly the sagging of the forestay, or maybe it is because the whole foresail has been made with the flow too far aft and the leach is thus too tight. Or possibly the leach is being kept too tight by sheeting the headsail too far forward.

As the wind increases the general rule is that you should sheet your headsail further and further aft. This has the effect of keeping some flow in the lower part of the headsail but mainly frees the leach in the upper part. This has the same effect as has bending the top of the mast aft on the mainsail, and also bending the end of the boom outwards and upwards.

This is a general rule which applies to most headsails which are made today but it is not the fastest combination. The fastest headsail is one which is built in such a way that you can sheet it farther forward in order to keep maximum flow in the foot and yet without tightening the leach so much that it disturbs the mainsail. The most important thing for the correct headsail design is to keep it full in the lower part which is the most effective part of its total area.

If the headsail is fluttering on the leach the reason can be that the cloth is too unstable or that the whole foresail has been made too flat. A headsail that flutters shakes the whole rig and I have found that the boat is then slowed down.

Since it is impossible to alter the shape of a headsail to any great extent as we have discussed, you will certainly have to change headsails in various wind conditions. You cannot have one headsail for all windspeeds.

In my experience, the deepest part of the curve of a headsail should be a little forward of the position of the centre of area. In the drawing on the next page the deepest part of the camber would be somewhere along the line marked 'a'. If the curve of the section of the sail is made so that it is too hollow near the luff you will find that you are not able to point so high and this extra area near the luff is wasted. This is shown by the pecked line 'b' on the upper drawing. If the sail has a tight or 'closed' leach as is shown by the pecked line 'c' it is just the same as moving the point of maximum flow aft and in my experience this just does not work.

If a headsail is very baggy it almost never flaps on the leach. Therefore the only way to stop this fluttering is to make it so that there is a slight hook on the leach as is shown at 'a' in the upper drawing. When you make a jib you must use a cloth stable enough so that it will just stop the flapping on the leach.

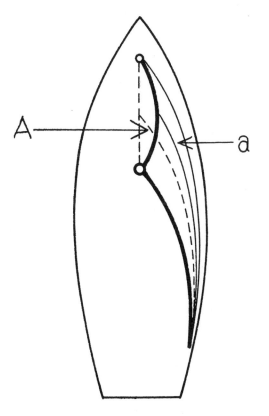

Beauvais-Nautisme

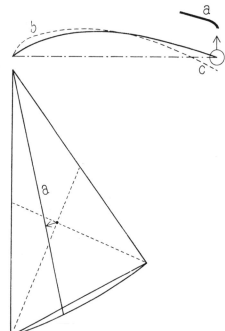

Here is a very good example which shows how flat the jib is at the bottom and how full it is in the area level with the lower batten. In my opinion the sail should be as full at the bottom as it is at the level of the lower batten.

Left:
The text on the previous page refers.

Spinnakers

The shape is put into spinnakers just like the mainsail by cutting curves on to every seam. There are certain classes like the Dragon that forbid the tapering of seams and the shape has to be introduced by curving the mitre seam only. In most classes the rules merely limit the lengths of the luffs and the maximum and minimum widths of the sail. In these classes the question is what is the most effective shape for the spinnaker.

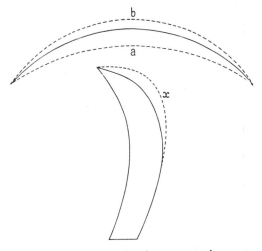

The upper drawing shows an effective cross sectional shape for the spinnaker. If you make a spinnaker too flat, in other words approximately as shown by the pecked line 'a' in the drawing, you will find that it is extremely fast on reaching but slower than the solid line on a dead run. You might think that if you made a spinnaker to the same rules flatter then the projected area presented to the wind would be greater but this is not so because, in order to make the 'ears' of the spinnaker stand, you have to curl the edges and this makes the ears slightly narrower. If you make the spinnaker baggier than the solid line then the projected area presented to the wind will be smaller. This baggy sail will not be any faster on a run and will be much slower on a reach.

Cutting a spinnaker looked at sideways as on the pecked line marked 'x' on the lower drawing is a big disadvantage on a reach but it also does not give you any extra speed on a run. The biggest disadvantage is on a close reach and the baggier it is the slower it becomes. There is no disadvantage to this shape on a dead run except in light airs when the 'uplifted' spinnaker will collapse earlier. This is because it will have the same projected area as a similar spinnaker without the 'uplift' but it will be heavier. Thus a greater wind pressure will be needed to keep the baggy spinnaker filled.

Where the class rules do not permit you to carry a genoa, such as in the 5·5-metre class, you have to use the spinnaker much more in order to take the place of a genoa. So in these classes you have to make a spinnaker which you are able to carry on a very close reach. This type of spinnaker has to be very narrow in the foot and with big ears but not too full so that it will remain filled when close reaching. At the same time you should make the sail out of very stable cloth so that you can use it in strong winds. If the spinnaker is too baggy you cannot adjust it to sail close to the wind.

The spinnaker shown by the solid line, if set at the sort of angle to the wind shown in the drawing, would collapse. If it had been made as in the pecked line then it would fill and stand on this point of sailing. The flatter spinnaker will also enable the air to be released out from the leach freely and the tiller pressure will be light.

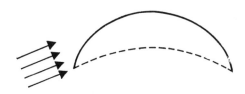

Aho & Vuorenjuuri

Opposite:

In the 5·5-metre class there are only three measurements for the medium sized spinnaker and these are the lengths of the luffs and the foot. In these two pictures it is easy to see how much bigger is spinnaker No. 36 than the other two across the width. This spinnaker will be a big advantage on a dead run and a broad reach but could be a disadvantage on a closer reach. Here you can easily see how the cloths are tapered in order to introduce the shape.

Above:

Here a spinnaker is tested on a special rig on a platform at the end of the harbour.

The Sheeting of Sails – Mainsails

The tension on the mainsheet varies in different wind strengths and also with different sails. The main rule is that you should try yourself to find out how your own boat goes best and the only thing I can do is to point out to you the various adjustments that you can try and their probable effect.

Let us take the sheeting of the mainsail first. In smooth water and light winds you are able to point very high by setting the mainsheet traveller, or any other system which you may be using, nearer to the centre of the boat. And the flatter the mainsail is, the nearer to the centre line can you sheet the boom. On the other hand, the fuller the mainsail is the further outboard the boom should be sheeted to avoid the wind being thrown off the leach to windward. This happens

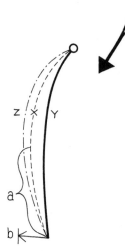

to the wind. So you can see that there is a perfect sail shape and a perfect sheeting position for every wind speed, but if your sail is not perfect you can improve your speed made good to windward by small adjustments to the sheeting.

This discussion is to help you to decide what to do with the sail you actually have with you. It may not necessarily be the best sail for the conditions. You may find that sail 'Z' will give you a higher speed if you free off when sailing to windward and it may pay to do this rather than try to point as high as sail 'X'. You may lose less in fact. Because sail 'Z' is fuller it may be faster reaching and thus you could gain back your loss and more.

The next drawing shows a boat. It would be unwise to sheet the sail so that the end of the boom came inside the pecked straight line since the leach would then begin to throw the escaping air to windward of the boat's course. If the sail is even baggier, as shown by the pecked curved line, then you can see that the wind will be thrown even more to windward and the boat will just be pulled mostly sideways and will slow down.

especially if the sail is very full near the boom.

In the drawing, the part of the sail marked 'a' on the pecked line of the full sail 'X' will catch the wind and throw it up to windward. Therefore this sail will have to be sheeted further outboard to the point 'b' so that the wind can leave it freely. In this case, if the sail 'X' is sheeted out to the point 'b' you will be able to point nearly as high as if you were using sail 'Y' but you will have a much higher speed because sail 'Y' is too flat for a light wind. Highest boat speed is the most important thing in light winds when the boats are not reaching their designed maximums. There can be very big differences in boat speed from very small adjustments in the sail sheeting, resulting also in only small differences in pointing.

If you have an even baggier mainsail as shown by 'Z' you have to sheet it even further outboard than sail 'X'. But even so you may not be able to increase speed enough to compensate if we assume that sail 'X' is the perfect shape for that wind speed. With sail 'Z' you can do two things. Either you can point as high as with 'X' and travel more slowly or free off and maybe only reach the same speed as 'X' can attain at a closer angle

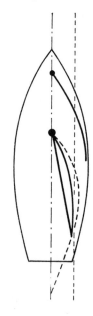

So far we have only been talking of the angle of the boom to the centreline of the boat. If you have to pull your mainsheet very tight in order to get the boom close enough inboard, for example if the distance between the traveller and the boom is too great, or if the position of the traveller on the boat is too far out to the lee side, you will tighten or 'close' or 'harden' the leach over its whole length which in my opinion is very bad in all conditions. My experience is that if you put too much tension on the leach the boat will be slowed in all kinds of winds. This is just a fact and do not ask me why it happens.

Therefore, the closer that you can get the traveller to the boom the greater the range of adjustment you will have. As the wind increases, the main rule is that you should sheet the boom further outboard. The same

In this picture the mainsail is not too tight on the leach. The batten has nearly the same direction as the centreline of the boat. However, the leach of the genoa should also be parallel to the centreline of the boat but this one is much too flat in the lower part.

thing goes in a strong wind as in a light wind but a flat sail can be sheeted further inboard than a baggy sail.

A useful point to remember in some conditions is that the looser you have your mainsheet the freer and looser will be the leach of the sail. Therefore in a strong wind if you sheet the traveller towards the centre of the boat and keep the sheets slack you will stop the lower part of the sail being backwinded by the genoa and in this way you will give the air coming off the leach of the genoa a freer passage. And you can do this without tightening the leach of the mainsail. You can also see this technique in some of the pictures.

Therefore, another general rule stemming from this is that the smaller the headsail is in area the farther outboard you can sheet the mainsail.

The reason for freeing off the leach of a sail in very strong winds is twofold. Firstly it is to ease the weather helm and secondly it is really the most effective way of reefing because it is this upper and leach area which you do not need when going to windward in strong winds. When you free off the leach completely only the shaded area marked 'X' is being used effectively. But it is very important that you do not make the shaded area too flat and ineffective.

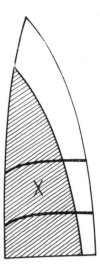

The Sheeting of Sails—Headsails

The main rule is the same as for mainsails, i.e. sheet inboard or outboard depending on the amount of flow built into the sail and the wind strength.

If you find that a headsail is too baggy for the wind conditions you can improve matters by sheeting it as far outboard as possible and move the fairlead aft. By pulling the foot of the sail tight in this way you can take a lot of the flow out of a sail without tightening the leach. A tight leach on a headsail is the worst possible thing for speed.

Another effect of moving the fairlead out and aft is that the wider gap between the headsail and the mainsail allows a greater volume of air to pass. If there is backwinding in the mainsail it means that the mainsail is stopping the genoa from passing the wind aft freely. The headsail sheeted as in the pecked line 'b' in the drawing will give a great deal of backwind to the mainsail but if the sheeting position is moved outboard and the headsail takes up shape 'a' this will give very little backwind. You will find that you are never able to get rid of all the backwind in

the mainsail because the rig is always a compromise between having a mainsail which is baggy enough to drive the boat on all points of sailing and being able to sheet the headsail close enough to be able to point high.

If the mainsail is lifting but you can see that the air is still passing smoothly then this is alright but if it is lifting and shaking it means that the air is turbulent and is not leaving the genoa freely. In this case, even in light winds, you must bend the mast to take away some of the flow in the mainsail. This will leave a wider passage for the air to leave the genoa. You can accomplish the mast bending in the manner we discuss in the section on mast tuning, by pushing the mast forward at the deck or by pulling it aft at the heel.

If you are unable to move the jib fairlead forward or aft, in an emergency you can move the whole jib on its stay upwards or downwards, which will have nearly the same effect. Or if you are unable even to do this you can make the leach freer by raking the mast more aft.

The Sheeting of Sails—Reaching

Here the kicking strap or boom vang comes into the picture and this is a very important piece of equipment, even in a keelboat.

You have to experiment with the amount of tension which you apply because if you pull your boom vang too tight perhaps the extra power brought into play from the top of the sail could cause the boat to heel too much. This in turn could cause excessive weather helm.

From a broad reach to a dead run you can never pull the kicking strap or boom vang too hard. The flatter you can get the sail the more projected area there will be and the faster you will go.

On a close reach in a keelboat, however, you can pull the boom vang too tight and lose the flexibility of the rig. You will then find that the rig is unable to absorb and smooth out the sudden shocks caused by gusts of wind and by the boat slamming into waves. This will have the effect of slowing you down.

This sail is sheeted correctly for these conditions and you can see that the lower batten is parallel to the centreline of the boat.

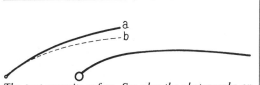

The text opposite refers. See also the photographs on pages 86 and 117.

The Sheeting of Sails – Spinnakers

On a run or a broad reach the main principle of sheeting a spinnaker is to obtain the greatest possible projected area. But when you come more nearly on to a beam reach you have to try to make the spinnaker flatter and to point the luff of the sail as close as possible to the wind. You have to think of it as if it was a big genoa.

On a beam or a close reach the spinnaker must be sheeted to a point as far aft as possible on the hull in order to get the leach as far to leeward as possible. In classes where the spinnaker shape is free you can make a spinnaker so narrow that you have to move the fairlead forward and sheet it like a genoa. If we have a very flat spinnaker and we want to point even higher there comes a stage when you cannot sheet the spinnaker in any tighter otherwise it will backwind the mainsail so much that the boat will stop.

Instead we can pull the spinnaker pole to windward approximately to a position similar to that marked 'a' in the drawing on the next page and in this way we can get a closer angle to the wind. The way this works is as follows— we take the whole spinnaker bodily closer to

119

the mainsail but at the same angle and then you can sheet the spinnaker home slightly more. This has the effect of flattening the whole spinnaker slightly at the same angle to the wind but because it is flatter you can point slightly higher without it collapsing.

Eventually there comes a point where you cannot get it any closer than a normal headsail but there are one or two other things that you can do to make a spinnaker even flatter. If you let the halyard down a few inches the spinnaker will move forward and to leeward slightly and this will have the effect of increasing the gap between it and the mainsail in the upper part. The other main way of altering spinnaker shape is by moving the pole up or down.

If the pole is too low then the luff has too much tension on it and this pulls the flow forward towards the luff. It is just the same effect as tensioning the luff of a mainsail. If the flow moves forward the sail cannot be pointed so high and the luff will curl in and the sail will collapse.

If you move the pole up, the luff will flatten out more and more and drop away to leeward enabling you to point higher. Eventually you reach a point where the curve built into the cloth cannot support the luff

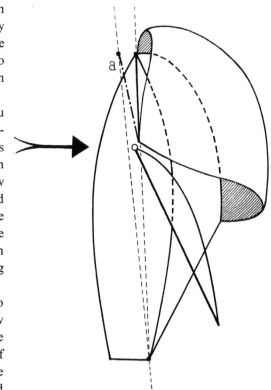

any longer and it will collapse outwards. It is very important to get the height of the pole adjusted correctly.

A useful guide to remember after you have rounded the weather mark and are trying to decide whether to hoist the spinnaker or not, is to look at the racing flag. If the apparent wind direction as shown by the flag is forward of the beam it is usually not worth trying to set a spinnaker though, once set, it is often possible by careful adjustment to sail closer than this in many classes. Single luffed, non-reversible sails of course behave in exactly the same way as a full, light genoa.

No. 174's spinnaker is made of dacron. This keeps the spinnaker flat even in strong winds. Therefore No. 174 can carry his spinnaker pole lower than he could have done had he been using a nylon spinnaker. The result in these conditions will be a more effective sail than one made in nylon. The Dragon No. 172 has a normal nylon spinnaker.

Flexible Dinghy Spars

The flexible mast must have a sail approximately shaped like a bird's wing, whereas the stiff mast must have a sail with a more even curve in order to make the dinghy go at its maximum speed.

The shape of the sail is of much greater importance than the positioning or rake of the mast. The shape of the sails has more effect on the helm balance than does the repositioning of the mast.

If, for example, the mainsail has a very hard leach, then the dinghy will carry a great deal of weather helm as the wind increases, and to prevent this you must move the mast nine inches further forward, but the weather helm can also be corrected with a new sail, which has not got a hard leach, instead of moving the mast.

In dinghies which use a flexible unstayed rig the top of the mast will come aft about three feet when going to windward, which will move the sail centre aft also, but the dinghy will not carry additional weather helm as you might think. The reason is that the bending of the mast alters the shape of the sail so that the leach is freed and this shows the relationship between sail and mast.

This relationship is one which you must really bear in mind. It is no good getting a fine new mast and then an expensive sail from a sailmaker because you are not sure that the mast and the sail will work together.

The mast on a Finn dinghy can be made as stiff or as flexible as you like. Personally

I prefer a mast which is flexible fore and aft, and stiff sideways, as this will give you good speed as well as enabling you to point high.

Supposing we have found in our experiments that the sail is too full for hard winds, this can be corrected in three ways. One, by making the sail out of a stiffer cloth; two, by cutting the sail flatter; three, by making the mast more flexible. If you think that the stiffer cloth will make sailing in light winds too difficult because it will not react quickly enough, then you must decide whether you should make the mast more flexible or the sail flatter. If you cannot make the sail any flatter because of its performance in light winds, then you must make the mast more flexible by planing timber off it on the front and back only. If, on the other hand, the sail is too flat in medium winds, then you must discover if the mast is too flexible, the cloth is too stiff, or the sail is cut too flat. If you are unable to point close enough when beating to windward do not forget that the boom could be too flexible.

In the Flying Dutchman, Five-O-Five and Snipe Classes aluminium masts are allowed. It has been found that the bending you can obtain from these masts coupled with a suitable sail can produce the fastest speeds. These masts should be fitted with diamond rigging

The flexibility of my Finn mast. For this Finn mast I have made a sail with cloth of a flexibility which matches that of the mast. When the mast bends under different wind conditions, the sail will be neither too flat nor too full. The mast is much stiffer sideways than fore-and-aft.

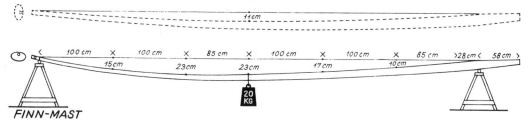

FINN-MAST

121

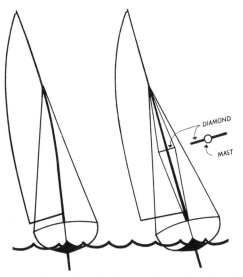

By using diamond rigging it is possible to straighten the mast completely and by adjusting the tension you have the possibility of being able to make the mast exactly suit the boat for gaining maximum speed. The ideal amount of mast bend depends on the type of boat and the shape of the sail. Diamond rigging is an advantage on a Snipe, Hornet, Five-O-Five and Flying Dutchman.

so that they can bend fore and aft and a controlled amount sideways.

If you have new sails you must make sure that they fit the mast, and also the weight of the crew, and for this you must use the experience which you have gained concerning this particular class.

The Finn and the O.K. Dinghy are very similar in their requirements for mast and sail. The lighter the helmsman the more flexible should be the mast so that the sail can flatten out in hard winds and free the wind better. The mast should be planed enough so that the leach of the sail is almost completely loose in the hardest puffs. A heavy man can use a stiffer mast, because he has more weight to counteract the pressure of the wind.

Below
Here is an example to show you how flat you can pull the sheets in a 5·5-metre and therefore how high it can point to the wind. This is only possible because of the very sharp hull shape.

Jibs

A good jib should be very full in the lower part and flatter higher up, but not too flat. I have always felt that it is really the jib which starts to get the boat moving again after tacking or after the boat has been stopped dead by hitting a wave. However, the jib must not be so full that you are unable to point close when going to windward.

Setting Mainsails

In order to be able to set a sail correctly you need, first and foremost, experience. In light weather you must not pull the sail out any farther than the point where the wrinkles just disappear, as you need to have the sail as full as possible. Take care not to stretch it too much. It is not correct, as many people do, to set the sail on the boom first, and then to hoist it on the mast.

No, hoist the sail first and then stretch it on the boom so that you can see how tight to make it. If the sail is stretched too much, a fold will appear along the mast and the boom, and this will pull the fullness away from the middle of the sail. In hard winds the sail would be able to blow out into a fair curve, but this will not happen in light winds.

Most sails are not affected by water but this is nullified by the presence of salt and therefore even synthetic sails must be washed in fresh water in order to bring back their water resistance. Do not be afraid to use soap on your synthetic sails. Do not let the sail remain damp in the sail bag for more than one week, or it will start to grow mildew, which will discolour the sail; whether this spoils the cloth we do not know.

Sail Battens

Sail battens function only to stiffen the cloth at the leach and to hold it steady. Sail battens must be light and stiff except that the top battens on a Flying Dutchman and Five-O-Five, and the long battens on a Hornet, must be thinner and more elastic the nearer they get to the mast. Wood is the stiffest and lightest material available. Plastic is too heavy and lifeless. If the sail battens are too heavy then the leach will shake in hard winds when going about and in light winds the roach may fall off.

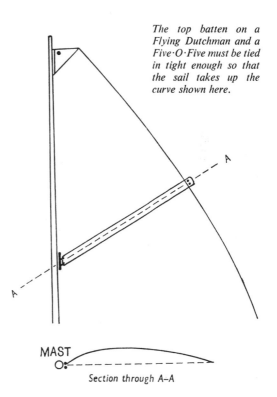

The top batten on a Flying Dutchman and a Five·O·Five must be tied in tight enough so that the sail takes up the curve shown here.

MAST

Section through A–A

TUNING THE RIG

Types of Rig

This shows a normal type of dinghy mast stayed with various types of spreader arrangements at position 'A'. The top of the mast in most classes is free to bend on its own but some classes such as the International 14-ft. have jumper stays to control the bend. The most important thing is to limit the bend in the lower part of the mast so that it does not become too great. This is done by means chiefly of the spreader arrangements, and their position, 'A', must be arranged so that the distance 'a' is shorter than the distance 'b'. You must arrange the position to suit your own rig and it will depend on whether your mast is deck-stepped or keel-stepped. In the latter case you can control the bend a great deal by chocking the mast at the deck. If you cannot do this for some reason in a keel-stepped mast then 'a' must be measured from the heel of the mast and still be shorter than the distance 'b'.

Sketch No. 1 shows the most normal type of spreaders which are held firmly at the stays and can either be fixed or swinging at the mast. The biggest disadvantage of this type of staying is that in order to adjust the rig you have to take the spreaders off and either make them shorter or put in longer ones. If you want to alter the angle in the horizontal plane you either have to change the holes in the root fitting or you can bend the spreaders.

Then in sketch No. 2 you have the normal diamond staying system. You can control the sideways bend of the mast very easily by means of adjustments on the ends of the wires near the heel. In a bendy mast the actual diamond spreaders must be made strongly of stainless steel, otherwise when the mast is at full bend they may collapse. In sketch No. 1 the spreaders can be made of aluminium if they are of the swinging type. If they are fixed they must be of stainless steel.

The more flexible the mast the more necessary it is to have a jumper strut as in sketch No. 3. This allows you to control the mast very accurately to match the sail you

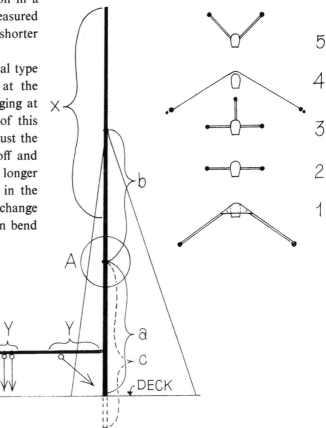

are using. In sketch No. 4 the control consists simply of wires leading from the shrouds to the mast. This system works in exactly the same way as for swinging spreaders when beating to windward with the added advantage that you can control the amount of bend by leading the wires through a little block on the mast and down to near the deck where you can adjust them. But when reaching this system does not help at all to push the middle of the mast forward. The stiff spreader in sketch No. 1 will push the mast forward and thus stops the top of the mast going forward and the middle back, a frequent cause of collapse of the rig when carrying a spinnaker in strong winds.

Sketch No. 5 shows the normal jumper struts. The disadvantage of this sytem is that you cannot control the forward bend and the sideways bend independently. It works on both at the same time. The only way you can adjust flexibility with this system is by making the fittings at the mast end adjustable so that you can alter the spreaders to a greater or smaller angle. This is the easiest system for controlling the bend at the top of the mast but it should not normally be necessary unless you have a mainsail with a very large roach on the leach. It might then be necessary to control the mast bend to avoid freeing the leach off too much.

You can adjust the flexibility of a wooden mast very easily by glueing on strips of wood or planing strips off as long as the class rules allow it. The situation is more difficult with a metal mast but it can be made softer very easily in the fore and aft direction by cutting slots in the luff track. But if you want to make a metal mast more flexible only do this over the distance marked 'X'.

As the wind speed increases nearly all dinghies carry increasing weather helm. You can feel this especially in strong puffs when the boat heels. Therefore it is very important that the boom is rigged in such a way that it can help to ease off the leach of the mainsail when the wind increases and this is accomplished by controlled bending. You can cut slots in the bolt rope groove of a metal boom, to increase the flexibility, in the same way that you can with the mast. But I would recommend that it is only done aft of the central sheet position. Of course if it is still too stiff you can cut some slots in front of the central main sheet but leave the areas marked 'Y' untouched and also be careful not to weaken the area round the kicking strap anchorage.

If you want to increase the sideways flexibility of a metal boom you can cut a long slot in the underneath side of the boom the whole way to the outer end. This slot must pass right through to the end of the boom because the two sides must be free to move slightly over each other. You can also use this same operation for increasing the sideways flexibility of the top of the mast.

It is very important to be able to chock the mast firmly at the deck because otherwise a very tight kicking strap could buckle or break the mast on a very broad reach in strong winds. And remember that a very tight kicking strap is essential for top speed when planing.

It is also important to have the mast as light as possible. The centre of gravity of an average dinghy mast is about 10 feet above the deck and if you imagine putting extra pounds up in that position when the boat is pitching and slamming into waves you can feel the effect of this will be to make the bows feel heavy and thus the boat will not have 'life'.

On a keelboat the tighter you can have the forestay the bigger you can make the genoa for that boat. The drawings show the rig of a

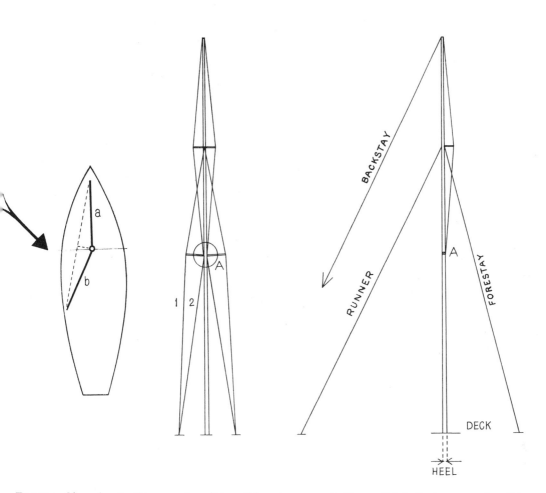

Dragon Class boat. We are describing this particular rig here because it is one of the most popular methods of rigging a keelboat and the problems encountered here are common to a very large proportion of keelboat classes. This is a description of how to adjust a mast. I have drawn the first sketch with the wind coming from the port side and you can keep the forestay 'a' as tight as possible by making the forestay and the runner 'b' take most of the strain. You can do this by loosening the lower and upper shrouds marked 1 and 2. Whether you have the top of your mast bending sideways or not, which is accomplished by loosening or tightening the jumpers, depends on whether the sail that you are using is very full at the

top or not. If you think that your mainsail is too full at the top it is worth while trying to make the mast bend sideways at the top by loosening the jumpers.

If your mast has been made so that it is too stiff you can improve the situation by having the jumpers slightly slack. Very tight jumpers cause a weakness in the mast at point 'A'. If your mainsail is too baggy for stronger winds you can bend your mast sideways by tightening the lower shrouds and easing off the upper shrouds and jumpers. In that way the mast will bend off to leeward from point 'A' upwards and you will get more space between the leach of the genoa and the mainsail. You can adjust the stiffness of the lower part of the mast by controlling it at the deck and the heel.

In light winds and a smooth sea you may find that your medium sail has too much flow near the mast and thus you cannot point high enough. In this case you can move the heel aft, which will bend the mast against the deck and take away some of the extra flow near the mast. You can accomplish the same thing by pushing the mast forward at the deck by putting chocks on the after side but some class rules have very tight tolerances on the hole in the deck and there may not be enough room to do this. In this case you have

to chock it at the heel. If you only bend the mast with the back-stay all that will happen is that you will open the mainsail leach too much which can be very bad in light winds, unless your jumpers are very tight. It may be that in strong winds you might want to free off the leach at the top of the sail because you cannot keep the boat on its feet, i.e. you want to flatten out the top of the sail. In this case you ought to do all of this by bending the top of the mast so that when the wind eases again you can straighten the mast and the flow comes back into the sail again.

This drawing shows how a Star boat is rigged. The top of the mast can be controlled in two ways. One is by means of a jumper-stay leading back to the mast at the lower hounds and down on to a Highfield lever at the bottom. By varying the tension on the High-field lever you can get more or less tension on the rest of the stay which is passing over the jumper. The other and better method of controlling the top of the mast is by rigging a separate topmast forestay to the stemhead.

The Star boat rig has double runners on each side. The upper one keeps the forestay tight and the lower one is intended to control the mast to suit the sail. The lower runner also avoids the mast breaking in a heavy sea.

But today you will find that we use lighter and lighter masts and that there will be more tension on the lower stay, B2, than on the upper stay when you are sailing.

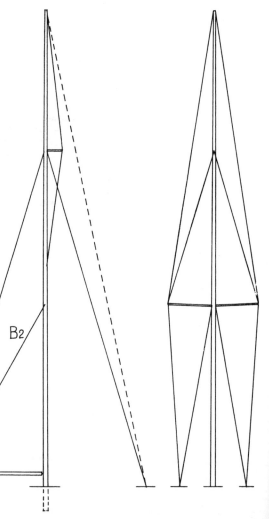

The next rig is very much used in cruising boats and is also the normal 5·5-metre rig but there is not very much room for adjustment. You can bend the mast by pulling harder on the backstay and by easing off the jumper stays and you can also alter the bend by moving the mast heel aft so that the aft side of the mast presses on the deck.

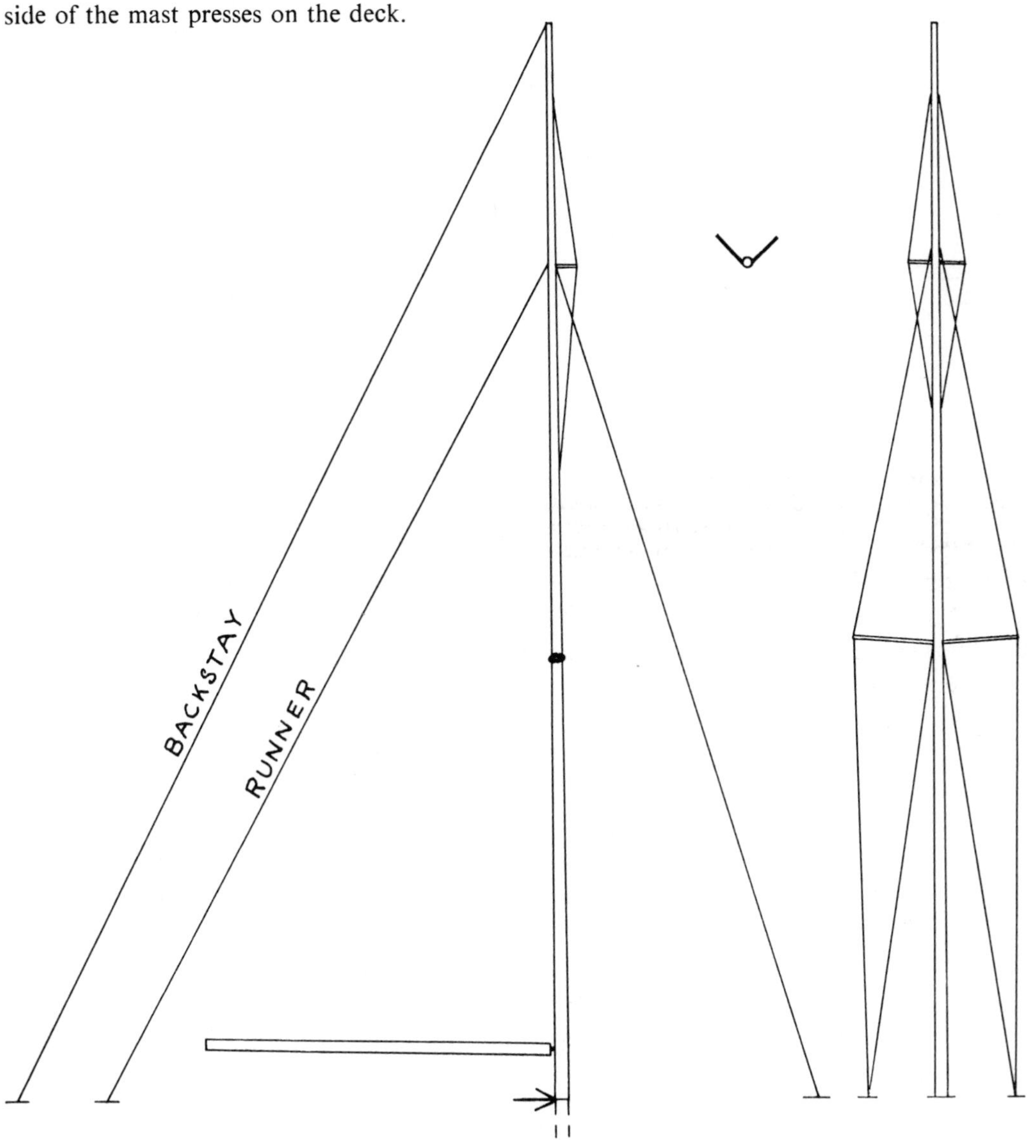

BACKSTAY

RUNNER

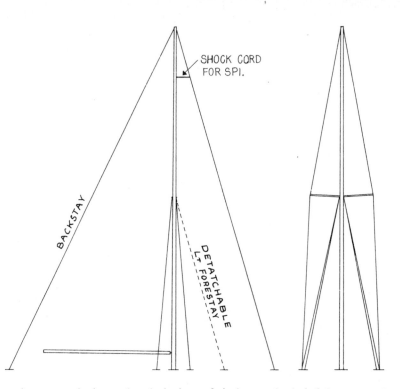

SHOCK CORD
FOR SPI.

BACKSTAY

DETATCHABLE
Lt. FORESTAY

This shows how a typical masthead rig is stayed. The amount one can let this type of mast bend is strictly limited otherwise it will collapse in a heavy sea. This is especially so if the mast is stepped on deck as is often the case. Therefore you have to make the sail for a straight mast and the only adjustments you can do are with the sail itself. With this type of rig it may be helpful to try softer or stiffer booms to get at least some form of adjustment. For example, you may find that you can gain a great deal with a sail which is very full in the lower part but this will be a disadvantage in strong winds and you may be able to correct this with a softer boom.

Boom Sheeting

If it is possible in the class of boat you are sailing for the traveller to be close to the boom then I would recommend that you sheet the boom from the centre and arrange it so that it will bend. If the distance between the traveller and the boom is too great you will find that you will have to pull down too hard in order to get the mainsail sheeted in close enough to be able to point well. The shorter the distance between the traveller and the boom the better. Therefore if the distance is too great you will have to sheet the mainsail from the end of the boom or somewhere near it. The shorter the distance between the traveller and the boom the more practicable it is to try various angles for the sheeting of the boom and various tensions for the mainsheet.

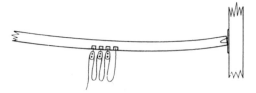

G. L. W. Oppenheim

This picture shows what a wonderful balance a free leach on a sail can give. The boat is an International 12 ft. dinghy of the type used in the Olympic Games of 1920 and 1928.

When does a Boat balance?

I believe that for really top speed a fully tuned dinghy or keelboat must not have any pressure on the rudder and hence has as nearly as possible neutral helm.

This state of perfect balance is only valid for periods when the boat has exactly the right angle of heel and trim and when the sails are at the most effective angle to the wind.

When the wind changes so that you can point higher the helm pressure should change to slight weather helm but this pressure should disappear again when you have reached the new course which the new wind direction allows you to steer.

On the other hand, when the wind heads, the boat should have a small tendency to bear away on its own. The most common mistake is for a boat to be tuned to have weather helm.

131

The Trimming of the Mast (*Dinghies*)

It is most important to discover the correct position and rake for the mast. The mast should be positioned so that the pressure on the helm is as small as possible. If you let go the tiller and the dinghy immediately luffs into the wind, then we call this 'weather helm'. If, on the other hand, the dinghy tries to fall off away from the wind, then this is called 'lee helm', and is bad. In a well designed boat which is sailing correctly trimmed there should be almost no weather helm. If there is too much weather helm then you will have to apply too much rudder which will thus slow the boat.

Particularly in dinghies which do not have complicated mast rigging you can reduce weather helm by using a more flexible mast. When the wind pressure bends the mast at the top this will free off the mainsail leach which will allow the wind to slide off more easily, and this will have the effect of lessening the tendency of the boat to luff. On the other hand, if the dinghy is carrying lee helm and the mast is flexible then it can help to use a stiffer mast.

Weather helm can also be corrected by moving the mast and with it the sail area forward in order to push the bow more to leeward. On the contrary, if the boat carries lee helm then you should move the mast and with it the sail area aft in order to push the stern more to leeward.

When altering the mast rake you must be careful not to allow the top to go too far forward. In some classes, where the mainsail is cut so that the boom is very high above the deck, then you should rake the mast aft to bring the boom lower and improve the effectiveness of the sail near the boom, if the boom cocks up in the air then the wind entering the sail cannot continue freely off the leach and has to go over, round and under

the boom. But if you rake the mast aft, and lower the boom, then the air stream will be able to pass right across the sail and off the leach. If, when you rake the mast aft, the dinghy carries weather helm, then you must move the heel of the mast as far forward as possible to restore the balance.

With the wind free, either dead aft or on the beam, it is an advantage to move the sail area as far forward as possible in the dinghy. If you leave the rigging slack, then the top of the mast will automatically drop forward since the mast will be pivoted at the heel. In this way you will be able to tune the dinghy to go its maximum speed either to windward or to leeward.

It is not the same with the Flying Dutchman rig. If the wind increases there is a danger that the mast will bend so much that it will collapse on the run. When sailing to windward there is less danger of the mast breaking. Under planing conditions the fore-

Above and left:

This O.K. Dinghy is going at top speed to windward and it is in perfect balance. The mast is apparently rather flexible in the lower part and that could be the reason why it was not going close enough to the wind.

Here D530 has a mast and sail which are working perfectly together and in the 1964 World Championship this boat was fastest to windward in stronger winds.

stay on a Flying Dutchman or a Five-O-Five should be tightened, otherwise the jib luff will shake from side to side; the stays on these types of boat therefore should be tightened up in strong winds.

The Positioning of the Sheets

The main sheet should be fixed to the boom immediately over the traveller when the boom is sheeted in the farthest outboard position. This will be neither too close nor too far away from the mast. The position of the jib sheets depends mainly on the shape of the jib. The jib must not throw too much back-wind into the mainsail and if this is the case the fairlead must be moved farther aft otherwise the actual cut of the jib must be altered to give a freer passage to the wind.

If it is impossible to move the fairleads any further aft and you still want to free the leach of the genoa more then the only way to do this is to rake the mast more aft.

Boom Vang or Kicking Strap

Every dinghy should have a boom vang made of wire or of rope led through two double blocks, the purpose of which is to hold the boom down, as near as possible to the horizontal. If you do not have a boom vang then the boom will lift causing the sail to twist and take up varying angles to the wind, only one of which will be the right one. If the boom vang is set up hard then the top of the sail and the boom will have the same angle to the wind, and when you trim the sail all parts of it will draw effectively.

The Boom and Boom Wedges

All classes will have rules controlling the size of the boom, and therefore you must try within these rules to obtain a boom which will resist the boom vang forces and at the same time remain elastic enough, especially at the outer end, to enable the wind to free off the sail easily.

133

The Finn, the O.K. Dinghy and some Moths cannot fit boom vangs and instead they have a wedge which is inserted in the foreside of the boom slot in the mast. The wedge, which is made of wood, plastic or hard rubber, prevents the outer end of the boom from lifting. Because the boom will have to resist great pressures at the mast end then I suggest you make this end out of ash or oak.

The stiffness of the boom depends on the cut of the sail, how full it is and the stiffness of the cloth. The boom must not be too flexible or you will be unable to point close enough to the wind.

It is just as important in proportion to its size to sheet the jib right out onto the rail as to have a kicking strap on the mainsail. You should have a snatch fairlead right on the gunwale into which you can clip the jib sheet when reaching.

Notice here that the very tight boom vang is holding the boom hard down in the right fashion whilst the sheets merely control the angle.

Left:

Here, the position of the fairlead can be adjusted fore-and-aft as well as athwartships. For reaching the sheet can be hooked into the open fairlead on the rail to obtain the best lead for this point of sailing.

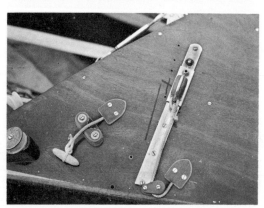

Opposite:

Here is a Finn with a very tight wedge and you can easily see how the sail is effective for the whole of its height.

Left:

This shows a very good idea for pulling the jib fairlead outboard whilst you are still hanging out from the opposite side of the boat. The toggle and cleat on the left operate the fairlead on the other side of the dinghy.

In the early days of Finn sailing no one used a mast wedge to hold the boom down. People did not like to do this in case the boom broke, but as the competition increased it became necessary to do so, and it was not long before people discovered that by glueing a hardwood end to the boom where it passed through the mast, it could be made much stronger.

The Trimming of the Mast (Keelboats)

The mast position in the boat depends on the shape of the mainsail and the headsail. The tighter that the leach is on the mainsail the further forward you have to place the mast in order to get the boat into balance. In addition you will find that the flatter the headsail is again the further forward you have to place the mast to get the boat into balance.

On the other hand the fuller that the headsail is and the flatter that the mainsail is on the leach the further aft you have to place the mast to obtain balance.

The problem is, therefore, to find the right compromise between the mast position and the shape of the sails. If the mainsail and the headsail have the shapes that we think are right to get the top speed from the boat and then the boat still carries weather helm we shall have to move the mast heel further forward.

In classes such as the Dragon and the 5·5-metre where we are able to move the forestay forward and aft as well then we can move this forward also so that we can keep the biggest distance possible between the forestay and the mast.

When correcting imbalance it is not sufficient to alter the rake of the mast. The use of this adjustment is only to obtain the very finest control over trim affecting the feel on the tiller and, of course, it has other effects on the leach tension and sheeting angle of the mainsail as explained elsewhere.

Let us now assume that the boat is in balance, and that it is pointing very well, but that the speed is not good enough. This can mean that the leach of the mainsail is too 'closed' or 'tight' in the lower part.

The answer to this problem is to open or 'ease' the seams in the lower part of the mainsail and then move the mast aft to retain the correct balance.

On the other hand, if the boat is balancing well, and yet it is not pointing at all well but the speed is good then you may find that the leach in the higher part of the sail is too 'open' or 'free' or perhaps the mast may be bending too much and has made the sail too flat.

In this case I would stiffen up the mast and move it further forward to retain the correct balance and if that is still not enough to enable me to point well I would 'close' or 'tighten' the leach of the mainsail a little and again move the mast even further forward to

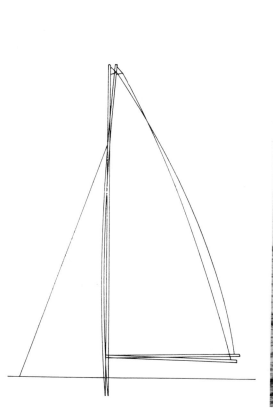

regain the correct balance which will have been affected by the newly tightened leach.

During all this time one must not forget the effect of the headsail on the balance of the boat.

If you bend the mast by only moving it forward in the deck you can see from the drawing how you also move the whole sail plan forward. Therefore if you find that your sail is very effective in light and medium winds but that you get a tremendous amount of weather helm in stronger winds you can try, by bending the mast as shown on the drawing, to correct this. In this way you will move forward and take away a part of the sail area which has the greatest effect in causing weather helm. You still need the area in this position in order to be able to point in light winds and you get this back by letting the mast come straight again.

This shows the normal type of Star jib, but I have found that it is better to make the jib shorter in the luff so that the clew comes as close as possible to the deck. You lose a little area but you gain a great deal in efficiency by having the foot of the sail close to the deck.

A mast which bends sideways excessively can also be a reason for the boat not pointing. The stiffer that the mast is in the sideways direction the better the boat will point but if the weather helm is excessive you can easily reduce this by letting the mast bend sideways more.

Generally speaking, in order to obtain the same balance in a boat which has a mast which bends sideways and you want to use the mast straighter, you will find that you will have to move the mast from two to five inches further forward.

RACING RULES

The most interesting thing about sailing races is to try to employ the right tactics but this ideal is frequently spoilt because competitors will not use the racing rules to the full, not because they are afraid of breaking the rules but because they do not know the rules properly.

Racing helmsmen can be divided into three groups. Firstly, there are those who like sailing and think it would be fun to sail their boat against others in a race; secondly, there are those who enjoy trying to make their boats go fast and to take the shortest way round the course and yet only know the most elementary of racing rules; and lastly there are those who know the rules absolutely thoroughly and are able to interpret them correctly, and they prefer to have all their competitors know the rules as well as they do and interpret them in the same way. This last group uses the racing rules to the full and manoeuvres which the other people might think to be rather sharp or questionable they consider to be completely legitimate.

The way in which I am going to explain the rules should give helmsmen a thorough working knowledge of them, so that quite

normal manoeuvres on the course conforming to the rules will not be taken to be somewhat unfair or sharp sailing. For example, gybing on the lee side of another competitor when you are running, even though you previously had no right to luff; but owing to the gybe a new overlap starts and therefore you are then allowed to luff. Another example: two boats are just approaching the finishing line with the wind aft; one dinghy gybes the main boom very fast, which makes the dinghy leap forward just enough to take the first gun.

In the bigger international regattas such as the European or World Championships or the Olympics, one has to sail very close to the rules, and you must always be prepared that some competitors will take every possible advantage; for example, the Argentinian was disqualified by the Italian in the Dragon Class in the Olympic Games at Naples two minutes before the start on account of the starboard tack rule.

In less important races, such as weekly afternoon regattas, you will have to race against people who do not know the rules thoroughly, and you will just have to put up with it. As well as this you must be careful not to shout at a less experienced competitor because you will not gain anything by this and all you will do will be to lose a friendly competitor for ever.

You should not learn racing rules solely to be able to hit at each competitor, but also to enable you to be able to work out the best tactics in general. The racing rules are the absolute basis of all tactics.

The 1965/1968 Racing Rules

Immediately after the Tokyo Olympic Games the racing rules were completely revised. Actually, the work had been going on for several years on this revision but it was finally completed at the I.Y.R.U. meeting in November, 1964. These rules are now 'frozen' for at least four years.

I think that we will have far less difficulty with these newly worded rules. They may look very long and complicated but this is only natural. It is not so bad when you start to study them and we have tried to present them to you in an easy way.

The rules are divided into six parts. The most important, and the part needing most explanation, is Part IV. These are the rules governing cases where yachts meet each other either on the open water or near marks or obstructions.

Nearly all the other rules are quite simple and easy to understand and deal with all the other problems of racing a yacht. You should read them through a few times so that you get familiar with them. Most of them you need not learn as long as you remember that they are there. Use the book for reference. But there are some of these rules which are very important or interesting and I have

explained the possibilities with notes and drawings.

The most important thing is to become very familiar with the sailing rules in Part IV. A beginner should read through all the easy rules several times and then concentrate on Part IV one rule at a time. Get thoroughly familiar with the basic rules in Part IV before going on to the others in detail. Use little models to help work out problems for yourself.

The actual text of the rules is here exactly as is printed in the I.Y.R.U. Rule Book and so it can be used by race committees. We have dealt with each rule in detail one at a time and on each page you will find at the top in **bold type** the number and name of the rule being discussed on that page.

When you meet a word in the rules printed in **bold type** this means that it is one of the terms defined in Part I of the rules.

The actual wording of the I.Y.R.U. rules is boxed in on each page so that you do not get this mixed up with my notes and the captions to my drawings. I have arranged the book so that each rule has its own explanations and drawings immediately following it and we complete one rule before we move on to the next.

Right of way when not subject to the racing rules

The rules of Part IV do not apply in any way to a vessel which is neither intending to race nor racing; such vessel shall be treated in accordance with the International Regulations for Preventing Collisions at Sea or Government Right-of-Way Rules applicable in the area concerned.

INDEX

141

PART I—DEFINITIONS

When a term defined in Part I is used in its defined sense it is printed in **bold** *type. All definitions and italicized notes rank as rules.*

Racing—A yacht is **racing** from her preparatory signal until she has either **finished** and cleared the finishing line and finishing **marks** or retired, or until the race has been **cancelled, postponed** or **abandoned,** except that in match or team races, the sailing instructions may prescribe that a yacht is **racing** from any specified time before the preparatory signal.

Starting—A yacht **starts** when, after her starting signal, any part of her hull, crew or equipment first crosses the starting line in the direction of the first **mark.**

Finishing—A yacht **finishes** when any part of her hull, or of her crew or equipment in normal position, crosses the finishing line from the direction of the last **mark.**

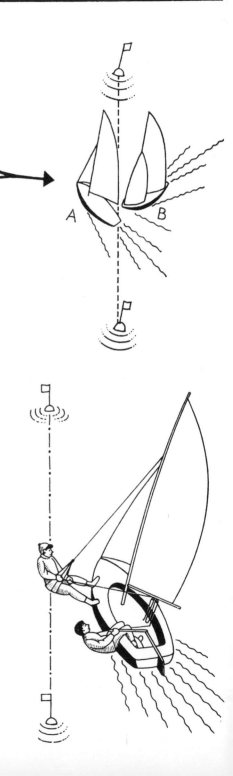

Note: RACING. *New to this rule is a sentence permitting boats to be governed by the racing rules before the preparatory signal (usually the 5-minute gun). This is meant to apply to some team or match races.*

RACING. *Even though A has received her winning gun she is still under the racing rules as long as any part of her hull or gear is still on the line, and in this case A would be disqualified by B.*

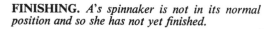

FINISHING. *A's spinnaker is not in its normal position and so she has not yet finished.*

FINISHING. *The racing rules say that the crew of the boat has to be in his normal position. B has not yet finished.*

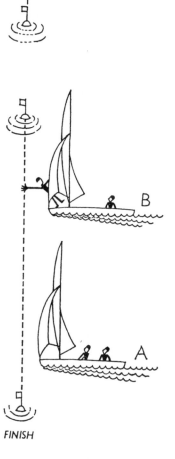

FINISHING. *This boat has finished.*

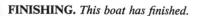

FINISH

Luffing—Altering course towards the wind until head to wind.

Tacking—A yacht is **tacking** from the moment she is beyond head to wind until she has **borne away**, if beating to windward, to a **close-hauled** course; if not beating to windward, to the course on which her mainsail has filled.

Bearing Away—Altering course away from the wind until a yacht begins to **gybe**.

Gybing—A yacht begins to **gybe** at the moment when, with the wind aft, the foot of the mainsail crosses her centre line and completes the **gybe** when the mainsail has filled on the other **tack**.

On a Tack—A yacht is **on a tack** except when she is **tacking** or **gybing**. A yacht is on the **tack** (**starboard** or **port**) corresponding to her **windward** side.

Close-hauled—A yacht is **close-hauled** when sailing by the wind as close as she can lie with advantage in working to windward.

Leeward and **Windward**—The **leeward** side of a yacht is that on which she is, or, if **luffing** head to wind, was, carrying her mainsail. The opposite side is the **windward** side.

When neither of two yachts on the same **tack** is **clear astern**, the one on the **leeward** side of the other is the **leeward yacht**. The other is the **windward yacht**.

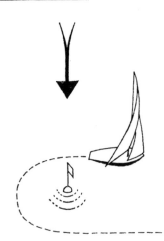

COURSE TO NEXT MARK

TACKING. *This boat finishes tacking when she reaches a close-hauled course on the new tack.*

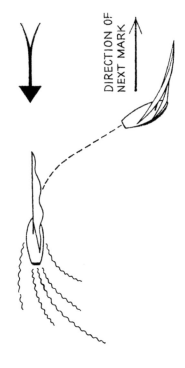

LUFFING *and* **TACKING.** *This yacht is luffing until she is head to wind. If she continues to turn she is tacking.*

WINDWARD *and* **LEEWARD.** *Because these yachts are not on the same tack neither complies with the definition of windward yacht or leeward yacht.*

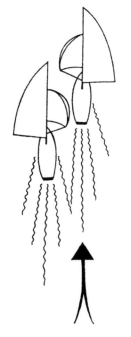

TACKING. *This boat finishes tacking when her mainsail fills, which might be on any course between close-hauled and a broad reach.*

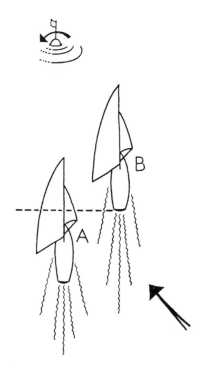

Clear Astern and Clear Ahead; Overlap— A yacht is **clear astern** of another when her hull and equipment are abaft of an imaginary line projected abeam from the aftermost point of the other's hull and equipment. The other yacht is **clear ahead.** The yachts **overlap** if neither is **clear astern;** or if, although one is **clear astern,** an intervening yacht **overlaps** both of them. The terms **clear astern, clear ahead** and **overlap** apply to yachts on opposite **tacks** only when they are subject to rule 42, Rounding or Passing Marks and Obstructions.

Proper course—A **proper course** is any course which a yacht might sail after the starting signal, in the absence of the other yacht or yacht affected, to **finish** as quickly as possible. The course sailed before **luffing** or **bearing away** is presumably, but not necessarily, that yacht's **proper course.** There is no **proper course** before the starting signal.

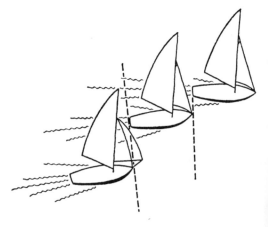

CLEAR ASTERN, CLEAR AHEAD, OVER-LAP. *Watch out because a foresail, a spinnaker or a boomed-out jib could establish an overlap.*

CLEAR ASTERN, CLEAR AHEAD, OVER-LAP. *A has not established an overlap because, the same as in the finishing definition, her spinnaker is not in the normal position.*

CLEAR ASTERN, CLEAR AHEAD. *A is clear astern, B is clear ahead.*

THE PROPER COURSE. *A is sailing the proper course.*

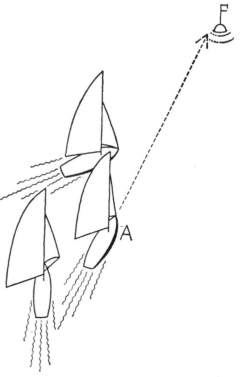

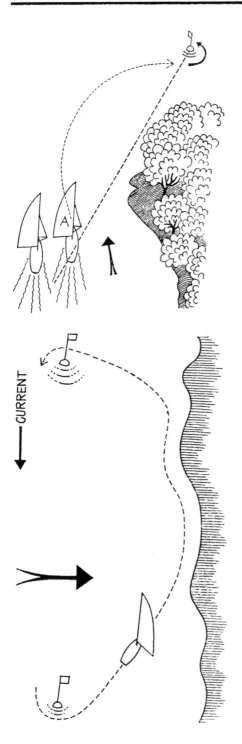

PROPER COURSE. *The proper course is not necessarily the shortest course.*

> **Mark**—A **mark** is any object specified in the sailing instructions which a yacht must round or pass on a required side.
>
> **Obstruction**—An **obstruction** is any object, including craft under way, large enough to require a yacht, if not less than one overall length away from it, to make a substantial alteration of course to pass on one side or the other, or any object which can be passed on one side only, including a buoy when the yacht in question cannot safely pass between it and the shoal or object which it marks.
>
> **Cancellation**—A **cancelled** race is one which the race committee decides will not be sailed thereafter.
>
> **Postponement**—A **postponed** race is one which is not started at its scheduled time and which can be sailed at any time the race committee may decide.
>
> **Abandonment**—An **abandoned** race is one which the race committee declares void at any time after the starting signal, and which can be resailed at its discretion.

PROPER COURSE. *The fastest course could be a very long way from the direct course, and this would be the proper course.*

Note: MARK. *Even though the starting line buoys do not have a required side until the starting signal is made, they still have to be regarded as marks of the course between the preparatory signal and the start. See rule 52.1 (a) (i).*

Note: OBSTRUCTION. *One only considers a change of course substantial when a boat would lose a substantial amount of ground by altering course. A small fishing buoy, for example, would not cause any obstruction because it would just slide along the side of the boat without stopping it.*

Note: 1.3. *This new rule now definitely states that it is the sole responsibility of the owner or crew whether they start or continue a race. This is especially important now that racing fleets are so large. It is impossible to be able to guarantee to rescue everybody and unless we have such a rule as this many race committees would not take the risk of starting big races in winds over Force 3. This would be ridiculous.*

PART II—MANAGEMENT OF RACES

Authority and Duties of Race Committee

The rules of Part II deal with the duties and responsibilities of the race committee in conducting a race, the meaning of signals made by it and of other actions taken by it.

1—General Authority of Race Committee and Judges

1. All races shall be arranged, conducted and judged by a race committee under the direction of the sponsoring organisation, except as may be provided under rule 1.2. The race committee may delegate the conduct of a race, the hearing and deciding of protests or any other of its responsibilities to one or more sub-committees which, if appointed, will hereinafter be included in the term 'race committee' wherever it is used.

2. For a special regatta or series, the sponsoring organisation may provide for a jury or judges to hear and decide protests and to have supervision over the conduct of the races, in which case the race committee shall be subject to the direction of the jury or judges to the extent provided by the sponsoring organisation.

3. All yachts entered or **racing** shall be subject to the direction and control of the race committee, but it shall be the sole responsibility of each yacht to decide whether or not to **start** or to continue to **race**.

4. Unless otherwise prescribed by the national authority, the race committee may reject any entry without stating the reason.

5. The race committee shall be governed by these rules, by the prescriptions of its national authority, by the sailing instructions, by approved class rules (but it may refuse to recognise any class rule which conflicts with these rules) and, when applicable, by the team racing rules of its national authority, and shall decide all questions in accordance therewith.

2—Notice of Race

The notice of a race or regatta shall contain the following information:

(*a*) That the race or races will be sailed under the rules of the I.Y.R.U. and the prescriptions of the national authority concerned.

(*b*) The date and place of the regatta and the time of the start of the first race and, if possible, succeeding races.

(*c*) The class or classes for which races will be given.

The notice shall also cover such of the following matters as may be appropriate:

(*d*) Any special instructions, subject to rule 3.1, which may vary or add to these rules or class rules.

(*e*) Any restrictions or conditions regarding entries and numbers of starters or competitors.

(*f*) The address to which entries shall be sent, the date on which they close, the amount of entrance fees, if any, and any other entry requirements.

(*g*) Particulars and number of prizes.

(*h*) Time and place for receiving sailing instructions.

(*i*) Scoring system.

(*j*) That for the purpose of determining the result of a race which is one of a series of races in a competition, decisions of protests shall not be subject to appeal if it is essential to establish the results promptly. A national authority may prescribe that its approval be required for such a procedure.

Note: 3.2. Many clubs do not take enough trouble over race notices and sailing instructions and this often results in confusion, disappointment and bad feeling. It is really very simple for clubs to go through Rules 2 and 3 and make out standard forms which can cover all races. Blanks can be left for the variable items to be filled in when the details of each race are known.

3—The Sailing Instructions

1. **Status**—These rules shall be supplemented by written sailing instructions which shall rank as rules and may alter a rule by specific reference to it, but except in accordance with rule 3.2 (*k*) they shall not alter Parts I and IV of these rules.

2. **Contents**—The sailing instructions shall contain the following information:

(*a*) That the race or races will be sailed under the rules of the I.Y.R.U. and the prescriptions of the national authority concerned.

(*b*) The course or courses to be sailed or a list of **marks** or courses from which the course or courses will be selected, describing all **marks** and stating the order in which and the side on which each is to be rounded or passed.

(*c*) The course signals.

(*d*) The classes to race and class signals, if any.

(*e*) Time of start for each class.

(*f*) Starting line and starting area, if used.

(*g*) Finishing line and any special instructions for shortening the course or for **finishing** a shortened course. (Where possible the sailing instructions for **finishing** a shortened course should not differ from those laid down for **finishing** the full course.)

(*h*) Time limit, if any, for **finishing**.

(*i*) Scoring system, if not previously announced in writing, including the method, if any, for breaking ties.

The sailing instructions shall also cover such of the following matters as may be appropriate:

(*j*) The date and place of the race or races.

(*k*) When the race is to continue after sunset, the time or place, if any, at which the International Regulations for Preventing Collisions at Sea, or Government Right-of-Way Rules, shall replace the corresponding rules of Part IV, and the night signals the committee boat will display.

(*l*) Any special instructions, subject to rule 3.1, which may vary or add to these rules, or class rules, and any special signals.

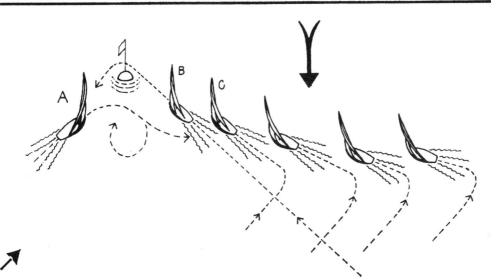

3.2 (b). *These drawings illustrate some of the problems for race committees. In this situation A is in reality just ahead of B but she has no chance of being able to keep her place and will eventually round behind C if she can find a hole. If you elect to come to the mark on starboard tack each succeeding boat has to tack further and further over to the starboard side in order to avoid backwind and thus loses that much more distance until the situation gets so bad that a boat decides to come in on port tack like A and hopes to lose less by taking a chance. But the eventual situation is just the same unless A is lucky and finds a hole. In this method of rounding everyone is afraid to come in from the port side of the course and therefore only the starboard side of the course is used instead of the whole area. This causes congestion.*

3.2 (b). *In large fleets if the weather mark is ordered to be rounded to starboard it is very much easier for boats to be able to round satisfactorily. In this case, if A overstands the mark by only about four boat-lengths she is almost certain to round in the clear. She will only have to sail six boat-lengths further than the boat which rounds in the best position. In this case the whole of the racing course is used because the boats can come in to the mark on starboard or port tack always with a good chance of being able to round. The following boats will be able to round the mark without losing nearly so much distance as if they were ordered to round the mark to port. In big fleets we do know that rounding marks to starboard seems to produce more protest situations but I still think that it is much better to order the mark to be rounded to starboard for the reasons I have given.*

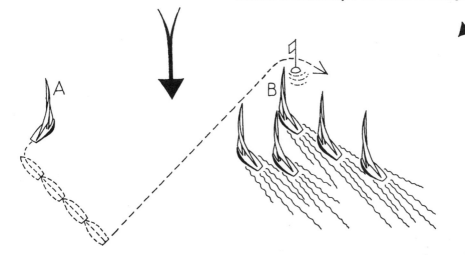

(*m*) Eligibility; entry; measurement certificate; declaration.

(*n*) Names, sail numbers and letters and ratings of the yachts entered.

(*o*) Any special instructions governing the methods of **starting** and recall.

(*p*) Recall numbers or letters, if used, of the yachts entered.

(*q*) Time allowances.

(*r*) Length of course or courses.

(*s*) Method by which competitors will be notified of any change of course.

(*t*) Prizes.

(*u*) Any special time limit within which, and address at which, the declaration that all rules have been observed, if required, or written protest shall be lodged, and the prescribed fee, if any, which shall accompany the latter.

(*v*) Time and place at which protests will be heard.

(*w*) That for the purpose of determining the result of a race which is one of a series of races in a competition, decisions of protests shall not be subject to appeal if it is essential to establish the results promptly. A national authority may prescribe that its approval be required for such a procedure.

(*x*) Whether races **postponed** or **abandoned** for the day will be sailed later and, if so, when and where.

(*y*) Disposition to be made of a yacht appearing at the start alone in her class.

3. **Distribution**—The sailing instructions shall be available to each yacht entitled to race.

4. **Changes**—The race committee may change the sailing instructions by notice, in writing if practicable, given to each yacht affected not later than the warning signal of her class.

5. **Oral Instructions** shall not be given except in accordance with procedure specifically set out in the sailing instructions.

4—Signals

1. **International Code Flag Signals**—Unless otherwise prescribed by the national authority or in the sailing instructions:

'AP'—Answering Pendant, Postponement signal.

When displayed alone over a class **signal** means:

'The scheduled time of the start of the designated race is **postponed** 15 minutes.'

(This **postponement** can be extended indefinitely in 15-minute intervals by dipping and rehoisting the signal.)

When displayed over 1 ball or shape over a class signal, means:

'The scheduled time of the start of the designated race is **postponed** 30 minutes.'

(This **postponement** can be extended indifinitely by the addition of 1 ball or shape for every 15 minutes.)

When displayed over one of the numeral pendants 1 to 9 over a class signal, means:

'The scheduled time of the start of the designated race is **postponed** 1 hour, 2 hours, etc.'

When displayed over the letter 'A' over a class signal, means:

'The designated race is **postponed** to a later date.'

When any of the above signals are displayed without a class signal below, means:

'The whole sailing programme is **postponed** in accordance with the signal made.'

'L'—When displayed means:
'Come within hail.'

'M'—Mark Signal.

When displayed on a buoy, vessel, or other object, means:

'Round or pass the object displaying this signal instead of the **mark** which it replaces.'

'N'—Abandonment Signal.

When displayed alone, means:
'All races are **abandoned**.'

When displayed over a class signal, means:
'The designated race is **abandoned**.'

'P'—Preparatory Signal.
When displayed means:
'The class designated by the warning signal
will **start** in 5 minutes exactly.'

'R'—Reverse Course Signal.
When displayed alone, means:
'Sail the course prescribed in the sailing
instructions in the reverse direction.'
When displayed over a course signal, means:
'Sail the designated course in the reverse
direction.'

'S'—Shorten Course Signal.
When displayed alone

(a) at or near the starting line, means:
'All classes shall sail the shortened course
prescribed in the sailing instructions.'

(b) at or near the finishing line, means:
'All classes shall **finish** the race either at
the prescribed finishing line at the end of
the round still to be completed by the
leading yacht, or in any other manner
prescribed in the sailing instructions
under rule 3.2 (g).'

(c) elsewhere, means:
'All classes shall **finish** between the
nearby **mark** and the committee boat.'
When displayed over a class signal, as in (a),
(b) or (c) above, means:
'The above signals apply to the designated
class only.'

'1st Substitute'—General Recall Signal.
When displayed, means:
'The class is recalled for a fresh start as
provided in the sailing instructions.'

2. **Signalling the Course**—Unless otherwise
prescribed by the national authority, the race
committee shall either make the appropriate
course signal or otherwise designate the course
before or with the warning signal.

3. **Changing the Course**—The course for a
class which has not **started** may be changed:

(a) by displaying the appropriate **postponement** signal and indicating the new course
before or with the warning signal to be
displayed after the lowering of the **postponement** signal; or

(b) by displaying a course signal or by removing and substituting a course signal before
or with the warning signal.
(The race committee should use method (a)
when a change of course involves either
shifting the committee boat or other starting
mark, or requires a change of sails which
cannot reasonably be completed within the
5-minute period before the preparatory signal
is made.)

4. **Signals for Starting a Race**

(a) Unless otherwise prescribed by the
national authority or in the sailing instructions, the signals for starting a race
shall be made at 5-minute intervals
exactly, and shall be either:

(i) *Warning Signal*—Class flag broken out
or distinctive signal displayed.
Preparatory Signal — Code flag 'P'
broken out or distinctive signal displayed.
Starting Signal — Both warning and
preparatory signals lowered, or

(ii) *Warning Signal*—White shape.
Preparatory Signal—Blue shape.
Starting Signal for first class to start—
Red shape.
In system (ii) each signal shall be
lowered 30 seconds before the hoisting
of the next, and in starting yachts by
classes, the starting signal for each
class shall be the preparatory signal for
the next.

(b) Although rule 4.4 (a) specifies 5-minute
intervals between signals, this shall not
interfere with the power of a race committee to start a series of races at any
intervals which it considers desirable.

(c) A warning signal shall not be given
before its scheduled time, except with the
consent of all yachts entitled to race.

(d) Should an error be made in the timing of
the interval between the warning and
preparatory signals, and a general recall
signal is not to be made, the race committee shall ensure that the correct
interval elapses between the preparatory
and starting signals.

5. **Finishing Signals**—Blue flag or shape. When displayed at the finish, means: 'The committee boat is on station at the finishing line.'

6. **Other Signals** — The sailing instructions shall designate any other special signals and shall explain their meaning.

7. **Calling Attention to Signals**—Whenever the race committee makes a signal, except 'R' or 'S' before the warning signal, it shall call attention to its action as follows:

Three guns or other sound signals when displaying 'N.'

Two guns or other sound signals when displaying the '1st Substitute,' 'AP,' or 'S.'

One gun or other sound signal when making any other signal.

8. **Visual Signal to Govern**—Times shall be taken from the visual starting signals, and a failure or mistiming of a gun or other sound signal shall be disregarded.

Note: 4.4 (a) (ii). *The White, Blue and Red system of starting races, much used in America, is really very simple. It also gives yachts 30 seconds extra warning of the start since each shape is lowered 30 seconds before the next is hoisted.*

Note: 4.4 (d). *There is here a very important change in timing the start. Now, if the race committee realises they have made the preparatory signal (usually we call this the '5-minute gun,' though it is really the visual signal which gives the time, and not the sound signal) either too late or too early by mistake, they can do one of two things. They can either signal a 'General Recall' and start again, or they can continue with the start. But if they do the latter they must make sure that there is exactly the right time interval between the preparatory signal and the start signal. In other words, if the start signal is supposed to be made five minutes after the preparatory then it must be made exactly this time after it, even if the preparatory was made late or early with reference to the warning signal (10-minute gun).*

Note: 4.8. *This is the very important matter of the visual signal. The timing is made from this and not from the gun, bell, whistle or hooter.*

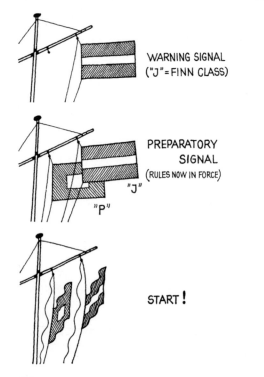

WARNING SIGNAL
("J"=FINN CLASS)

PREPARATORY
SIGNAL
(RULES NOW IN FORCE)

"J"

"P"

START !

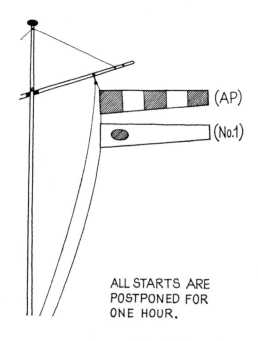

(AP)

(No.1)

ALL STARTS ARE
POSTPONED FOR
ONE HOUR.

International Flag Signals and Morse Code

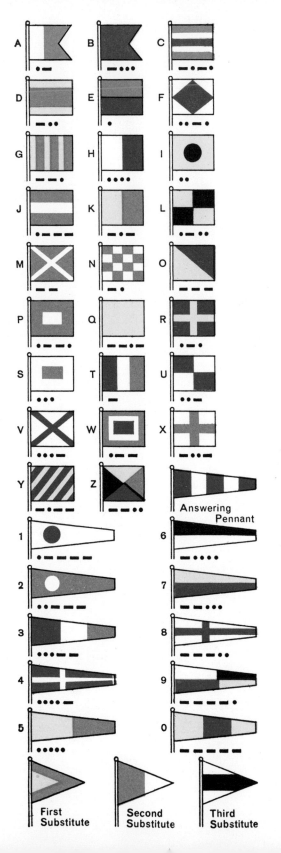

First Substitute

Second Substitute

Third Substitute

155

Here are two different types of starting boat used for international racing. Above is a small warship at Kiel. It has to be moored bow and stern to stop it swinging on the current. They have used a dan buoy to keep boats away from the mooring cables.

Below is the Thorpe Bay boat used for the Catamaran Challenge Match. It is a catamaran itself and can be moored so that no cables project fore and aft. It is a very good stable platform. The man on the top deck can see the line perfectly.

5—Cancelling, Postponing or Abandoning a Race and Shortening Course

1. The race committee:

(*a*) before the starting signal may shorten the course or **cancel** or **postpone** a race for any reason, and

(*b*) after the starting signal may shorten the course by **finishing** a race at any rounding mark or **cancel** or **abandon** a race because of foul weather endangering the yachts, or because of insufficient wind, or because a **mark** is missing or has shifted, or for other reasons directly affecting safety or the fairness of the competition.

2. After a **postponement** the ordinary starting signals prescribed in rule 4.4 (*a*) shall be used, and the postponement signal, if a general one, shall be hauled down before the first warning or course signal is made.

3. The race committee shall notify all yachts concerned by signal or otherwise when and where a race **postponed** or **abandoned** will be sailed.

Note: 5.1. *Always be prepared in case the committee stops the race at one of the marks.*

6—Starting and Finishing Lines

The starting and finishing lines shall be either:

(*a*) A line between a **mark** and a mast or staff on the committee boat or station clearly identified in the sailing instructions;

(*b*) a line between two **marks**; or

(*c*) the extension of a line through two stationary posts, with or without a **mark** at or near its outer limit, inside which the yachts shall pass.

For types (*a*) and (*c*) of starting or finishing lines the sailing instructions may also provide a **mark** at or near the inner end of the line, in which case yachts shall pass between it and the outer **mark**.

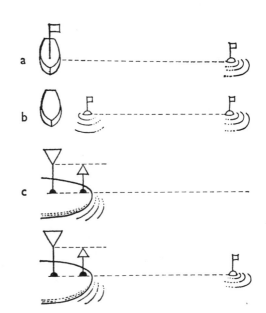

Rule 6 Starting Lines

Note: 6. *I would advise race committees always to lay the starting line between two fixed marks or buoys so that the limit and direction of the line is fixed. This sort of line is the most precise one for competitors. In the drawings, example 'B' is the best. With a windward start, race committees should always lay the line at right angles to the wind and not at right angles to the course to the next mark. In addition they can give a slight bias to the port end of the line. This will give a slight advantage in distance to the boats starting at the port end but to compensate for this there is a slight disadvantage in that it is dangerous for the port end boats to tack. This will ensure that the whole length of the line will be used because it evens out the advantages and disadvantages of starting in various places.*

The 5-minute rule should be used for all starts right from the very beginning because it saves a lot of time and a lot of work for the committees. In championships there should be a checking boat at the opposite end of the line to the committee boat.

I am also sure that even with the 5-minute rule competitors that are over the line early ought to be able to make a new start by going to the committee boat and passing their number and getting an acknowledgement. This will give them some penalty and of course they may have to wait to get their number acknowledged if there are a large number of boats over the line.

In a windward start if the wind shifts permanently the committee must realise this and abandon the start immediately and then re-start the race from another starting line. It can spoil the whole race if the committee continues with a start when the wind has shifted so that boats cannot cross the line on starboard, for example.

6. *A is a distance-mark as described in the sailing instructions but it only has a required side after a yacht has started (i.e. first touches the line after the starting gun) and even then, only if the mark begins, bounds or ends a leg of the course (rule 51.3). If the distance-mark had been in position B it would never legally have a required side for starting purposes even though the sailing instructions might have said that yachts shall start on only one side of it, since it is the starting line which begins this leg of the course and distance-mark B would not have been on the leg which the starting line begins. Therefore you could, in this case, start anywhere between mark B and the committee boat should you wish.*

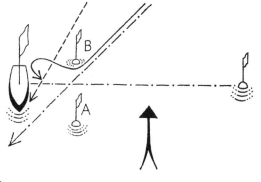

6. *Trouble could possibly be avoided if the sailing instructions describe an imaginary point on the starting line where a line from B to the starting line cuts it at right angles. It could then have been ordered that boats shall not start outside this point. In case of dispute, however, the facts would be very difficult to establish.*

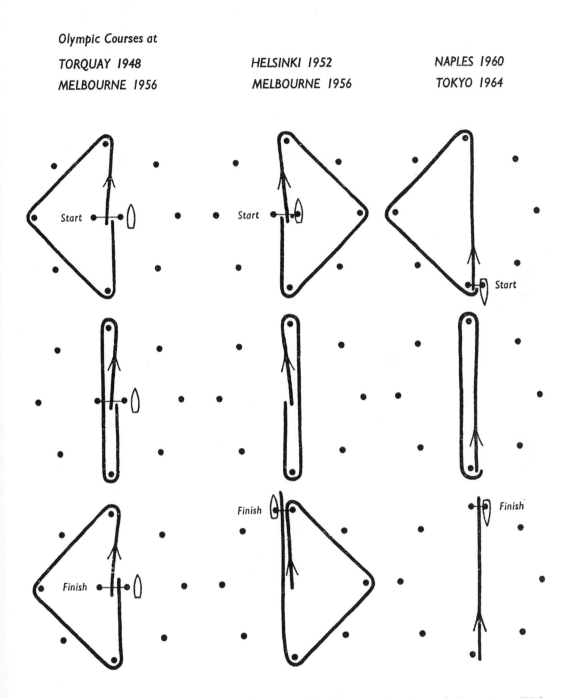

Olympic Courses at

TORQUAY 1948
MELBOURNE 1956

HELSINKI 1952
MELBOURNE 1956

NAPLES 1960
TOKYO 1964

Start

Start

Start

Finish

Finish

Finish

With the starting boat at the centre it was very easy to alter the course direction at the last minute. With the course used at Naples and Tokyo there were cases of the first leg which was not a beat at all and it was too difficult for the committee to move the whole line to another buoy after a wind shift at the last minute. I consider that the fixed ring of eight buoys ought to be abandoned and in the future the committee should lay a windward and a reaching buoy at the ten-minute gun. This would be easy to do accurately with modern radar and radio telephones. Also, an equilateral triangle or any other shape could be laid which would give better racing for planing boats.

7—Start of a Race

1. **Starting Area**—The sailing instructions may define a starting area which may be bounded by buoys. If so, they shall not rank as **marks**.

2. **Timing the Start**—The **start** of a yacht shall be timed from her starting signal.

8—Recalls

1. Unless otherwise prescribed by the national authority or in the sailing instructions, the race committee shall allot a recall number or letter to each yacht. When practicable, yachts' sail numbers should be used as recall numbers, otherwise the race committee shall allot a suitable recall number or letter to each yacht, in which case see rule 3.2 (*p*).

2. (*a*) When any part of a yacht's hull, crew or equipment is over the starting line or its extensions when her starting signal is made, either:

   (i) her recall number or letter shall be displayed as soon as possible and a suitable sound signal shall be given, or

   (ii) such other procedure shall be followed as may be prescribed by the national authority or in the sailing instructions.

   (*b*) When there is either a number of un-identified premature starters, or an error in starting procedure, the race committee may make a general recall signal in accordance with rules 4.1, '1st Substitute,' and 4.7. Unless otherwise prescribed by the national authority or in the sailing instructions, a fresh warning and preparatory signal shall be given. Rule infringements before the preparatory signal for the new start shall not be cause for disqualification.

3. As soon as a recalled yacht has wholly returned to the right side of the starting line or its extensions, the race committee shall so inform her by removing her recall number if displayed; if not, by hail if practicable or in some other manner prescribed in the sailing instructions.

9—Marks

1. **Mark Missing**

   (*a*) When any **mark** either is missing or has shifted, the race committee shall, if possible, replace it in its stated position, or substitute a new one with similar characteristics or a buoy or vessel displaying the letter 'M' of the International Code—the **mark** signal.

   (*b*) If it is impossible either to replace the **mark** or to substitute a new one in time for the yachts to round or pass it, the race committee may, at its discretion, act in accordance with rule 5.1.

2. **Mark Unseen**—When races are sailed in fog or at night, dead reckoning alone should not necessarily be accepted as evidence that a **mark** has been rounded or passed.

10—Finishing

Unless otherwise prescribed by the national authority or in the sailing instructions, in races where there is a time limit, one yacht **finishing** within the prescribed limit shall make the race valid for all other yachts in that race.

11—Ties

When there is a tie at the finish of a race, either actual or on corrected times, the points for the place for which the yachts have tied and for the place immediately below shall be added together and divided equally. When two or more yachts tie for a trophy or prize in either a single race or a series, the yachts so tied should, if possible, sail a deciding race; if not, either the tie shall be broken by a method established under rule 3.2 (i), or the yachts so tied shall either receive equal prizes or share the prize.

12—Yacht Unduly Prejudiced

When the race committee decides that, through no fault of her own, the finishing position of a yacht has been materially prejudiced, by rendering assistance in accordance with rule 58, Rendering Assistance, by being disabled by another yacht which should have kept clear, or by an action of the race committee, it may **cancel** or **abandon** the race or make such other arrangements as it deems equitable.

8.2 (a). *In this case at the moment the starting gun fires the crew, whether he be the helmsman or the trapeze hand, is considered as part of the gear of the boat and the boat A is therefore starting too soon.*

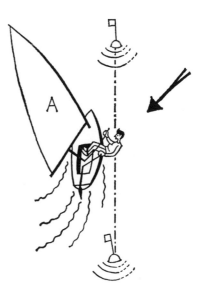

Note: 8.2 (b). *If you were disqualified in one start this is annulled if the start is abandoned and an official new start is ordered.*

Note: 8.3. *This rule has been reworded and seems to mean that the race committee is now compelled to inform a returning yacht when she has reached the right side of the line for a re-start. Previously it seemed to mean that if it was too difficult to do this then the committee need not do so. In large fleets in fact it has been general practice not to allot recall numbers at all and to put the onus on all yachts that they not only start correctly (see also rule 51.1) but also return correctly if they are over too early. Therefore, if an extra gun is fired at the start it means that at least one boat is over early and it becomes the committee's duty to inform each boat when it has returned correctly.*

Note: 10. *You must look carefully at the sailing instructions because there are many different ideas about time limits. It is very seldom, in fact, that this I.Y.R.U. method is used.*

Note: 11. *There are also many different tie-breaking systems but you are not allowed to spin a coin. For example, in the case of a dead heat in a race, the leeward of the two boats could be declared the winner because he was the last previous leader.*

Note: 12. *You will find it quite hard to win a protest under this rule, but it has been done successfully. The race committee will have to decide just how dangerous the situation had been. Of course, if there had been a real risk of a person drowning then there would have been a good case for re-sailing the race.*

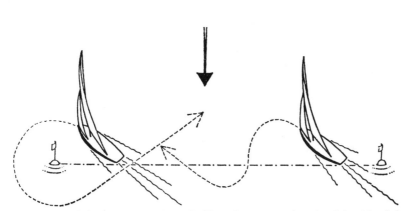

8.3. *In rule 8.3 it is stated that as soon as a recalled boat has returned to the right side of the line, or its extensions . . . this could be interpreted literally as meaning that if you are over the line you could go round and across the continuation of the line to get to the right side, and then start again across the continuation, but rule 51.1 (b) specifically says that this is not allowed.*

13—Re-Sailed Races

When a race is to be re-sailed:

1. All yachts entered in the original race shall be eligible to sail in the re-sailed race.

2. Subject to the entry requirements of the original race, and at the discretion of the race committee, new entries may be accepted.

3. Rule infringements in the original race shall not be cause for disqualification.

4. The race committee shall notify the yachts concerned when and where the race will be re-sailed.

14—Award of Prizes

Before awarding the prizes, the race committee shall be satisfied that all yachts whose finishing positions affect the awards have complied with the racing rules and sailing instructions. It is recommended that the sailing instructions require the member in charge of each yacht to submit within a stated time after she has **finished** a race a signed declaration to the effect that 'all the rules and sailing instructions were obeyed in the race (or races) on (date or dates of race or races)'.

(Numbers 15, 16 and 17 are spare numbers)

PART III—GENERAL REQUIREMENTS

Owner's Responsibilities for Qualifying his Yacht

A yacht intending to **race** *shall, to avoid subsequent disqualification, comply with the rules of Part III before her preparatory signal and, when applicable, while* **racing**.

Note: 14. *You will often find that you will have to sign a declaration that all the rules have been observed correctly. If you forget to sign you will be disqualified. I would like to ask race committees not to go to the trouble of asking for a declaration to be signed because the fact that a boat crossed the finishing line correctly meant in effect that it had obeyed all the rules of the race.*

18—Entries

Unless otherwise prescribed by the national authority or by the race committee in either the notice or the sailing instructions, entries shall be made in the following form:

FORM OF ENTRY

To the Secretary...Club
Please enter the yacht................................ for
the...........................race, on the.....................
Her distinguishing flag is.................................
her sail numbers and letters are............, her rig is..........
the colour of her hull is....................................
and her rating or class is..................................

I agree to be bound by the rules of the I.Y.R.U., by the prescriptions of the national authority under which this race is sailed and by the sailing instructions.

Signed................................. Date...............
(Owner or owner's representative)
    Name..
    Address...
    Telephone No...
    Club..
Entrance fee enclosed.

19—Measurement Certificates

Every yacht entering a race shall hold such valid measurement or rating certificate as may be required by the national authority or other duly authorised body, by her class rules, by the notice of the race, or by the sailing instructions and she shall adhere to the conditions upon which such certificate was based.

20—Ownership of Yachts

1. Unless otherwise prescribed in the conditions of entry, a yacht shall be eligible to compete only when she is either owned by or on charter to and has been entered by a yacht or sailing club recognised by a national authority or a member or members thereof.

2. Two or more yachts owned or chartered wholly or in part by the same body or person shall not compete in the same race without the previous consent of the race committee.

21—Member on Board

Every yacht shall have on board a member of a yacht or sailing club recognised by a national authority, to be in charge of the yacht as owner or owner's representative.

22—Shifting Ballast

1. **General Restrictions**—Floorboards shall be kept down; bulkheads and doors left standing; ladders, stairways and water tanks left in place; all cabin, galley and forecastle fixtures and fittings kept on board; all movable ballast shall be properly stowed under the floorboards or in lockers and no dead weight shall be shifted.

2. **Shipping, Unshipping or Shifting Ballast; Water**—No ballast, whether movable or fixed, shall be shipped, unshipped or shifted, nor shall any water be taken in or discharged except for ordinary ship's use, from 9 p.m. of the day before the race until the yacht is no longer **racing**, except that bilge water may be removed at any time.

23—Anchor

Unless otherwise prescribed by the national authority or by her class rules, every yacht shall carry on board an anchor and chain or rope of suitable size.

24—Life-Saving Equipment

Unless otherwise prescribed by her class rules, every yacht, except one which has sufficient buoyancy to support the crew in case of accident, shall carry adequate life-saving equipment for all persons on board, one item of which shall be ready for immediate use.

25—Sail Numbers, Letters and Emblems

1. Every yacht of an international class recognised by the I.Y.R.U. shall carry on her mainsail:

    (a) When **racing** in foreign waters a letter or letters showing her nationality, thus:

A	Argentine	CY	Ceylon
AR	United Arab Republic	CZ	Czechoslovakia
		D	Denmark
B	Belgium	E	Spain
BA	Bahamas	EC	Ecuador
BL	Brazil	F	France
BU	Bulgaria	G	West Germany
CA	Cambodia	GO	East Germany

GR	Greece	MX	Mexico
H	Holland	N	Norway
HA	Netherlands Antilles	NK	Democratic People's Republic of Korea
I	Italy		
IR	Republic of Ireland	OE	Austria
		P	Portugal
J	Japan	PH	The Philippines
K	United Kingdom	PR	Puerto Rico
KA	Australia	PU	Peru
KB	Bermuda	PZ	Poland
KC	Canada	RC	Cuba
KG	British Guiana	RI	Indonesia
KGB	Gibraltar	RM	Roumania
KH	Hong Kong	S	Sweden
KI	India	SA	South Africa
KJ	Jamaica	SE	Senegal
KK	Kenya	SR	Union of Soviet Socialist Republics
KR	Zambia and S. Rhodesia and Malawi		
KS	Singapore	T	Tunisia
KT	West Indies	TH	Thailand
KZ	New Zealand	TK	Turkey
L	Finland	U	Uruguay
LE	Lebanon	US	United States of America
LX	Luxembourg		
M	Hungary	V	Venezuela
MA	Morocco	X	Chile
MO	Monaco	Y	Yugoslavia
		Z	Switzerland

Note: 22. *This rule is mainly worded for ocean racers. Of course, in a dinghy, the helmsman is himself ballast, and the shifting of his weight is absolutely necessary to get maximum speed. But the crew must wear normal clothes. It is not allowed to wear lead belts. It has become accepted that wet sweaters without limits are not ballast for the purpose of this rule. I agree with this because if you wear too many wet sweaters you become too slow moving about the boat.*

Note: 24. *Now we have special life-jackets for dinghy racing which do not stop you moving about quickly and it is foolish not to wear them. The buoyancy in a racing boat is chiefly to save the boat and to allow you to right it and continue the race. You still need a life-jacket because the boat may blow away from you or you may be too tired and cold to climb in.*

(b) A number, letter or emblem showing the class to which the yacht belongs.

(c) Number of yacht:

A distinguishing number allotted by her own national authority. In the case of a self-administered international class, the number may be allotted by the class owners' association.

Assuming a five-point-five metre yacht belonging to the Argentine Republic to be allotted number 3 by the Argentine national authority, her sail shall be marked:

$$\frac{5.5}{A3}$$

When there is insufficient space to place the letter or letters showing the yacht's nationality in front of her allotted number, it shall be placed above the number.

(d) The sail numbers, letters and emblems shall be placed on both sides of the mainsail, at approximately two-thirds of the height of the sail above the boom, so that the lowest number shows when the sail is fully reefed. Sail numbers, letters and emblems shall sharply contrast in colour with the sail and shall be placed at different heights on the two sides of the sail, those on the starboard side being uppermost, to avoid confusion owing to translucency of the sail. The sail numbers only, shall be similarly placed on both sides of the spinnaker, but at approximately half height.

(e) The following sizes for numbers and letters are prescribed:

Class	Minimum height of figure and letters		Minimum width occupied by each figure except Figure 1		Minimum thickness of every portion of each figure or letter		Minimum space between adjoining figures	
	Metres.	Ins.	Metres.	Ins.	Metres.	Ins.	Metres.	Ins.
12 Metre	0.66	(26)	0.46	(18)	0.10	(4)	0.15	(6)
15 and 13.5 Metre Cruiser Racer ..	0.66	(26)	0.43	(17)	0.10	(4)	0.15	(6)
12 and 10.5 Metre Cruiser Racer ..	0.56	(22)	0.35	(14)	0.10	(4)	0.12	(5)
9 Metre Cruiser Racer	0.50	(20)	0.33	(13)	0.075	(3)	0.10	(4)
8 and 7 Metre Cruiser Racer ..	0.45	(18)	0.30	(12)	0.075	(3)	0.10	(4)
8 Metre	0.50	(20)	0.36	(14)				
6 Metre								
5.5 Metre								
30 sq. Metre	0.46	(18)	0.30	(12)	0.075	(3)	0.10	(4)
22 sq. Metre								
Dragon								
'C' Catamaran	0.38	(15)	0.25	(10)	0.064	(2½)	0.10	(4)
Star								
Flying Dutchman								
Five-O-Five								
12 sq. Metre Sharpie	0.30	(12)	0.20	(8)				
Lightning								
Finn								
14 ft. Dinghy								
Vaurien								
Cadet	0.23	(9)	0.15	(6)				
Snipe								

(f) Sail makers' marks, if any, shall be placed near the tack of the sail and shall not exceed 15 × 15 cms. (6 × 6 ins.).

as they may be applicable, conform to the above requirements.

2. Other yachts shall comply with the rules of their national authority or class in regard to the allotment, carrying and size of sail numbers, letters and emblems, which rules should, so far

3. A yacht shall not be disqualified for failing to comply with the provisions of rule 25 without prior warning and adequate opportunity to make correction.

26—Forestays

Unless otherwise prescribed in the class rules, the forestay or forestays shall be fixed approximately in the centre-line of the yacht.

27—Flags

A national authority may prescribe the flag usage which shall be observed by yachts under its jurisdiction.

(Numbers 28, 29 and 30 are spare numbers)

Note: 25.3. This is a new rule. One or two cases of disqualification have happened when it was found that sail letters were too small after a race. It is stupid to disqualify yachts straight away for such a small thing.

Note: 27. National authorities now have to say whether they need racing flags in their waters. The old British attitude of 'Distinguishing Flag etiquette,' now wholly out of keeping with modern sailing conditions, especially for dinghies, is gradually dying out. Most countries have never required a distinguishing flag at the masthead (usually called a Racing Flag). The British argument for lowering the racing flag upon retirement has almost nothing in its favour and much against it. The alternative of putting an ensign at the stern is much more sensible from almost all points of view.

Part IV   Sailing Rules

PART IV—SAILING RULES WHEN YACHTS MEET

Helmsman's Rights and Obligations Concerning Right of Way

The rules of part IV apply only between yachts which either are intending to **race** or are **racing** in the same or different races, and, except when rule 3.2 (k) applies, replace the International Regulations for Preventing Collisions at Sea or Government Right-of-Way Rules applicable to the area concerned, from the time a yacht intending to **race** begins to sail about in the vicinity of the starting line until she has either **finished** or retired and has left the vicinity of the course.

SECTION A—RULES WHICH ALWAYS APPLY

31—Disqualification

1. A yacht may be disqualified for infringing a rule of Part IV only when the infringement occurs while she is **racing**, whether or not a collision results.

2. A yacht may be disqualified before or after she is **racing** for seriously hindering a yacht which is **racing**, or for infringing the sailing instructions.

Note: PART IV – Sailing Rules when Yachts Meet.

This is the most tricky part of the racing rules and so we will spend some time in examining cases in detail.

A point to remember is that, if you are racing and meet another yacht racing, these racing rules apply. It does not matter if the boats are in different races. But if you are not sure if the other yacht is racing then the International Regulations for Preventing Collisions at Sea apply (otherwise known as the 'Rule of the Road at Sea'), which all normal shipping has to recognise. These regulations always take precedence if there is doubt.

In order to settle any damage claims the result of a yacht racing protest is normally binding on two yachts racing. If one or both boats are not racing then liability depends on the 'Rule of the Road at Sea.'

Note: 31. Before you go afloat you should study the sailing instructions very carefully (see rule 3) because you can be disqualified if you fail to keep any of the special rules for this particular race. For example, you may be required to carry some special flag in your rigging, or you may be required to wear life-jackets or there may be some special starting instruction such as the 5-minute rule or you may have to carry extra buoyancy.

32—Avoiding Collisions

A right-of-way yacht which makes no attempt to avoid a collision resulting in serious damage may be disqualified as well as the other yacht.

33—Retiring from Race

A yacht, which realises she has infringed a racing rule or a sailing instruction, should retire promptly; but, if she persists in racing, other yachts shall continue to accord her such rights as she may have under the rules of Part IV.

34—Misleading or Baulking

1. When one yacht is required to keep clear of another, the right-of-way yacht shall not (except to the extent permitted by rule 38.1, Luffing after Starting), so alter course as to:

    (*a*) prevent the other yacht from keeping clear; or

    (*b*) mislead or baulk her while she is keeping clear.

2. A yacht is not misleading or baulking another if she alters course by **luffing** or **bearing away** to conform to a change in the strength or direction of the wind.

35—Hailing

A right-of-way yacht, except when **luffing** under rule 38.1, Luffing after Starting, should hail before or when making an alteration of course which may not be foreseen by the other yacht or when claiming room at a **mark** or **obstruction**.

Note: 32. *This rule is now greatly simplified and its effects will now surely be changed. It seems that collisions are now officially approved of except where they result in 'serious damage.' If the right of way yacht tries to avoid a collision and fails, and this collision results in 'serious damage,' then she seems to be in the clear.*

But the problem is to decide what is 'serious damage.' I consider that there is very little that racing dinghies can do to each other which would come under this heading. But the intention is that, if the damaged boat is unable to complete the race at normal speed, then the damage can be considered as 'serious.'

Note: 33. *If you are absolutely sure that you have broken a racing rule then you should, of course, retire immediately, but the racing rules have no way of stopping a man who has broken the rules from continuing. This is especially important in points racing where you could interfere with another competitor and force him to get a bad placing when your own placing does not matter.*

If you really have doubts as to who was right then you should put up your protest flag. If there was a collision one or both yachts must have been wrong and it is best to find out so that you will know next time. Read again the foreword to this racing rules section.

Note: 35. *This is not so much a rule as a recommendation. A new provision – Claiming room at Marks and Obstructions – is added to the situations when a hail is recommended.*

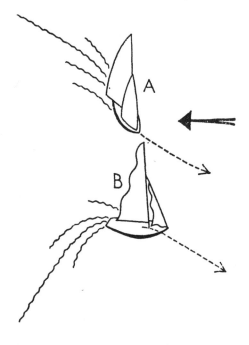

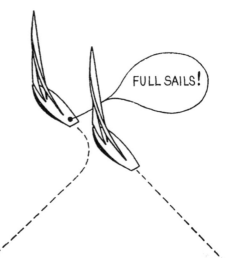

35. *This is not really a rule but it is trying to say that a hail is often very helpful in clarifying a situation.*

——————————————————▶

34.1. *B tacks and A gybes at the same time. Rule 41.1 cannot apply and therefore B, who held right of way originally, must be disqualified under rule 34.*

——————————————————▶

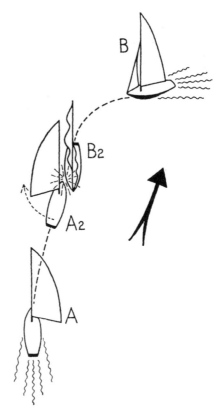

34. *This is a situation which many people would like to include under this rule where a port tack boat is attempting to fall off and pass under the stern of a boat tacking from starboard to port. But this situation can only come under rule 41.1 (Tacking or Gybing). The reason for this is that B always has the right to tack and A must watch out for this.*

◀——————————————————

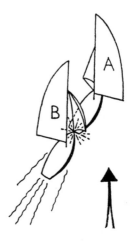

SECTION B—OPPOSITE TACK RULE

36—Fundamental Rule

A **port-tack** yacht shall keep clear of a **starboard-tack** yacht.

SECTION C—SAME TACK RULES

37—Fundamental Rules

1. A **windward** yacht shall keep clear of a **leeward** yacht.

2. A yacht **clear astern** shall keep clear of a yacht **clear ahead.**

3. A yacht which establishes an **overlap** to **leeward** from **clear astern** shall allow the **windward yacht** ample room and opportunity to keep clear, and during the existence of that **overlap** the **leeward yacht** shall not sail above her **proper course.**

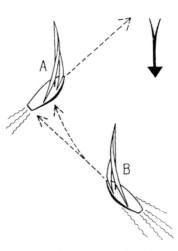

36. *As A has the wind coming from the starboard side, and B the wind from the port side, then B should give way to A.*

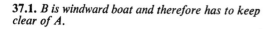

37.1. *B is windward boat and therefore has to keep clear of A.*

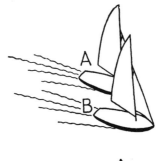

36. *Even though B is overtaking A and is clear astern, A must give way because B is sailing on starboard tack. Rule 36 applies because they are on opposite tacks.*

37.2. *B must keep clear of A and must not sail into A's stern if they are on the same tack. If they are on opposite tacks rule 36 applies.*

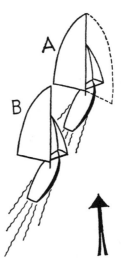

36. *B may not luff to try to hit A, who would otherwise have been able to keep clear. This case comes under Rule 34.1 (b).*

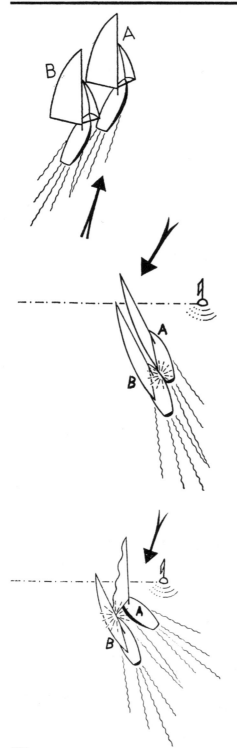

37.3. *B is overtaking A but has given too little room for A to be able to luff and keep clear.*

37.3. *B establishes her overlap by diving through A's lee but may not luff above her proper course.*

37.3. *B, coming from astern with better speed, obtains an overlap but is too close and collides with A, who had just luffed close hauled in order to cross the starting line. Therefore, B obtained the overlap too close to A, who was not given enough room by B to luff. A is right according to rule 37.3.*

37.3. *In this situation A must keep clear as she is windward boat (37.1) and can only rely on 37.3 if she can show that she had not been given ample room and opportunity to keep clear. In this case all she had to do was immediately to pull in her boom slightly when the overlap had been established.*

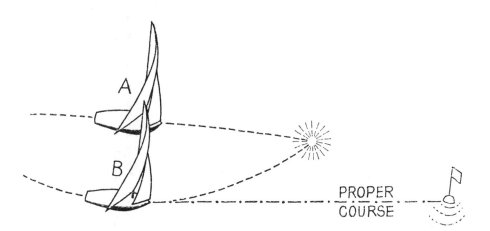

PROPER
COURSE

Rule 38　　Luffing after Starting

38—Right-of-Way Yacht Luffing after Starting

1. **Luffing Rights and Limitations.** After she has **started** and cleared the starting line, a yacht **clear ahead** or a **leeward yacht** may **luff** as she pleases, except that:

A **leeward yacht** shall not sail above her **proper course** while an **overlap** exists if, at any time during its existence, the helmsman of the **windward yacht** (when sighting abeam from his normal station and sailing no higher than the **leeward yacht**) has been abreast or forward of the mainmast of the **leeward yacht**.

2. **Overlap Limitations.** For the purpose of this rule: An **overlap** does not exist unless the yachts are clearly within two overall lengths of the longer yacht; and an **overlap** which exists between two yachts when the leading yacht **starts**, or when one or both of them completes a **tack** or gybe, shall be regarded as a new **overlap** beginning at that time.

3. **Hailing to Stop or Prevent a Luff**—When there is doubt, the **leeward yacht** may assume that she has the right to **luff** unless the helmsman of the **windward yacht** has hailed 'Mast Abeam,' or words to that effect. The **leeward yacht** shall be governed by such hail, and, if she deems it improper, her only remedy is to protest.

4. **Curtailing a Luff**—The **windward yacht** shall not cause a **luff** to be curtailed because of her proximity to the **leeward yacht** unless an **obstruction**, a third yacht or other object restricts her ability to respond.

5. **Luffing Two or More Yachts**—A yacht shall not **luff** unless she has the right to **luff** all yachts which would be affected by her **luff**, in which case they shall all respond even if an intervening yacht or yachts would not otherwise have the right to **luff**.

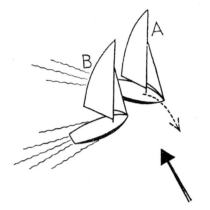

38.1 *B is overtaking. A has the right to luff because she was ahead and is now to leeward and still ahead of B's 'mast abeam' position.*

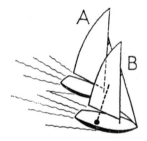

38.1. *B's helmsman during the luffing match has reached a point ahead of A's mast. When B's helmsman calls 'mast abeam' A must no longer steer above his proper course. A regains her luffing rights only when there is more than two overall lengths of the longest boat of clear water between them, or she is clear ahead.*

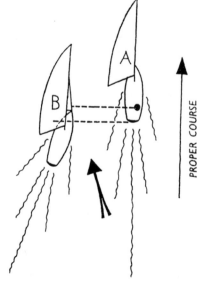

38.1. *B is overtaking A, but on a course which is slightly higher than the proper course. We cannot talk about luffing here, but nevertheless A's helmsman should call 'mast abeam,' and thus B is obliged to turn back on to the proper course.*

Two Five-O-Fives going at absolutely top speed during the World Championship in 1966 at Adelaide, South Australia.

*This is a Scandinavian Folkboat, which is the most popular racing keelboat class in Sweden, Denmark and Finland,
and they have a Gold Cup competition every year. This class is also growing very fast in Germany. In many other
places there are Folkboats and in San Francisco for example they start around forty at a time.*

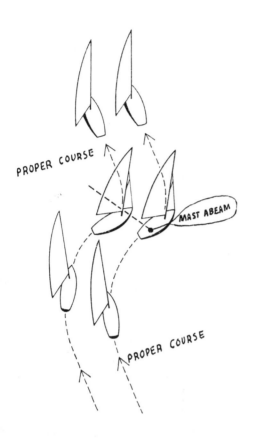

PROPER COURSE

PROPER COURSE

MAST ABEAM

PROPER COURSE

38.1. *Remember not to luff again after this situation without gaining new luffing rights.*

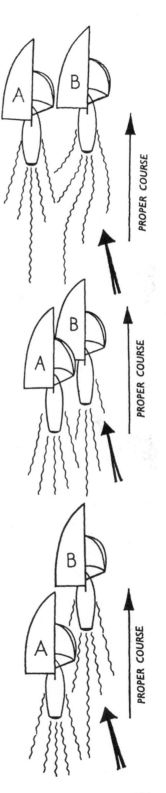

38.1. *A is overtaking and B must luff far enough so that A does not touch her boom, but she need not luff any further because A must not luff above her proper course.*

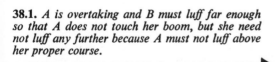

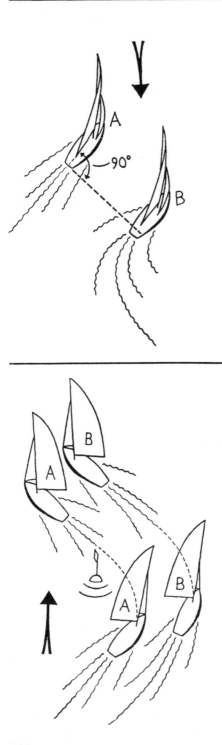

38.2. *The measurement of the two boats' length distance is taken from hull to hull as shown.*

38.2. *B's overlap starts from the moment when she completes her tack.*

38.2. *At the start the moment of the beginning of the overlap is taken from the time when the leading boat actually crosses the starting line.*

38.2. *The overlap starts from the moment when A and B have completed their gybes.*

38.2. *A is overtaking B, and as soon as her mast goes forward of B's helmsman, she may gybe and then gains luffing rights. If A is overtaking on the same gybe as B, then she can gain her luffing rights by doing two quick gybes.*

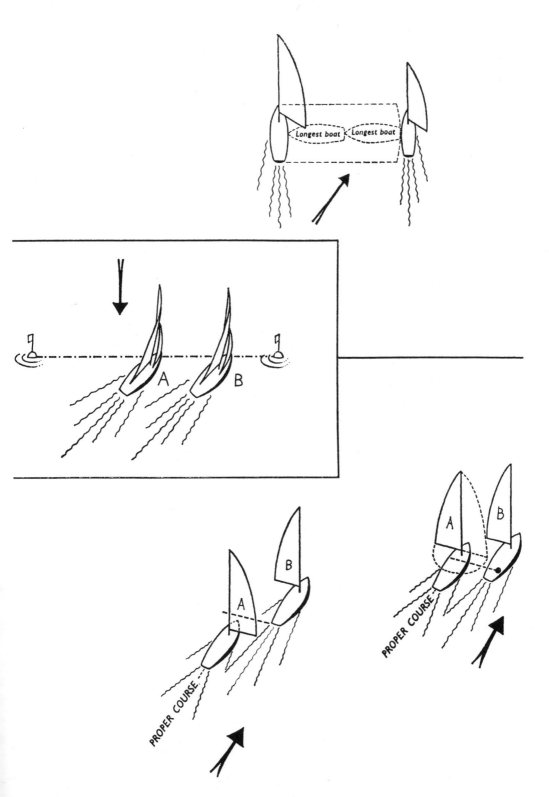

38.3. *Remember to call 'mast abeam' or something similar, because this is the only way you can take away the luffing rights of the leeward boat. After this the leeward boat must pay off on to her proper course and will only regain luffing rights if she breaks the overlap by drawing clear ahead or more than two lengths abeam and then re-establishes it again with her mast forward of the windward boat's helmsman.*

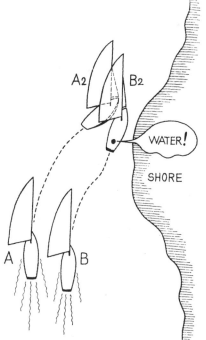

38.4. *A may luff and does so. B can now stop the luff by calling 'Water' and A does not have to return to her proper course but need only just give enough room.*

38.5. *C must respond to a luff from A, and also give room to B, even though B may have no luffing rights of her own over C.*

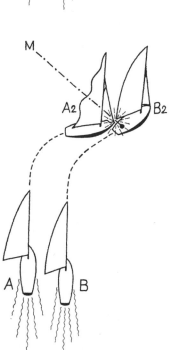

38.3. *A luffs correctly but if she hits B when she is obviously behind the 'mast abeam' position, A will be wrong. If there is doubt and B has not called 'mast abeam,' A would be right.*

38.5. *In this instance, A has luffed B, C and D, but loses luffing rights over D, and thus D can call 'mast abeam,' and force A to go back on to her proper course.*

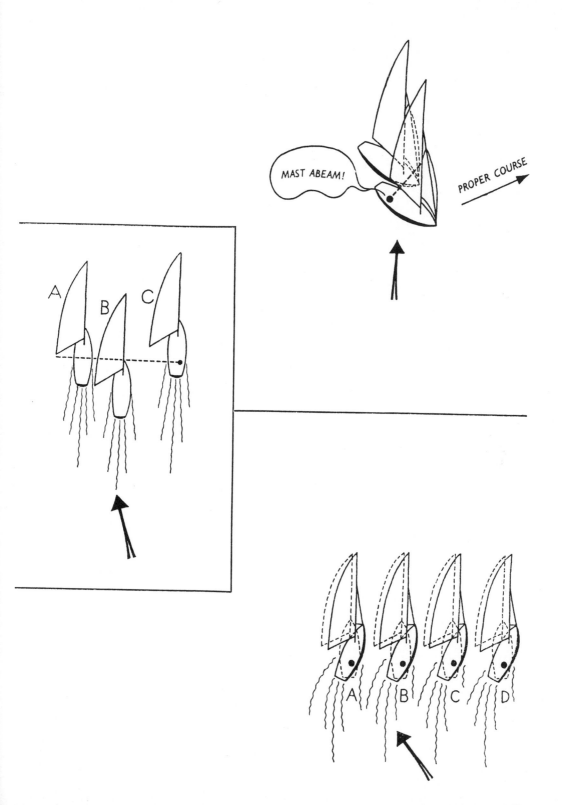

39—Sailing Below a Proper Course after Starting

A yacht which is on a free leg of the course after having **started** and cleared the starting line shall not sail below her **proper course** when she is clearly within three of her overall lengths of either a **leeward yacht** or a yacht **clear astern** which is steering a course to pass to **leeward**.

Note: 39. *This is one of the main alterations in principle in the 1965 revision and it takes the old American viewpoint again. It means that you may not bear away to throw your dirty wind on to another yacht if the leg is a free one and if you are within three lengths of her. On the other hand, if you are both on a windward leg you may do so. Presumably, if a tack will have to be made to reach the next mark this is evidence that the leg is 'to windward.'*

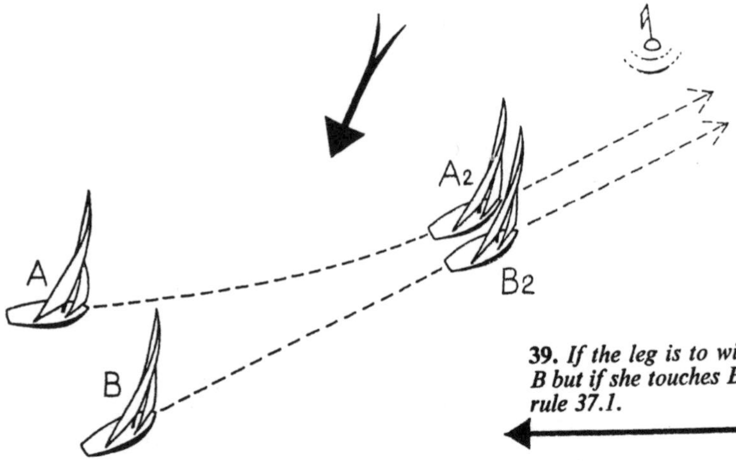

39. *If the leg is to windward A may bear away on B but if she touches B she will be disqualified under rule 37.1.*

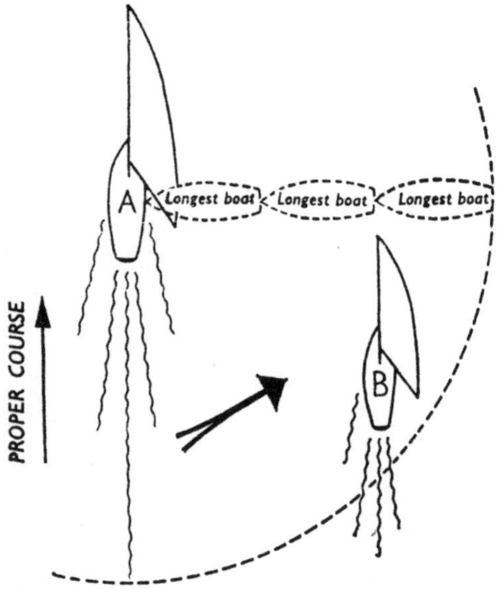

39. *As long as B is inside a distance of three boats' lengths from A, then A may not bear away out of her proper course to interfere with B on a free leg of the course.*

Rule 40   Luffing before starting

40—Right-of-Way Yacht Luffing before Starting

Before a yacht has **started** and cleared the starting line, any **luff** on her part which affects another yacht shall be carried out slowly. A **leeward yacht** may so **luff** only when the helmsman of the **windward yacht** (sighting abeam from his normal station) is abaft the mainmast of the **leeward yacht.** However, after her starting signal the **leeward yacht** may **luff** slowly to assume her **proper course** even when, because of her position, she would not otherwise have the right to **luff.** Rules 38.3, Hailing to Stop or Prevent a Luff; 38.4, Curtailing a Luff; and 38.5, Luffing Two or More Yachts, also apply.

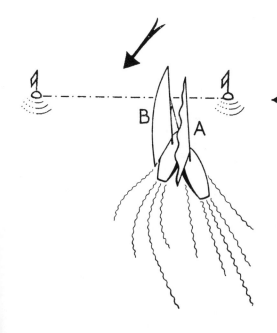

40. *Rule 40 is very difficult as it is hard to define what it is to alter course 'slowly.' The intention with this rule must be to avoid collisions when boats are closest to each other at the start, and consequently have difficulty in keeping clear when a leeward boat is luffing. The more boats there are the slower the leeward boat must luff. If only two boats are involved it is all right to luff as shown in the sketch. A has a fair chance to keep clear.*

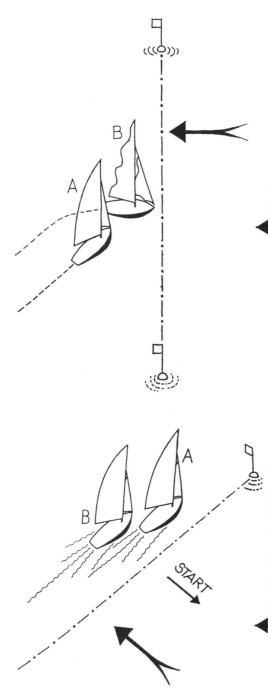

40. *B has luffing rights and can luff head to wind before the start. She cannot be forced to bear away at any time before or after the starting signal.*

40. *B overlaps A before the starting signal. She may only continue in the same direction she had when she obtained the overlap. A must hail 'Mast abeam' in order to protect herself from being luffed. Also, if B is travelling faster, A must pull in her boom because she will be wrong if B touches it.*

If the same situation occurred after the starting signal, A must immediately luff on to her proper course. B must remember rule 37.3 and allow A ample room and opportunity to do this. Because of the use of the word 'ample' in this rule, if there is any doubt it must be resolved in favour of the windward boat. It is also easier for B to bear away.

SECTION D—CHANGING TACK RULES

41—Tacking or Gybing

1. A yacht which is either **tacking** or **gybing** shall keep clear of a yacht **on a tack**.

2. A yacht shall neither **tack** nor **gybe** into a position which will give her right of way unless she does so far enough from a yacht **on a tack** to enable this yacht to keep clear without having to begin to alter her course until after the **tack** or **gybe** has been completed.

3. A yacht which **tacks** or **gybes** has the onus of satisfying the race committee that she completed her **tack** or **gybe** in accordance with rule 41.2.

4. When two yachts are both **tacking** or both **gybing** at the same time, the one on the other's **port** side shall keep clear.

41.3. *A puts in a protest. It will be easy for B to satisfy the committee because there was no collision. A must remember that she must touch B in order to have a good chance of winning the protest. This is a sensible interpretation because it is too easy for A to put in a protest in cases like this. If A touches B without A bearing away there is very little chance that she will lose the protest.*
A does not have to begin to give way until B's tack is complete.

41.2. *B is coming on port tack and is tacking on to starboard tack. B has not completed her tack and therefore A does not have to start to luff yet and is therefore right.*

Note: 41.3. *It is now clearly stated in this rule, and it seems to apply also to all rules, that what used to be called 'proving' that your manoeuvre was correct is the same thing as 'satisfying the race committee.' Unless you can succeed in this your whole case will fail.*

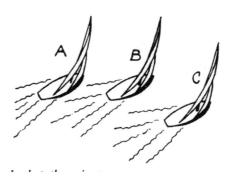

41.2. *In this situation D tacks but there is no possibility of C being able to clear her and therefore D has not satisfied rule 41.2. If D wants to tack on to starboard she will have to bear away under C.*

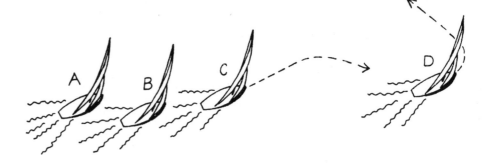

41.2. *In this situation the rules are not clear about whether D can insist on her starboard tack rights after tacking. But my interpretation is that if D tacks C must bear away because there is no time for C to hail B and A for room to tack herself before a collision would occur with D.*

41.1, .2 and .3. B tacks on to starboard and must have completed her tack before she can claim right of way over A. The onus of proof is on B, to show that the tack was not too close. A does not have to begin to give way until B's tack is complete.

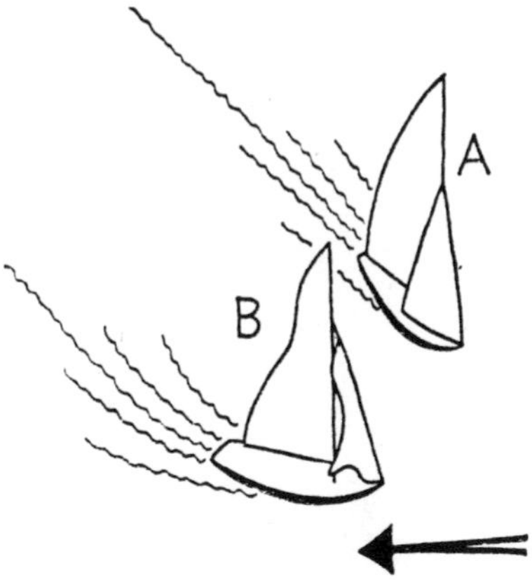

41.1 and **.3.** B must complete her gybe before she can force A to alter course. Here B has gybed too late to gain right of way over A, because A has no possibility of being able to keep clear. In case of doubt the onus of proof is on B. In practice this means that B must have a witness from a third boat.

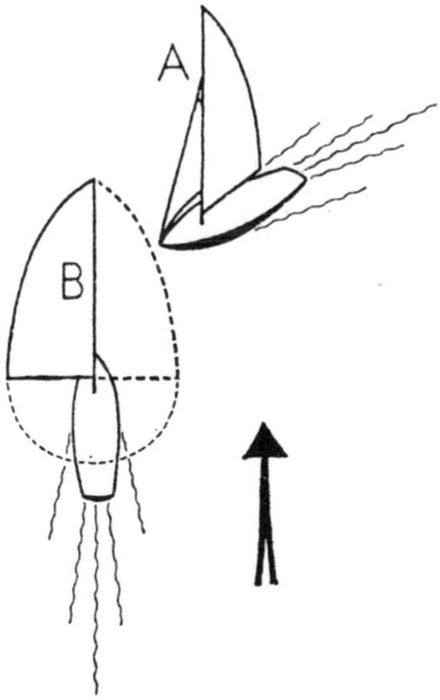

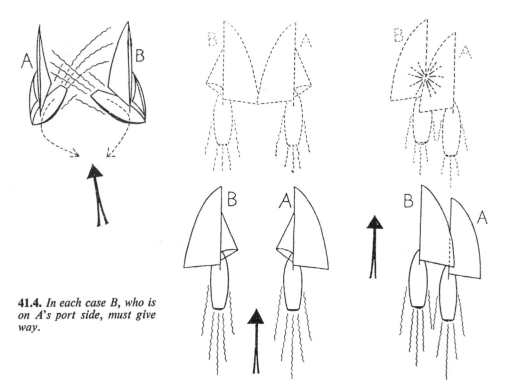

41.4. *In each case B, who is on A's port side, must give way.*

SECTION E—RULES OF EXCEPTION AND SPECIAL APPLICATION

When a rule of this section applies, to the extent to which it explicitly provides rights and obligations, it over-rides any conflicting rule of Part IV which precedes it, except the rules of Section A— Rules Which Always Apply.

42—Rounding or Passing Marks and Obstructions

When yachts either on the same **tack** or, after **starting** and clearing the starting line on opposite **tacks,** are about to round or pass a **mark** on the same required side or an **obstruction** on the same side:

When Overlapped

1. (*a*) An outside yacht shall give each yacht **overlapping** her on the inside room to round or pass it, except as provided in rules 42.1 (*c*), (*d*) and (*e*). Room includes room to **tack** or **gybe** when either is an integral part of the rounding or passing manoeuvre.

(*b*) When an inside yacht of two or more **overlapped** yachts on opposite **tacks** will have to **gybe** in rounding a **mark,** in order most directly to assume a **proper course** on the next leg, she shall **gybe** when she has obtained room.

(*c*) When two yachts on opposite **tacks** are either on a beat or when one of them will have to **tack** either to round the **mark** or to avoid the **obstruction,** as between each other rule 42.1 (*a*) shall not apply and they are subject to rules 36, Opposite Tack, Fundamental Rule, and 41, Tacking or Gybing.

(*d*) An outside **leeward yacht** with luffing rights may take an inside yacht to windward of a **mark,** provided that she hails to that effect and begins to **luff** before she is within two of her overall lengths of the **mark** and provided that she also passes to windward of it.

Note: SECTION E (Rules 42–45). *All the rules in this section cover special cases and when these cases apply they override all the basic rules which precede them in Part IV, with the exception of those in Section A which always apply.*

The rules which always apply (31–35) concern mainly one's 'conduct and manners' during racing and do not describe the sort of boat-to-boat situations covered in Sections B to E (36–45).

Note: 42. *This is one of the most important rules to understand and is divided into three parts.*

First there are instructions for rounding and passing marks and obstructions when boats are overlapped. These are 42.1 (a) to (e).

Secondly there are instructions for cases where boats are <u>not overlapped</u>. 42.2 (a) and (b).

Thirdly there are instructions on the vital point of establishing and breaking overlaps. 42.3 (a) to (d).

(*e*) When approaching the starting line to **start,** a **leeward yacht** shall be under no obligation to give any **windward yacht** room to pass to leeward of a starting **mark** surrounded by navigable water; but, after the starting signal, a **leeward yacht** shall not deprive a **windward yacht** of room at such **mark** either:

(i) by heading above the first **mark**; or

(ii) by **luffing** above **close-hauled.**

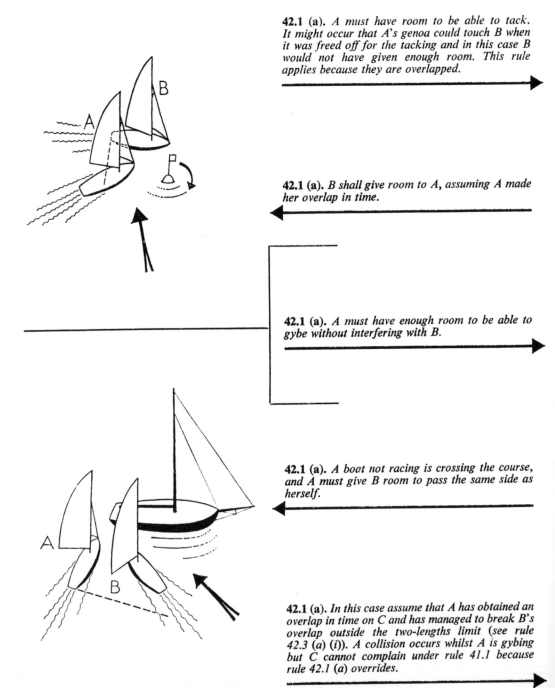

42.1 (a). *A must have room to be able to tack. It might occur that A's genoa could touch B when it was freed off for the tacking and in this case B would not have given enough room. This rule applies because they are overlapped.*

42.1 (a). *B shall give room to A, assuming A made her overlap in time.*

42.1 (a). *A must have enough room to be able to gybe without interfering with B.*

42.1 (a). *A boat not racing is crossing the course, and A must give B room to pass the same side as herself.*

42.1 (a). *In this case assume that A has obtained an overlap in time on C and has managed to break B's overlap outside the two-lengths limit (see rule 42.3 (a) (i)). A collision occurs whilst A is gybing but C cannot complain under rule 41.1 because rule 42.1 (a) overrides.*

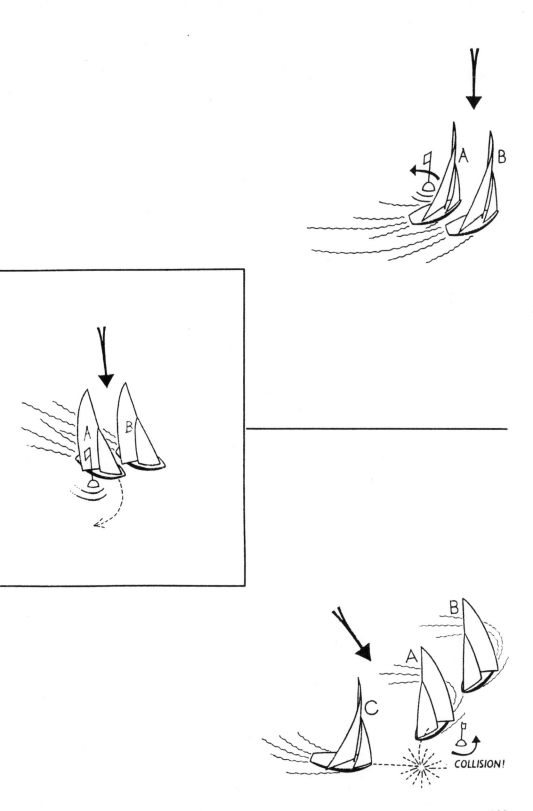

COLLISION!

Rule 42.1 (b)   *Rounding when overlapped*

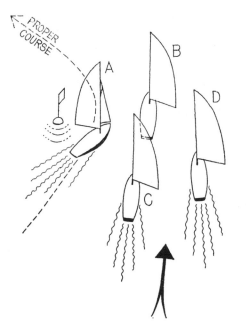

42.1 (b). *A must gybe on to the new proper course at the earliest opportunity. She is not allowed to continue and force B, C and D to keep clear under rule 36.*

Opposite: Absolute concentration is the secret of success in light weather. Here, Silver Medallists Tony Morgan and Keith Musto are determined that their spinnaker shall not collapse.

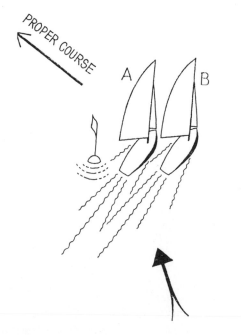

42.1 (b). *Because A and B are on the same tack A does not have to gybe on to her new proper course.*

Rule 42.1 (c)   Rounding when overlapped

42.1 (c). *Rule 42.1 (a) does not apply in this situation because the two boats are sailing to windward on opposite tacks. Rules 36 applies, and so B does not have to give room.*

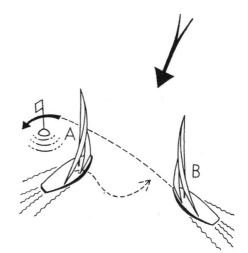

Opposite: Lowell North's Dragon, which won the Bronze Medal at Tokyo, had double-runners to control the very flexible mast. These are not now allowed in the class but are a very effective way of staying a mast. Note the powerful sails for this light-to-medium wind.

42.1 (c). *B cannot claim room during her tacking manoeuvre. It is exactly the same as if they were on the open sea with no mark anywhere near.*

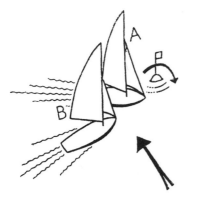

42.1 (d). *If A has the right to luff then she can take B to the wrong side of the mark and she must also go the wrong side with her, but in this case she has luffed too late. (See the next drawing.)*

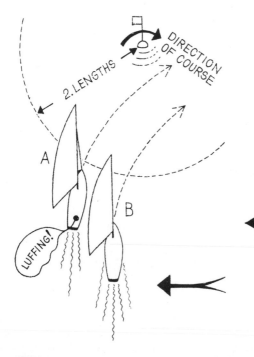

42.1 (d). *A must hail and must also start to luff when she is still outside her two-length radius of the mark. She must also go to windward of the mark as well as B.*

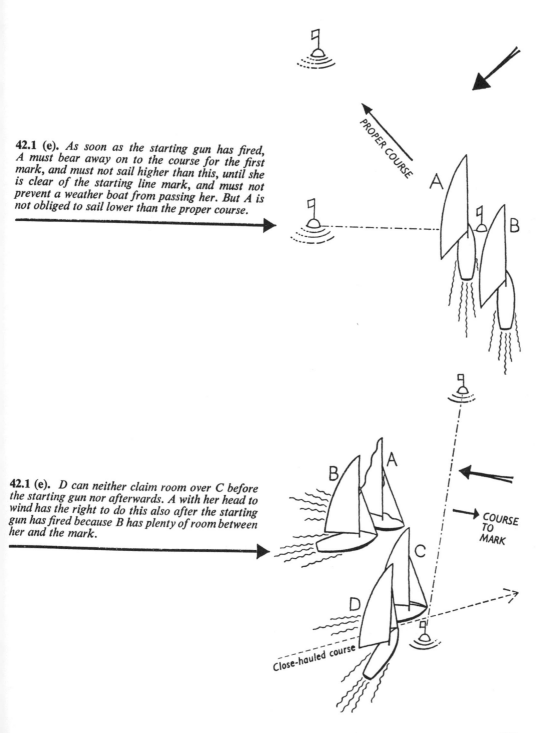

42.1 (e). *As soon as the starting gun has fired, A must bear away on to the course for the first mark, and must not sail higher than this, until she is clear of the starting line mark, and must not prevent a weather boat from passing her. But A is not obliged to sail lower than the proper course.*

42.1 (e). *D can neither claim room over C before the starting gun nor afterwards. A with her head to wind has the right to do this also after the starting gun has fired because B has plenty of room between her and the mark.*

PROPER COURSE

COURSE TO MARK

Close-hauled course

195

When Clear Astern and Clear Ahead

2. (*a*) A yacht **clear astern** shall keep clear in anticipation of and during the rounding or passing manoeuvre when the yacht **clear ahead** remains on the same **tack** or **gybes**.

(*b*) A yacht **clear ahead** which **tacks** to round a **mark** is subject to rule 41, Tacking or Gybing, but a yacht **clear astern** shall not **luff** above **close-hauled** so as to prevent the yacht **clear ahead** from **tacking**.

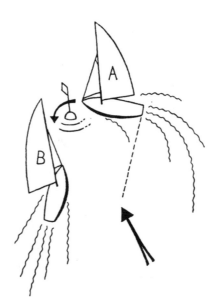

42.2 (a). *A who is clear ahead has the right to gybe as this is part of the rounding manoeuvre.*

→

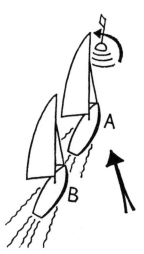

42.2 (a). *B must keep clear even though she now has an overlap because this was not made in time (see rule 42.3 (a) (i)). Neither can B claim her starboard tack rights.*

←

NOT 42.2 (a) *or* **(b).** *A shall not have room to tack because they are beginning a beat to windward and rule 41.1 applies.*

→

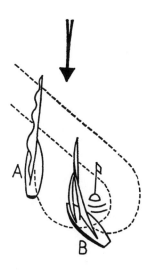

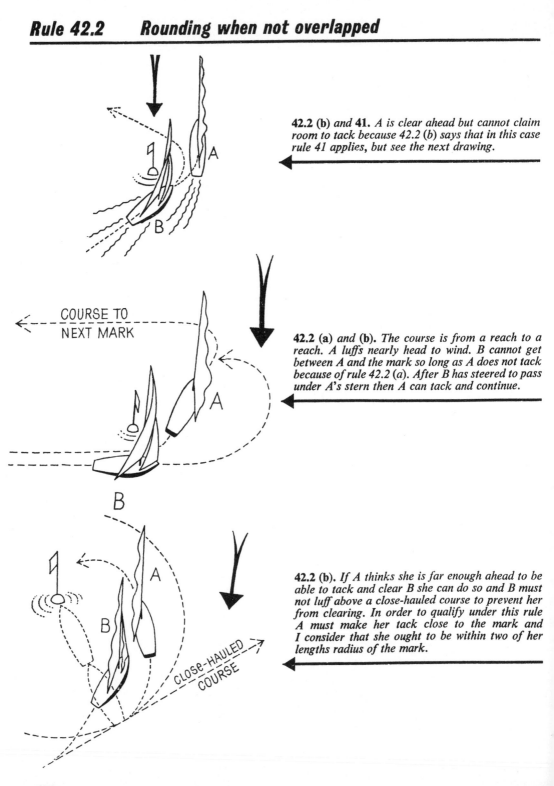

42.2 (b) and 41. *A is clear ahead but cannot claim room to tack because 42.2 (b) says that in this case rule 41 applies, but see the next drawing.*

COURSE TO
NEXT MARK

42.2 (a) and (b). *The course is from a reach to a reach. A luffs nearly head to wind. B cannot get between A and the mark so long as A does not tack because of rule 42.2 (a). After B has steered to pass under A's stern then A can tack and continue.*

42.2 (b). *If A thinks she is far enough ahead to be able to tack and clear B she can do so and B must not luff above a close-hauled course to prevent her from clearing. In order to qualify under this rule A must make her tack close to the mark and I consider that she ought to be within two of her lengths radius of the mark.*

CLOSE-HAULED
COURSE

Restrictions on Establishing and Breaking an Overlap

3. (*a*) A yacht **clear astern** shall not establish an inside **overlap** and be entitled to room under rule 42.1 (*a*) when the yacht **clear ahead**:

   (i) is within two of her own lengths of the **mark** or **obstruction**, except as provided in rule 42.3 (*b*); or

   (ii) is unable to give the required room.

(*b*) A yacht **clear astern** may establish an **overlap** between the yacht **clear ahead** and a continuing **obstruction** such as a shoal or the shore, only when there is room for her to do so in safety.

(*c*) A yacht **clear ahead** shall be under no obligation to give room before an **overlap** is established. The onus will lie upon the yacht which has been **clear astern** to satisfy the race committee that the **overlap** was established in proper time.

(*d*) When an **overlap** exists at the time the outside yacht comes within two of her lengths of the **mark**, she shall be bound by rule 42.1 (*a*), even though the **overlap** may thereafter be broken.

Note: 42.3 (a). *This is a completely new rule which I suggested to the I.Y.R.U. at Tokyo. Up till now it has been impossible to decide how late you can leave the claiming of room. We all know how boats surge back and forth relative to each other on waves. Often in the past you have been able to claim room at the very last moment as you surge down a wave. This can be quite dangerous. Now you have to claim your overlap before the leading boat is within two lengths of the mark, which gives her a better chance of giving room.*

Look out for part (ii) of this rule. There will be cases when you can establish an overlap in time but it may still be impossible for the outside boat to give you room. If you hit the mark or obstruction or if you hit the outside boat you may find that you have no rights at all.

42.2 (a) (i). *B is too late in claiming room. She is surfing on a wave at twice the speed of A who has no chance of giving room. B must establish her overlap before A gets within two lengths of the mark and even then this may be too late in some conditions for A to be able to give room (see 42.3 (a) (ii)).*

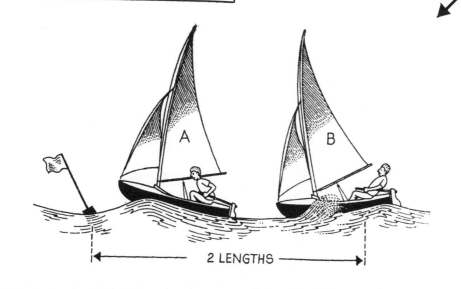

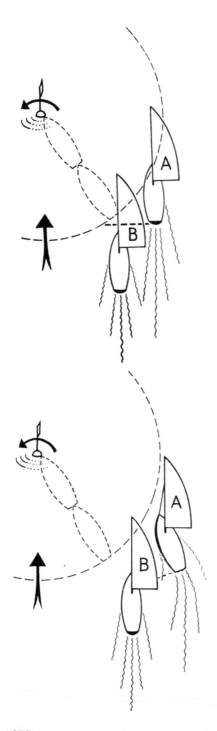

42.3 (a) (i). *The intention of this rule is that a leeward yacht is not compelled to go close to the mark in order to deny a windward boat water. A is allowed to make a normal smooth rounding. This distance is to be more than two boat lengths. It means that A, who is within this distance and clear ahead of B, does not have to give room when she is altering course to round the mark.*

42.3 (a) (i). *A is not within the required distance of two boat lengths from the mark when she is altering her course, so she cannot refuse to give B room.*

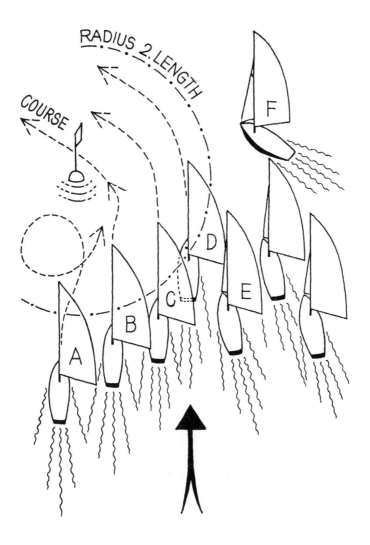

42.3 (a). *Even though A has established an overlap in proper time on B, the latter may not be able to give room because of the delay in response from the outside boats. If she has been given too little room she ought not to risk making a protest under rule 42.1 (a).*

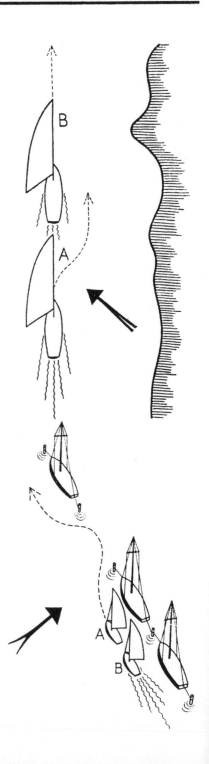

Note: 42.3 (b). *This is an awkward rule to interpret. Presumably the leading boat is already as close to the obstruction as she thinks she can go with safety. Therefore it is difficult for the overtaking boat to show that she can go safely closer. However, rule 42.3 (c) says that the leader does not have to begin to give room until the overlap is actually established. If the overtaking boat runs aground or hits the obstruction before she has established her overlap and also given the overtaken boat time to give room then obviously she has not satisfied this rule.*

42.3 (b). *If A is of the opinion that B could safely go closer to the shore, then A has the right to try to pass between B and the shore. B loses her right to luff owing to A's overlap if they are so close to the shore that there is danger of grounding.*

42.3 (b). *A must be careful when arriving at a break in the obstruction. This is B's chance to establish an overlap.*

Note: **42.3 (d).** *This is the logical extension of 42.3 (a). You must therefore make absolutely sure that you have established your overlap before entering the 'two-lengths' zone and that you have got an acknowledgement from the other boat.*

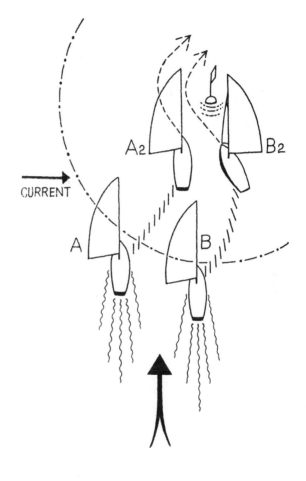

42.3 (d). *B has an overlap in time. The gybe breaks the overlap but this rule says that in this situation B can still claim room to round inside.*

43—Close-Hauled, Hailing for Room to Tack at Obstructions

1. **Hailing**—When safe pilotage requires one of two **close-hauled** yachts on the same **tack** to make a substantial alteration of course to clear an **obstruction**, and if she intends to **tack,** but cannot **tack** without colliding with the other yacht, she shall hail the other yacht for room to **tack.**

2. **Responding**—The hailed yacht at the earliest possible moment after the hail shall either:

(*a*) **tack,** in which case, the hailing yacht shall begin to **tack** either:

  (i)   before the hailed yacht has completed her **tack,** or

  (ii)   if she cannot then **tack** without colliding with the hailed yacht, immediately she is able to **tack,** or

(*b*) reply 'You **tack,**' or words to that effect, if in her opinion she can keep clear without **tacking** or after postponing her **tack.** In this case:

  (i)   the hailing yacht shall immediately **tack,** and

  (ii)   the hailed yacht shall keep clear.

  (iii)   The onus shall lie on the hailed yacht which replied 'You **tack**' to satisfy the race committee that she kept clear.

3. **Limitation on Right to Room**

(*a*) When the **obstruction** is a **mark** which the hailed yacht can fetch, the hailing yacht shall not be entitled to room to **tack** and the hailed yacht shall immediately so inform the hailing yacht.

(*b*) If, thereafter, the hailing yacht again hails for room to **tack,** she shall, after receiving it, retire immediately.

(*c*) If, after having refused to respond to a hail under rule 43.3 (*a*), the hailed yacht fails to fetch, she shall retire immediately.

Note: **43.1.** *This is one of only two cases where a hail is compulsory (the other is 42.1 (d)). For some reason rule 35 says that a hail should be made, which is not compulsory and therefore you almost certainly could not be disqualified under that rule. However, there are many other occasions, such as claiming room at marks, where you ought to hail for your own good since you will need evidence to support any protest which might result from any incident.*

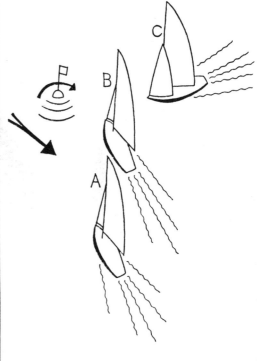

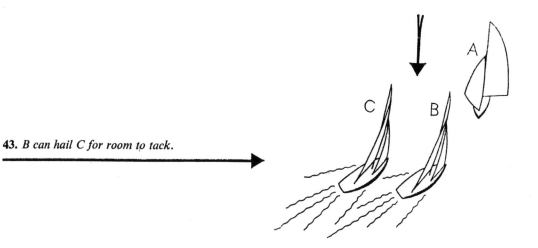

43. *B can hail C for room to tack.*

→

43.1. *B can hail for room to tack and A must keep clear.*

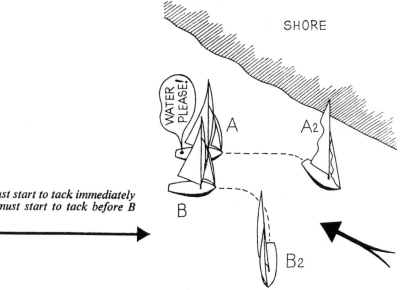

SHORE

WATER PLEASE!

A

A₂

B

B₂

43.1 *and .2 (a) (i). B must start to tack immediately she hears A's hail. A must start to tack before B reaches position B2.*

→

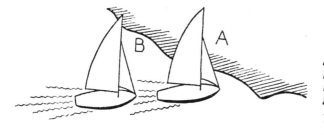

43.1 *and* **.2 (b).** *A has the right to call for water, but B can reply 'you tack,' and then must pass clear under A's stern, if she is of the opinion that she can go closer to the shore or the obstruction than A. B must remember that in the case of a protest, she will have to prove that she has kept clear of A during this manoeuvre.*

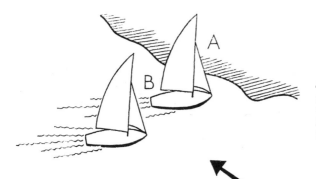

43.1 *and* **.2 (a).** *When A can no longer continue with reasonable safety she can call for room to tack. B must then give A room to tack by tacking herself, and thereafter A is obliged to tack immediately.*

43.1 *and* **.2 (b).** *In this case where A is easily able to tack and keep clear of B, she has no right to call for water. She only has the right to call for water when she is certain that she cannot clear B by falling away under her stern.*

43.3 (a). *B cannot call A for room to tack if A can fetch the mark. It would be exactly the same as if the mark was not there. If B has luffing rights she may be able to use these and in this way be able to clear the mark.*

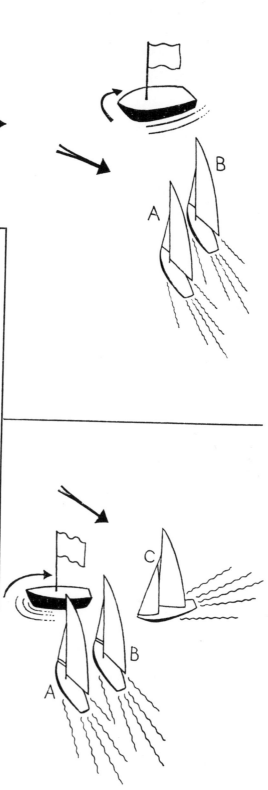

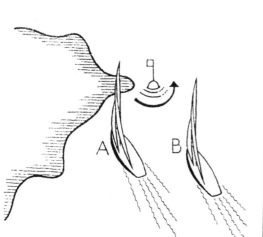

43.3 (a). *In this case B can lay the mark but as the mark is so close to the shore then A can call for room to tack, because of the obstruction.*

43.3 (a). *Here B can hail and A must tack not because she cannot lay the mark, but because C is coming in on starboard tack.*

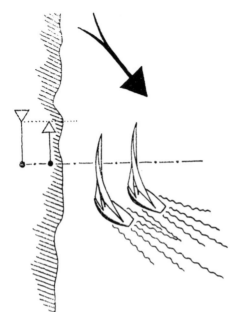

43. *The starting boat forms one end of the line and is therefore a mark of the course after a yacht starts since it then has a required side. It is not clear from the rules whether the starting boat in this case should be regarded as a mark or an obstruction for the purpose of this rule before a yacht starts. I consider that the ship must be regarded as a mark to avoid difficult situations arising with boats to lee of the line asking for water legally and boats to windward of the line unable to obtain room. A must foresee this situation and pull out of the line to find another hole. B may be able to claim room for the mooring chain which is not part of the mark.*

43.3 (a). *In the case of a starting line transit which is completely on the shore, both before and after the start A can hail B for water to tack because the shore is an obstruction.*

43. *A and B cannot fetch the mark and therefore A can hail B for room to tack. But C can fetch it, and therefore B has no right to hail for room. Both A and B must retire.*

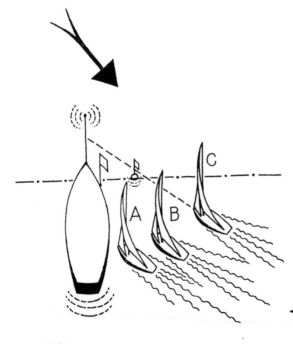

43. *The case of a large starting boat. If there is no inner distance mark then this boat ranks as a mark and has a 'required side' only after a yacht starts (i.e. first cuts the line after the gun). If there is an inner distance mark the starting boat, under most normal sailing instructions, would not have a required side and would therefore not qualify as a mark under the definition of a mark.*

In this situation A can hail B for room to tack at any time. B can only hail C for room to tack because of the starting boat and not to pass the right side of the inner distance mark. If A were not there she might have been forced to sail over the line between the mark and the starting boat before she could claim room.

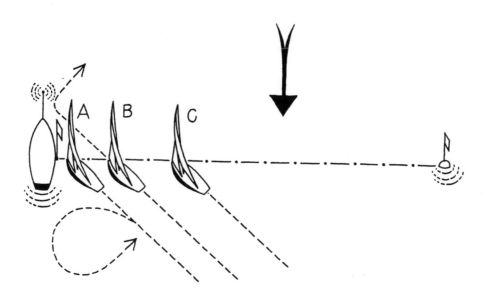

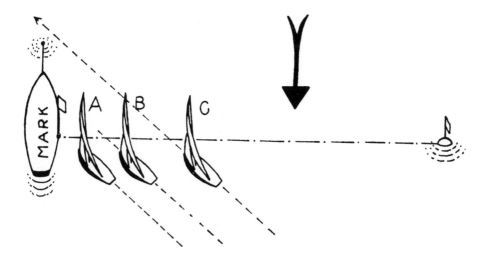

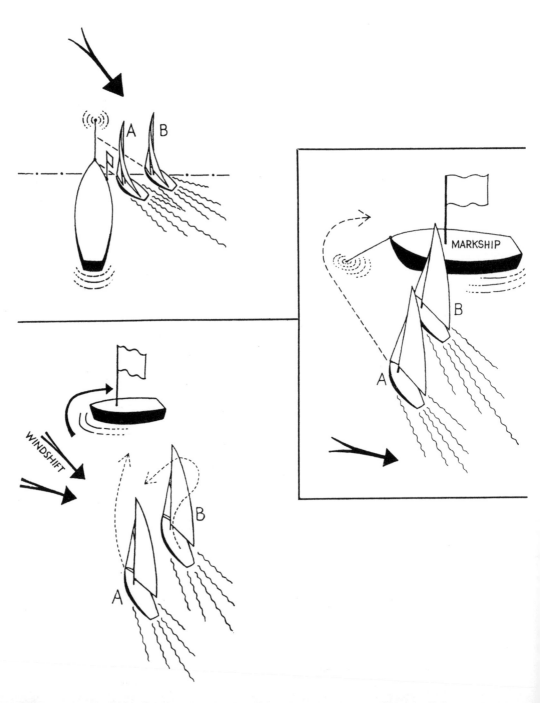

43.3 (b). *In this case the starting boat forms one end of the line and A forces B to tack. She must retire even though B subsequently did not clear the mooring chain.*

43.3 (b). *If A can fetch the mark she need not give B room to tack unless B cannot avoid a collision either with A or the mark. Then B should hail a second time and immediately she is clear she must retire. If B had been slightly more to windward she would have been able to hail for water on the mooring rope.*

43.3 (c). *After A has declined B's call to tack, the latter bears away in order to tack and pass under A's stern. Now the wind shifts and A cannot any longer lay the mark. Because of this A must immediately retire.*

44.1. *Even though a boat which has started too early is on starboard tack, she has to keep clear of all others – even port tack boats.*

44—Yachts Returning to Start

1. (*a*) A premature starter when returning to **start,** or a yacht working into position from the wrong side of the starting line or its extensions, when the starting signal is made, shall keep clear of all yachts which are **starting,** or have **started,** correctly, until she is wholly on the right side of the starting line or its extensions.

   (*b*) Thereafter, she shall be accorded the rights under the rules of Part IV of a yacht which is **starting** correctly; but if she thereby acquires right of way over another yacht which is **starting** correctly, she shall allow that yacht ample room and opportunity to keep clear.

2. A premature starter while continuing to sail the course and until it is obvious that she is returning to **start,** shall be accorded the rights under the rules of Part IV of a yacht which has **started.**

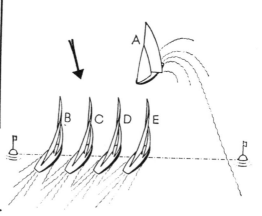

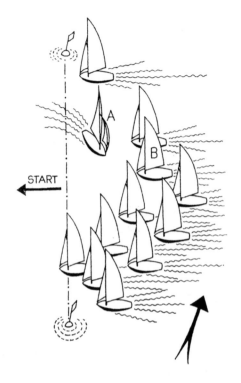

44.1 (b). *A must tack or bear away because the rule says that she has to give B ample room and opportunity to keep clear, and it will be impossible for B to comply in this situation.*

44. *A has started too early but the only thing she can do is let go the jib and the mainsail without affecting any of the other boats around her. A can slow down by backing the sails if she can do it without affecting the other boats.*

44. *A has started too early and luffs into the wind in order to slow down so that she can drop back and start again. But if she affects C, then C will have to respond and A will be disqualified.*

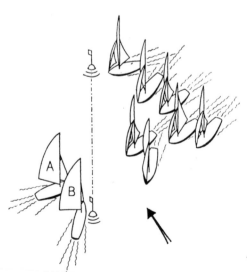

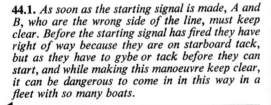

44.1. *As soon as the starting signal is made, A and B, who are the wrong side of the line, must keep clear. Before the starting signal has fired they have right of way because they are on starboard tack, but as they have to gybe or tack before they can start, and while making this manoeuvre keep clear, it can be dangerous to come in in this way in a fleet with so many boats.*

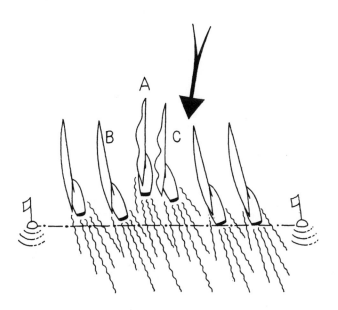

44. *B has started too early and because of the starboard tack boat A, she has to call upon C for room to tack. B has the right to do this because she is not yet returning to make her restart. After tacking she can then begin to slow down as long as this does not affect A and C.*

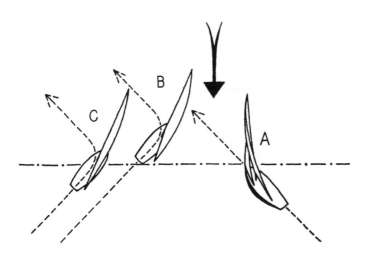

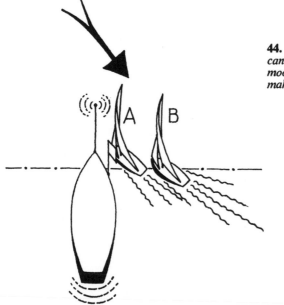

44. *In this situation A is over the line too early but can still claim room to tack on account of the mooring chain because she is not yet returning to make her restart.*

45—Anchored, Aground or Capsized

1. A yacht under way shall keep clear of another yacht **racing** which is anchored, aground or capsized. Of two anchored yachts, the one which is anchored later shall keep clear, except that a yacht which is dragging shall keep clear of one which is not.

2. A yacht anchored or aground shall indicate the fact to any yacht which may be in danger of fouling her. Unless the size of the yachts or the weather conditions make some other signal necessary, a hail is sufficient indication.

3. A yacht shall not be penalised for fouling a yacht in distress which she is attempting to assist nor a yacht which goes aground or capsizes immediately ahead of her.

(Numbers 46, 47 and 48 are spare numbers)

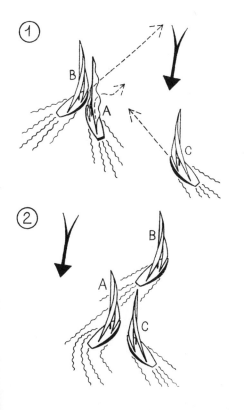

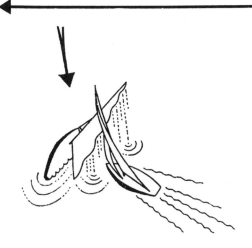

45.2. *A, on starboard, was hit by B, on port, and knocked on to the other tack. A is now nearly stopped on port tack and is hit by C who is on starboard. A should have hailed 'Out of control' under rule 45.2, and C should treat her as an obstruction.*

45. *You have to keep clear of a capsized dinghy. Under the rules it is the same as if it was an obstruction.*

PART V—OTHER SAILING RULES

Obligations of Helmsmen and Crew in Handling a Yacht

Except for rule 49, a yacht is subject to the rules of Part V only while she is **racing.**

49—Fair Sailing

A yacht shall attempt to win a race only by fair sailing, superior speed and skill, and, except in team races, by individual effort. However, a yacht may be disqualified under this rule only in the case of a clear-cut violation of the above principles and only if no other rule applies.

50—Ranking as a Starter

A yacht which sails about in the vicinity of the starting line between her preparatory and starting signals shall rank as a starter, even if she does not **start.**

51—Sailing the Course

1. (*a*) A yacht shall **start** and **finish** only as prescribed in the starting and finishing definitions, even if the committee boat is anchored on the side of the starting or finishing **mark** opposite to that prescribed in the sailing instructions.

   (*b*) Unless otherwise prescribed in the sailing instructions, a yacht which either crosses prematurely, or is on the wrong side of the starting line at the starting signal, or at any other prescribed time before the starting signal, shall return and **start** in accordance with the definition.

   (*c*) Failure of a yacht to see or hear her recall notification shall not relieve her of her obligation of **starting** correctly.

Note: PART V – Other Sailing Rules. *For an example of rule 49 applying when not racing a crew might deliberately damage a boat between races. Because you can be disqualified between races it also means that you could be disqualified for a whole series.*

Note: 49. *Except for team racing a yacht is not allowed to receive outside help. There was a recent case where it was suspected that a crew was using a walkie-talkie radio with another on the shore. If it had been proved then the yacht would have been disqualified.*

2. A yacht shall sail the course so as to round or pass each **mark** on the required side in correct sequence, and so that a string representing her wake from the time she **starts** until she **finishes** would, when drawn taut, lie on the required side of each **mark.**

3. A **mark** has a required side for a yacht as long as she is on a leg which it begins, bounds or ends. A starting **mark** begins to have a required side for a yacht when she **starts.** A finishing **mark** ceases to have a required side for a yacht as soon as she **finishes.**

4. A yacht which rounds or passes a **mark** on the wrong side may correct her error by making her course conform to the requirements of rule 51.2.

5. It is not necessary for a yacht to cross the finishing line completely. After **finishing** she may clear it in either direction.

51.3. *A has just rounded mark 'b,' and therefore mark 'a' no longer is considered as a mark for her. Both mark 'a' and 'b' are marks of the course for boat B. C has not yet rounded mark 'a,' and therefore she can please herself which side of mark 'b' she goes.*

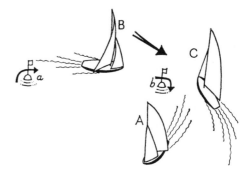

51.2 *and* **.4.** *A has rounded incorrectly. B is right. You have to unwind yourself before rounding properly.*

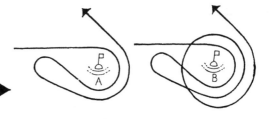

51.5. *A, who has crossed the finishing line, can go under B's stern and still maintains her finishing position.*

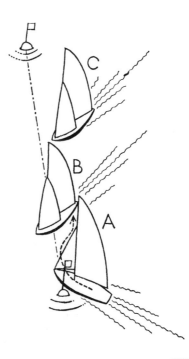

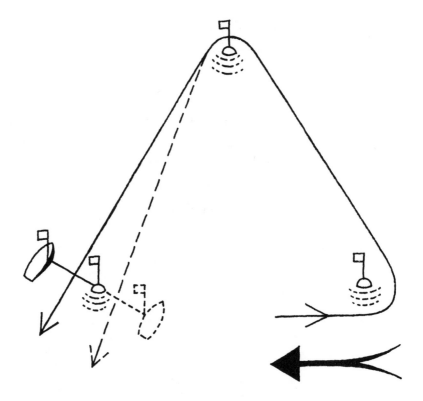

51.1 (a). *Normally the sailing instructions say that you finish from the direction of the last mark but if they put the committee boat inside the course you should follow the finishing definition exactly and you must be right.*

52—Touching a Mark

1. A yacht which either:

(*a*) touches:

    (i)   a starting **mark** before **starting**;

    (ii) a **mark** which begins, bounds or ends the leg of the course on which she is sailing; or

    (iii) a finishing **mark** after **finishing**; or

(*b*) causes a **mark** vessel to shift to avoid being touched,

shall retire immediately, unless she claims that she was wrongfully compelled to touch it by another yacht, in which case she shall protest.

2. For the purposes of rule 52.1: Every ordinary part of a **mark** ranks as part of it, including a flag, flagpole, boom or hoisted boat, but excluding ground tackle and any object either accidentally or temporarily attached to it.

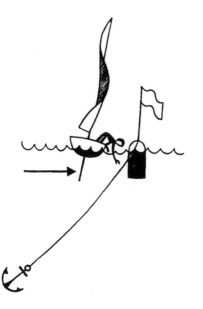

52.2. *Even though the mooring rope is not considered part of the mark, it is still forbidden, under rule 60, to use the anchor line as a means of avoiding touching the mark.*

52.2. *However, touching the rope with the keel is permitted.*

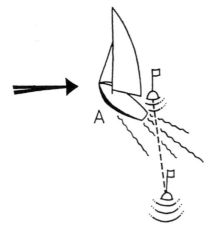

52.1. *If A touches the mark even after she has crossed and cleared the finishing line, she shall be disqualified.*

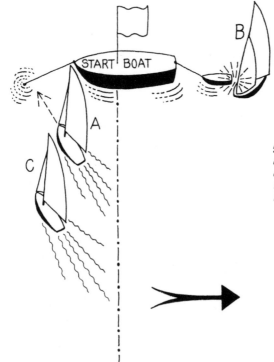

52.2. *If the starting boat is a starting mark, A is allowed to touch the mooring cable, even the part above water. She can also hail C to give room to tack since the cable is an obstruction. B can also hit the dinghy tied up at the stern.*

53—Fog Signals and Lights

Every yacht shall observe the International Regulations for Preventing Collisions at Sea or Government Rules for fog signals and, as a minimum, the carrying of lights at night.

54—Setting and Sheeting Sails

1. **Changing Sails**—While changing headsails and spinnakers a replacing sail may be fully set and trimmed before the sail it replaces is taken in, but only one mainsail and, except when changing, only one spinnaker shall be carried set.

2. **Sheeting Sails to Spars**—Unless otherwise prescribed by the national authority or by the class rules, any sail may be sheeted to or led above a boom regularly used for a working sail and permanently attached to the mast to which the head of the working sail is set, but no sails shall be sheeted over or through outriggers. An outrigger is any fitting so placed, except as permitted in the first sentence of rule 54.2, that it could exert outward pressure on a sheet at a point from which, with the yacht upright, a vertical line would fall outside the hull or deck planking at that point, or outside such other position as class rules prescribe. For the purpose of this rule: Bulwarks, rails and rubbing strakes are not part of the hull or deck planking. A boom of a boomed foresail which requires no adjustment when **tacking** is not an outrigger.

3. **Spinnaker, Spinnaker Boom**—A spinnaker shall not be set without a boom. The tack of a spinnaker when set and drawing shall be in close proximity to the outboard end of a spinnaker boom. Any head sail may be attached to a spinnaker boom provided a spinnaker is not set. A sail tacked down abaft the foremost mast is not a head sail. Only one spinnaker boom shall be used at a time and when in use shall be carried only on the side of the foremost mast opposite to the main boom and shall be fixed to the mast. Rule 54.3 shall not apply when shifting a spinnaker boom or sail attached thereto.

Note: **54.2.** *Be careful how you fix your jib fairleads so that they do not contravene this rule. But a hand holding out a sheet is not an 'outrigger.'*

55—Owner Steering another Yacht

An owner shall not steer any yacht other than his own, in a race wherein his own yacht competes, without the previous consent of the race committee.

56—Boarding

Unless otherwise prescribed by the national authority or in the sailing instructions, no person shall board a yacht except for the purpose of rule 58, Rendering Assistance, or to attend an injured or ill member of the crew or temporarily as one of the crew of a vessel fouled.

Note: 56. *In the Tokyo Olympics the Swedish Flying Dutchman crew picked up the Australian crewman. They could have carried him to the finish and this would have been legal.*

57—Leaving, Man Overboard

Unless otherwise prescribed by the national authority or in the sailing instructions, no person on board a yacht when her preparatory signal was made shall leave, unless injured or ill, or for the purpose of rule 58, Rendering Assistance, except that any member of the crew may fall overboard or leave her to swim, stand on the bottom as a means of anchoring, haul her out ashore to effect repairs, reef sails or bail out, or help her to get clear after grounding or fouling another vessel or object, provided that this person is back on board before the yacht continues in the race.

Note: 58. *It looks as though a yacht could be disqualified for not going to the help of another in trouble. Normally in dinghy racing there are rescue boats about, but even if there are, you should always watch out for other boats in difficulty. The rescue boats may be busy already.*

58—Rendering Assistance

Every yacht shall render all possible assistance to any vessel or person in peril, when in a position to do so.

59—Outside Assistance

Except as permitted by rules 56, Boarding, 58, Rendering Assistance, and 64, Aground or Foul of an Obstruction, a yacht shall neither receive outside assistance nor use any gear other than that on board when her preparatory signal was made.

60—Means of Propulsion

A yacht shall be propelled only by the natural action of the wind on the sails, spars and hull, and water on the hull, and shall not check way by abnormal means, except for the purpose of rule 58, Rendering Assistance, or for the purpose of recovering a man who has accidentally fallen overboard. An oar, paddle or other object may be used in emergency for steering. An anchor may be sent out in a boat only as permitted by rule 64, Aground or Foul of an Obstruction.

61—Sounding

Any means of sounding may be used provided rule 60, Means of Propulsion, is not infringed.

62—Manual Power

A yacht shall use manual power only, except that if so prescribed by the national authority or in the sailing instructions, a power winch or windlass may be used in weighing anchor or in getting clear after running aground or fouling any object.

63—Anchoring and Making Fast

1. A yacht may anchor. Means of anchoring may include the crew standing on the bottom and any weight lowered to the bottom. A yacht shall recover any anchor or weight used, and any chain or rope attached to it, before continuing in the race, unless after making every effort she finds recovery impossible. In this case she shall report the circumstances to the race committee, which may disqualify her if it considers the loss due either to inadequate gear or to insufficient effort to recover it.

2. A yacht shall be afloat and off moorings before her preparatory signal, but may be anchored, and shall not thereafter make fast or be made fast by means other than anchoring, nor be hauled out, except for the purpose of rule 64, Aground or Foul of an Obstruction, or to effect repairs, reef sails or bail out.

Note: 60. *During the Olympic Games at Naples there was a protest on 'Pumping' and as a result the I.Y.R.U. say that 'Pumping sails or rocking a yacht are considered to be an infringement of rule 60. Pumping consists of frequent rapid trimming of sails with no particular reference to a change in the true or apparent wind direction. To promote planing or surfing rapid trimming of sails need not be considered as pumping.'*

64—Aground or Foul of an Obstruction

A yacht, after grounding or fouling another vessel or other object, is subject to rule 62, Manual Power, and may, in getting clear, use her own anchors, boats, ropes, spars and other gear; may send out an anchor in a boat; may be refloated by her crew going overboard either to stand on the bottom or to go ashore to push off; but may receive outside assistance only from the crew of the vessel fouled. A yacht shall recover all her own gear used in getting clear before continuing in the race.

(Numbers 65, 66 and 67 are spare numbers)

PART VI—PROTESTS
DISQUALIFICATIONS AND APPEALS

68—Protests

1. A yacht can protest against any other yacht, except that a protest for an alleged infringement of the rules of Part IV can be made only by a yacht directly involved in, or witnessing an incident.

2. A protest occurring between yachts competing in separate races sponsored by different clubs shall be heard by a combined committee of both clubs.

3. (a) A protest for an infringement of the rules or sailing instructions occurring during a race shall be signified by showing a flag (International Code flag 'B' is always acceptable, irrespective of any other provisions in the sailing instructions) conspicuously in the rigging of the protesting yacht at the first reasonable opportunity and keeping it flying until she has **finished** or retired, or if the first reasonable opportunity occurs after **finishing**, until acknowledged by the race committee. In the case of a yacht sailed single-handed, it shall be sufficient if the flag (whether displayed in the rigging or not) is brought to the notice of the yacht protested against as soon as possible after the incident and to the race committee when the protesting yacht **finishes**.

(b) A yacht which has no knowledge of the facts justifying a protest until after she has **finished** or retired may nevertheless protest without having shown a protest flag.

(c) A protesting yacht shall try to inform the yacht protested against that a protest will be lodged.

(d) Such a protest shall be in writing and signed by the owner or his representative, and should state:

(i) The date, time and whereabouts of the incident.

(ii) The particular rule or rules or sailing instructions alleged to have been broken or infringed.

(iii) A statement of the facts.

(iv) Unless irrelevant, a diagram of the incident.

(e) Unless otherwise prescribed in the sailing instructions, the protest shall be delivered, or if that is impossible, mailed to the race committee within two hours of the **finish** of the protesting yacht, or should she not **finish**, within two hours of her arrival in port, or within such special time limit and with such fee, if any, as may have been prescribed in the sailing instructions under rule 3.2 (*u*). But the race committee shall have power to extend this time should it have reason to do so.

(*f*) The race committee shall allow any omissions in the details required by rule 68.3 (*d*) to be remedied at a later time.

4. (a) A protest that a measurement, scantling or flotation rule has been infringed while **racing**, or that a classification or rating certificate is for any reason invalid, shall be lodged with the race committee not later than 6 p.m. on the day following the race. The race committee shall send a copy of the protest to the yacht protested against and, should there appear to be reasonable grounds for the protest, it shall refer the question to an authority qualified to decide such questions.

(b) The race committee, in making its decision, shall be governed by the determination of such authority. Copies of such decision shall be sent to all yachts involved.

5. (a) A yacht which claims that her chances of winning a prize have been prejudiced by an action or omission of the race committee, may seek redress from the race committee in accordance with the requirements for a protest provided in rules 68.3 (*d*), (*e*) and (*f*).

K. Hashimoto

381, Andromeda, *which finished 4th in the Olympic Regatta here in Japan, is just about to gybe around the wing mark. 166*, White Lady, *was the Gold Medal winner.*

An international regatta for the Finn class in Holland.

> (b) When the race committee decides that such action or omission was prejudical, and that the result of the race was altered thereby, it shall **cancel** or **abandon** the race, or make such other arrangement as it deems equitable.
>
> 6. A protest made in writing shall not be withdrawn, but shall be decided by the race committee, unless prior to the hearing full responsibility is acknowledged by one or more yachts.

Note: 68.1. *There was a case in the Tokyo Olympics where a competitor protested against another over an incident which he first heard about when ashore after the race. You cannot now protest under any of the rules in Part IV – Sailing Rules when Yachts Meet – unless you actually saw the incident or were directly involved in it. (N.B.: Not – directly* affected *by it.)*

Note: 68.3 (a). *It is best for all yachts to carry a protest flag, made like flag 'B,' always on board. You may never need it but you would be very angry if, as a result of a collision, you lost the race simply because the other boat would not retire and you had no protest flag.*

Note: 68.3 (d), (e) and (f). *The formalities of putting in a protest are for the protection of everyone and to save time. Race committees do not like protests and it often happens that they have thrown out a protest on some small technical matter connected with the way it was written out. Now, if the protest has been written out wrongly they must still accept it after allowing it to be amended.*

R.Y.A. PROTEST FORM

To the Race Committee of..Club

Race No..................... Class...

Protest lodged by............................ Sail No.................

Against.. Sail No.............
(whose helmsman I have/have not informed)

Date of incident..................... Time of incident.................

Whereabouts of incident..

Rule or rules considered infringed...............................

Wind direction............................... Strength.................

Direction of tidal stream or current.......... Strength.........

Depth of water (if relevant)..

Time at which protest flag was shown...........................

Signed......................... Helmsman of..........................

Member of...Club

Address..

.... Tel. No....................

Enclosed £   :   :   Protest fee

Witnesses...

....

....

Protest flag seen by....................................(Race officer)

at...

Protest committee...................................(Chairman)

....

....

Facts found

....
....
....
....

Rule or rules judged applicable...................................
Yacht holding right-of-way..

Decision and ground for decision

....
....
....
....
....
....

Signed...

(Chairman)

Diagram submitted by..

(N.B.—Boats should be shown sailing from the bottom of the diagram towards the top)

Scale: 1 square = one boat's length

DESCRIPTION OF THE INCIDENT

69—Refusal of a Protest

1. When the race committee decides that a protest does not conform to the requirements of rule 68, Protests, it shall inform the protesting yacht that her protest will not be heard and of the reasons for such decision.

2. Such a decision shall not be reached without giving the protesting yacht an opportunity of bringing evidence that the requirements of rule 68 were complied with.

70—Hearings

1. When the race committee decides that a protest conforms to all the requirements of rule 68, Protests, it shall call a hearing as soon as possible. The protest, or a copy of it, shall be made available to all yachts involved, and each shall be notified, in writing if practicable, of the time and place set for the hearing. A reasonable time shall be allowed for the preparation of defence. At the hearing, the race committee shall take the evidence presented by the parties to the protest and such other evidence as it may consider necessary. The parties to the protest, or a representative of each, shall have the right to be present, but all others, except one witness at a time while testifying, may be excluded. A yacht other than one named in the protest, which is involved in that protest, shall have all the privileges of yachts originally named in it.

2. A yacht shall not be penalised without a hearing, except as provided in rule 73.1 (a), Disqualification without Protest.

3. Failure on the part of any of the interested parties or a representative to make an effort to attend the hearing of the protest may justify the race committee in deciding the protest as it thinks fit without a full hearing.

71—Decisions

The race committee shall make its decision promptly after the hearing. Each decision shall be communicated to all parties involved, in writing if required by them, and shall state fully the facts and grounds on which it is based and specify the rule or rules, if any, infringed. The findings of the race committee as to the facts involved shall be final.

72—Disqualification after Protest

1. When the race committee or any appeal authority decides after a protest and the hearing thereon:

> (a) that a yacht has been shown to the race committee's satisfaction to have infringed any of these rules or the sailing instructions, or
>
> (b) that in consequence of her neglect of any of these rules or the sailing instructions she has compelled other yachts to infringe these rules or the sailing instructions,

she shall be disqualified unless the sailing instructions applicable to that race provide some other penalty. Such disqualification or other penalty shall be imposed, irrespective of whether the rule or sailing instruction which led to the disqualification or penalty was mentioned in the protest, or the yacht which was at fault was mentioned or protested against, e.g. the protesting yacht or a third yacht might be disqualified and the protested yacht absolved.

2. A retirement after an infringement of any rule or sailing instruction shall not rank as a disqualification. This penalty can be imposed only in accordance with rules 72, Disqualification after Protest, and 73, Disqualification without Protest.

3. When a yacht either is disqualified or has retired, the next in order shall be awarded her place.

4. The question of damages arising from any infringements of these rules shall be governed by the prescriptions, if any, of the national authority.

73—Disqualification without Protest

1. (*a*) A yacht which fails either to **start** or to **finish** may be disqualified without protest or hearing, after the conclusion of the race, except that she shall be entitled to a hearing, provided she satisfies the race committee that an error may have been made.

   (*b*) A yacht so penalised shall be informed of the action taken, either by letter or by notification in the racing results.

2. When the race committee:

   (*a*) sees an apparent infringement by any yacht of these rules or the sailing instructions (except as provided in rule 73.1), or

   (*b*) receives a report not later than the same day from a witness who was neither competing in the race, nor otherwise an interested party, alleging such an infringement, or

   (*c*) has reasonable grounds for supposing from the evidence at the hearing of a valid protest, that any yacht involved in the incident may have committed such an infringement,

it may notify such yacht thereof in writing, delivered or mailed not later than one day after:

   (i)   the finish of the race, or

   (ii) the receipt of the report, or

   (iii) the hearing of the protest.

Such notice shall contain a statement of the pertinent facts and of the particular rule or rules or sailing instructions believed to have been infringed, and the race committee shall act thereon in the same manner as if it had been a protest made by a competitor.

74—Penalties for Gross Breach of Rules

1. If a gross breach or infringement of any of these rules is proved against the owner, the owner's representative, the helmsman or sailing master of a yacht, such persons may be disqualified by the national authority, for any period it may think fit, from either steering or sailing in a yacht in any race held under its jurisdiction.

2. Notice of any penalty adjudged under this rule shall be communicated to the I.Y.R.U. which shall inform all national authorities.

75—Persons Interested not to Take Part in Decision

No member of either a race committee or of any appeals authority shall take part in the discussion or decision upon any disputed question in which he is an interested party, but this does not preclude him from giving evidence in such a case.

76—Expenses Incurred by Protest

Unless otherwise prescribed by the race committee, the fees and expenses entailed by a protest on measurement or classification shall be paid by the unsuccessful party.

Note: 72.1. *Other forms of penalty than disqualification ought to be used more often in yacht racing because it is only in this sport that there is such a severe penalty for such a very small transgression of the rules.*

Note: 72.2. *There is a difference between 'retirement' and 'disqualification.' The first is voluntary and most sailing instructions give a higher series points award to a boat retiring compared to a boat thrown out after a full protest hearing.*

77—Appeals

1. Unless otherwise prescribed by the national authority which has recognised the sponsoring organisation concerned, an appeal against the decision of a race committee shall be governed by rules 77, Appeals, and 78, Particulars to be Furnished in Appeals.

2. Unless otherwise prescribed by the national authority or in the sailing instructions (subject to rule 2 (*j*) or 3.2 (*w*)), a protest which has been decided by the race committee shall be referred to the national authority solely on a question of interpretation of these rules, within such period after the receipt of the race committee's decision, as the national authority may decide:

(*a*) when the race committee, at its own instance, thinks proper to do so, or

(*b*) when any of the parties involved in the protest makes application for such reference.

This reference shall be accompanied by such deposit as the national authority may prescribe, payable by the appellant to be forfeited to the funds of the national authority in the event of the appeal being dismissed.

3. The national authority shall have power to uphold or reverse the decision of the race committee, and if it is of opinion, from the facts found by the race committee, that a yacht involved in a protest has infringed an applicable rule, it shall disqualify her, irrespective of whether the rule or sailing instruction which led to such disqualification was mentioned in the protest.

4. The decision of the national authority, which shall be final, shall be communicated in writing to all interested parties.

5. In the Olympic Games and such other international regattas as may be specially approved by the I.Y.R.U. the decisions of the race committee, jury or judges shall be final.

6. An appeal once lodged with the national authority shall not be withdrawn.

78—Particulars to be Furnished in Appeals

1. The reference to the national authority shall be in writing and shall contain the following particulars, in order, so far as they are applicable:

(*a*) A copy of the notice of the race and the sailing instructions furnished to the yachts.

(*b*) A copy of the protest, or protests, if any, prepared in accordance with rule 68.3 (*d*), and all other written statements which may have been put in by the parties.

(*c*) The observations of the race committee thereon, a full statement of the facts found, its decision and the grounds thereof.

(*d*) An official diagram prepared by the race committee in accordance with the facts found by it showing:

   (i) The course to the next **mark**, or, if close by, the **mark** itself with the required side;

   (ii) The direction and force of the wind;

   (iii) the set and strength of the current, if any;

   (iv) the depth of water, if relevant; and

   (v) the positions and courses of all the yachts involved.

   (vi) Where possible, yachts should be shown sailing from the bottom of the diagram towards the top.

(*e*) The grounds of appeal, to be supplied by either:

   (i) the race committee under rule 77.2 (*a*); or

   (ii) the appellant under rule 77.2 (*b*).

(*f*) Observations, if any, upon the appeal by the race committee or any of the parties.

2. The race committee shall notify all parties that an appeal will be lodged and shall invite them to make any observations upon it. Any such observations shall be forwarded with the appeal.

The Spirit of Racing

The racing rules must be observed but you must also be reasonable about this. When starting in a race with a large number of boats they will often be so close together that small touchings will occur between booms or sails – and other such errors can occur – and there is no reason to worry the jury or racing committee with such small matters. But if people break the rules on purpose, then you must put in a protest.

It is very difficult to make rules to enable starting to be really good and therefore we must try to help each other to make the start as fair as possible; but in open waters the rules must be observed meticulously. In any case, in my opinion, there is really no need to protest except over a gross breach of the rules or if a dinghy has deliberately broken a rule.

During a race a boat on starboard tack is passed by another on port tack whilst going to windward, if the starboard tack boat is not actually affected by this boat then there is no need for there to be a protest. If there is some doubt whether the port tack boat can cross, he can shout to him 'Pass ahead, if you like,' for if he does this, he will interfere less than if he had tacked under your lee bow. If a dinghy touches a mark and it is his own fault, then he must retire immediately. It is not necessary to go so close to the mark that there is a danger of fouling it. During racing we should always act with good sportsmanship.

Why Do We Race?

A race is, and always must be, only a game. Hard competition only gives more excitement to the game, and it is really exciting to find out who can win.

It is quite a problem that some people are able to spend a great deal of time and money on tuning their boats and making them go fast whereas other people are unable to do this. But remember that a man cannot get the speed only because of time and money. He must also be clever in order to get the best out of his new gear. Very many skippers have the best possible new boats and sails and yet do not know how to make them go fast.

If a yachtsman cannot afford to spend the same amount of time and money as his competitors it is not a reason for spoiling this man's pleasure in racing but it does, of course give him a very good reason why he may be slower.

We all ought to be friends, and be glad we are sailing together in the same class. A helmsman in the Finn Class ought to be extremely glad to hear of any newcomer coming into the class – he will thus have one more friend to race with.

Before the Olympic Games there is usually a long series of trial races in each of the participating countries, and jealousy and feeling between the contenders can be very fierce – so fierce in fact that the favourites hardly speak to each other, sometimes.

Therefore, it seems we ought to be pleased to have other competitors to race with, but the opposite is sometimes the case. It is quite normal to talk to yourself about beating the other competitors, but you must do this in a sporting manner.

I am sure that it is more important to compete and enjoy yourself than to win.

After a race you cannot tell by looking at some people's faces whether they have won or lost because the sailing alone gives them so much pleasure that their position does not matter to them greatly.

With other people you do not need to ask if they have won or lost. You can see it in their faces straight away. To them I would like to give some advice. It is difficult to change your nature but you can help yourself by remembering that it is a greater satisfaction to give than to receive, and here you have a chance to give the best form of compliment to the winner by your smile and also by your words 'well done.'

Remember that if you show in your face that you do not like it when certain of your competitors win, then they will have the same feelings for you when you win, and that spoils the racing for both of you.

When you feel that none of your competitors are afraid to lose to you then you also will not mind losing to them. When your competitors are happy to see you win, you are naturally happy when their turn comes to win. This is an unwritten law common to all sports.

Also, do not forget to show your enjoyment during the race. For example, you only need to make just the smallest friendly gesture when you pass near one of your competitors such as when crossing on port or starboard whether you pass ahead or astern. If you do not show that you are enjoying the competition you can spoil the pleasure for your competitors.

RACING

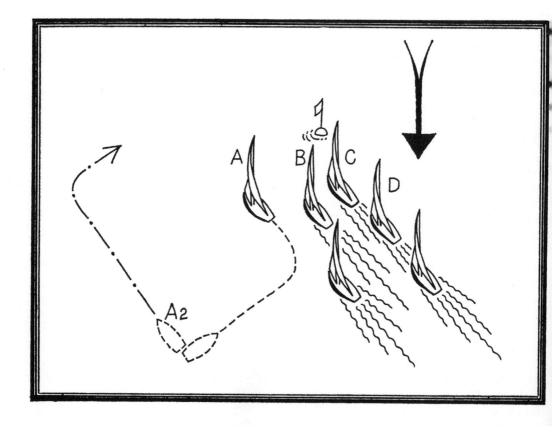

TACTICS

The most interesting part of racing is the tactics, and by this I mean the way the competitor places himself in relation to the other competitors, the marks, the course, the current and the wind. You can sail as fast as you like and have the best possible technique, but if you do not know your tactics you will not do any good. Therefore I have given a great deal of room in the book to tactics, because this is for me, and always has been, the most interesting thing about racing. A really clever tactician can often win against helmsmen who are actually sailing their boats faster.

When I was a boy it was generally thought that races were won by chance, and unfortunately this idea still exists today. But as you improve you begin to realise that it is quite wrong to think this. Here in Denmark we have fairly steady winds but on racing courses in France, Switzerland and Germany– that is to say on lakes and rivers – the winds are fluky and luck, both good and bad, is quite normal. The worst example that I have seen is on a course on the Seine near Paris, where the wind goes right round the compass which, to a Dane coming on to such a course

for the first time seems to be hopelessly fluky. But by studying the results of races on such courses you can see that it is the same helmsmen that win each time. When I first raced on the Seine in 1953 I thought that it was completely hopeless to study the course and work out tactics in advance. Later I said to myself, 'But it is the same people, even though they come from different parts of the world, who win each time. Therefore I must be able to learn this myself.'

To get used to foreign waters is difficult, but it is certainly possible if you are prepared to concentrate and really learn the local conditions. I have sailed on many race courses around the world with a good deal of success because I have trained myself to take the trouble to learn the local wind and current conditions.

Many Danes come back from foreign regattas excusing their bad placings by saying it was all luck and the conditions were fluky, but I think that is a stupid attitude, because I know from experience that it is not so. In 1958 Denmark sent five men to Wannsee in Berlin for an international team match against five German sailors. The Danish boats took the last five places and told on coming home how the Germans were much faster and that the Danes had no chance of winning on such a fluky course, where they were sailing amongst water lilies, etc. I did not think much of this excuse. It is impossible to go straight from home waters to entirely new conditions and think that you can still go as fast as the local experts. To do this you either must be very good or you must be used to sailing under these particular conditions. One more example: in 1958 there was a big international Finn regatta on the Muckelsee in Berlin where the Frenchmen Pinaud and Poullain were first and second, because they had the good fortune to find exactly the same conditions on the Muckelsee as they were used to at home.

In order to be a successful tactician you must train yourself to sense in advance the type of situation that is likely to develop. You have to weigh up instantly the various possibilities and then select your own tactics from the answers.

The greatest advantage is experience. The reason why so many older helmsmen are so hard to beat is that they have stored up so many race course situations in their minds that they automatically make the right decisions.

Unless you are always thinking ahead you may tack, for example, on a heading shift, as one is often taught to do, when this would put you immediately in the wind-shadow of another boat. Then you would have to tack back again and, whilst this would certainly slow your boat, it might also put you in an even worse situation. In fact, lack of forethought could lose you ten places in as many seconds in a hot fleet.

Another example – the wind heads slightly and you cannot decide whether to tack or to carry on. The result is that you pinch and the boat slows down. You must know in advance whether you are going to tack or to bear away when the wind heads you.

You must also keep track of shifts so that you know at any one moment which side of the mean wind direction is the shift. A compass can be helpful sometimes but it is better to keep your eyes outside the boat.

Note: *When studying the following tactical situations I have assumed that all the boats are tuned to the same standard and therefore have the same boat speed unless I specifically state otherwise.*

The Start

Before you go out to a regatta you must study the sailing instructions very carefully so that you are absolutely clear over the start and finishing line, the course, the time of the start, and after that make sure that the dinghy is completely ready to go afloat with the sails set on the mast and boom. Go round every shackle and make sure that it is tight. When you and the dinghy are completely ready, go afloat and sail to the starting line so that you are there in plenty of time and are not flustered.

Be prepared for the start, and start the watch at the ten-minute gun, check the time again at the five-minute gun, and after that take note of the direction and strength of the wind and the direction of the first mark. If you cannot see the first mark you must go and ask the committee boat. You cannot make a good start unless you know where you are going. I only point this out because I know from experience how very often helmsmen start without thinking. Before the start take your dinghy onto the line and point it head to wind, noting the direction of the wind in relation to the direction of the line. You can then tell which end of the line to start.

You must sail out beyond the end of the line to discover whether it is absolutely fixed or if it is moving slightly. This may be due to the committee boat not being moored fore-and-aft, or to the wind being against the current. Then you must try to decide the position of the distance mark relative to the shore or some other object so that you have a guide.

If there are not many boats you can start at the most favourable end but if the advantage is not very great it may pay you to start at the other end of the line and in clear wind. In a start with a large number of boats and a short starting line it is so crowded that you cannot guarantee to hit the line exactly on the gun and with full speed. In starts like this you must be careful to avoid getting competitors close under your lee so that you cannot bear away and get full speed just before the starting gun. On the other hand, it does not matter how many dinghies there are close to you to windward, because you are in the safe leeward position. Here, as well as in the whole race, you should have a perfect knowledge of the racing rules because this is the basis of all tactics. For example, I have seen that the starboard starting mark has a grass-line attached to it and reaching for four yards from it, so that it is impossible to pass close to the mark. The rules say that such an obstruction is not part of the mark and this means that boats which previously could not ask for room at the mark can now claim room to pass the obstruction.

If you are too far to windward of the windward mark and do not want to go closer to the line, you must pull the centreboard right up so that you slide sideways and then when you come to the right position you drop the centreboard again. Also push the tiller completely down to leeward.

If it is obvious that, after the start, you are going to have to tack onto port, either because this is the most favourable tack, or because of the tide, then you must work it out beforehand and put yourself in such a position that you can tack afterwards.

If you are starting in very strong winds and are sailing a class of boat which is difficult to gybe easily, for example the Finn or the Star which have very long booms, then take care that you do not start early too close to the port end mark. You may be forced to make a rapid gybe.

When planning your start you must always

avoid getting yourself into such a position that you are unable to sheet in and gather full speed just before the gun fires. You must always position yourself so that you can accelerate and steer in the direction you want to go. This should be your main starting tactic.

It could happen that the boats covering you are a little early so that, after the start, they are nearly stopped and then you are unable to start either. Never get yourself into a dead position like this. It is astonishing how much distance people lose at the start because they try to get just half a boat's length closer to the line than the others.

At the start you must have a firm hold over your nerves because you can easily get yourself into a position where you would be disqualified. For example, tacking onto port just in order to try to gain five boat's lengths when you could not possibly clear the starboard tack boats. It is stupid to spoil the whole race for a small possible gain.

If you are getting too close to the starting line and you have boats on both sides of you so that you cannot manoeuvre, you can back your sail to stop you so that you can drop back into the right position. If you are unable to drop back you must pull in the sheets, go across the line, turn back to find a hole, and get back the right side. The sooner that you realise that you are going to make an early start the easier it will be to get across the line and come back and find a hole. It is dangerous just to wait and hope that you will not be too early. If the gun fires the boats will be coming up on you from behind and it will be very difficult to turn and find a hole to get back across.

If you feel that there was a chance that you were over the line too early and you hear the recall signal, your action depends on whether it is a single race or a series. If it is a series, where you would lose little were you disqualified, or if you would gain a lot should you win the race, then you must continue. But if you need only to finish in a medium position to retain a high position in a series, then you should return.

Then there is the problem as to how you should make your re-start. The main point is that you must not interfere with boats that have started correctly. Remember that you may not even luff another boat that has started correctly after you have started to return.

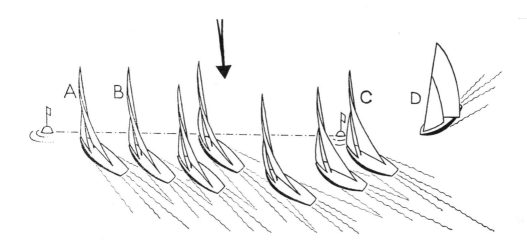

A makes the best start, because she has her wind clear and is able to sail free and fast after the start. All the other boats are being lee-bowed by one of the others and will drop back in succession. A is thus the only boat which is not being interfered with by the others.

B has two possibilities, either to wait until the wind-ward boats tack or to fall off through the lee of A. The latter is the best possibility, if the wind is tending to free on the starboard tack. On the other hand, if the wind starts to head she must wait and tack at the earliest opportunity. She must tack immediately the windward boat tacks as long as she avoids being lee-bowed.

C makes a good start especially if the wind is heading at the moment of the starting gun because she has the possibility of getting completely clear of the fleet as soon as it frees again. Apart from that she is lucky that the boat to leeward is not farther ahead where it would be in safe leeward position. On the other hand, if the wind remains heading, she will be given back wind by the boat to leeward of her, and she must then immediately tack, taking care that she does not interfere with D by tacking too close.

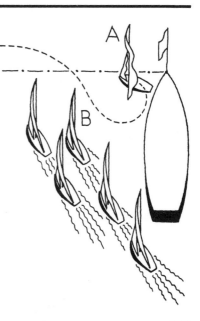

The use of a big committee boat or even a warship at the starboard end of the line is meant to stop barging and is sometimes used in championships and the Olympic Games. Boats coming round the stern of the committee boat to start will cross the line many lengths away from the end. (see photo on page 245)

A comes in on port reach from the other side of the line and tacks as close to the committee boat as possible. She can remain for quite a long time with flapping sails in the corner by the starboard end. Then, as the gun fires, she can pull in her sails and gather full speed and will be several lengths to windward of the next boat.

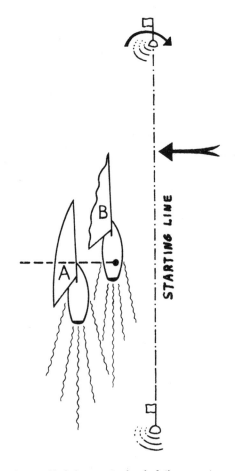

The main part of the fleet gathers at the starboard end of the starting line just before the gun when the wind shifts to make the port end more favourable . . .

. . . A is the first to realise the significance of the wind shift and should take a chance, free off and sail fast to the port end of the line . . .

As long as B's helmsman is ahead of A's mast, A cannot force B to point higher.

. . . then tacking on to port tack and making a start with the gun and with her wind clear. If the wind shifts back to its original direction, she can tack back on to starboard and be even farther ahead of the fleet. If she had started on starboard, and had then tacked after the start, she would have lost the amount lost in the actual tack. It does not cost anything to tack before the start, but it does not pay to tack unnecessarily afterwards.

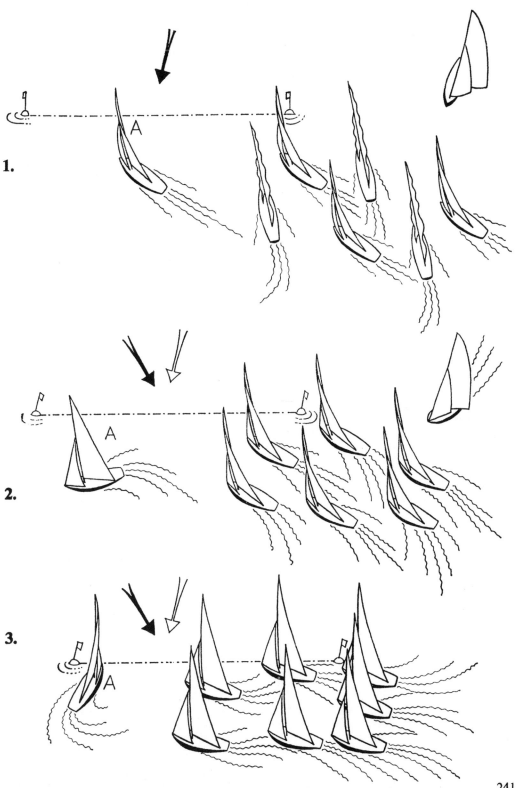

1.

2.

3.

241

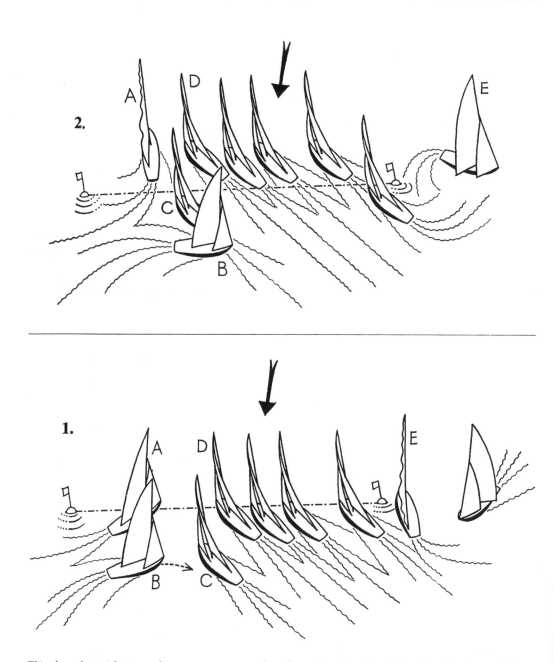

This shows how risky it can be to start on port tack. A has started on port and can go ahead of C because this boat is late. But D has started with the gun and cannot pass, and therefore A must tack to leeward of her. If A is quick enough she may be able to get safe leeward position, but failing this, A's only possibility is to fall off to leeward and get a free wind. B, who started later than A, has to pass under the stern of the entire fleet and will cross the line last, even later than E, who was unable to find room at the windward mark.

Oslo Aftenposten

This picture is from one of the starts during the 1963 Finn Gold Cup and it shows what can happen in a shifting wind. The wind has changed to give a very big advantage to the committee boat end of the line. When the wind changes like this it is almost certain that it will change back again shortly afterwards, and in this case it is very important that you should start with a clear wind and continue on starboard tack. Do not start like K37, who is coming up on port tack towards the stern of the committee boat.

The START

It can be dangerous to slow down too much whilst starting. G935 is too close to the lee mark and is stopped. She may find that she cannot cross the line at all when the others take her wind as they pass. G1173 is also in a difficult position since she is going too fast and may be forced over the line early if G688 luffs or if she overtakes G1122 before gunfire.

The camera is exactly on the start line. The port-end mark is on the extreme right in the top picture 15 seconds before the start. The mark is just to the right of the centre of the lower picture 15 seconds after the start. The committee boat is a big warship and note that N50 is the only boat at this end that has made a good start. The skipper placed himself there one minute before the start by coming in on port tack, then tacking and lying hove-to. Apart from N50, only the boats in the far distance have made good starts. There was no transit mark and this shows how important it is to be able to judge exactly where the line is.

Tactics after the start. In this case just after the start if they are sailing on a heading puff then 2366 should tack immediately to consolidate her advantage because it will almost certainly shift back again soon afterwards.

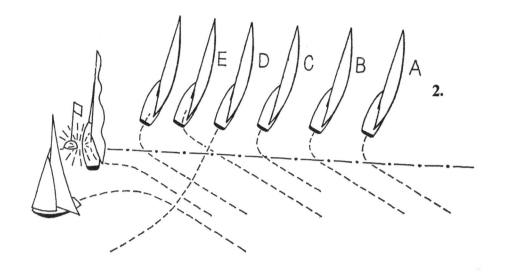

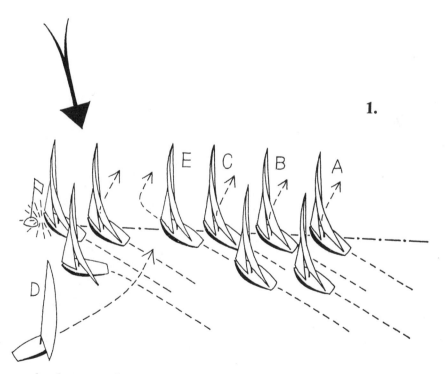

This is a case where boats can only just, or not at all, lay the line on starboard tack. As soon as you realise that this will be so you ought to put yourself in the position shown for boat D.

A will tack immediately and all the others will follow in quick succession and there will always be a hole through which D can dive and pass the tacking boats which will have lost most of their speed. The boats near the mark will have no speed on either tack.

This tactic is especially valuable when sailing keelboats which are heavy and gather speed only slowly. The second drawing shows the position immediately after the start with D pulling through to a clear wind.

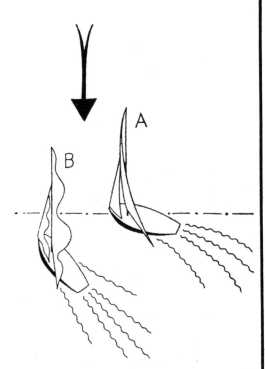

B has full speed and would like to place herself on the empty lee side of A. A must watch out for this and immediately she sees that it is about to happen she must bear away hard and try to persuade B to go on her weather side instead.

A must try to keep her lee side clear so that she can bear away just before the gun to gather full speed for crossing the line. This will also help to avoid her being lee-bowed after starting.

In this drawing B is excellently placed with her lee side completely clear. Her problem is whether to try to stop A sailing across her bow and gaining this lee position.

Here, the faster that A crosses the better it will be for B. After this manoeuvre A would never be able to place herself closer than 1½ lengths to leeward of B whatever she did and this would not harm B.

If B tries to prevent A from crossing she will almost certainly cross the line and, in trying to spoil A's start, she will also spoil her own.

The starting gun is just about to fire. C should have already hailed A and B that they will not be allowed room at the mark.

If A and B ignore the warning and still try to force a passage at the mark, C should not hold her course and insist on her rights but should free off also and keep her wind clear and gain speed. C will thus only lose one or two lengths whereas otherwise she might get involved in a messy collision which could end in C getting boxed in without speed or wind. In a Star, for example, it would be easy to lose the whole rig in such a situation.

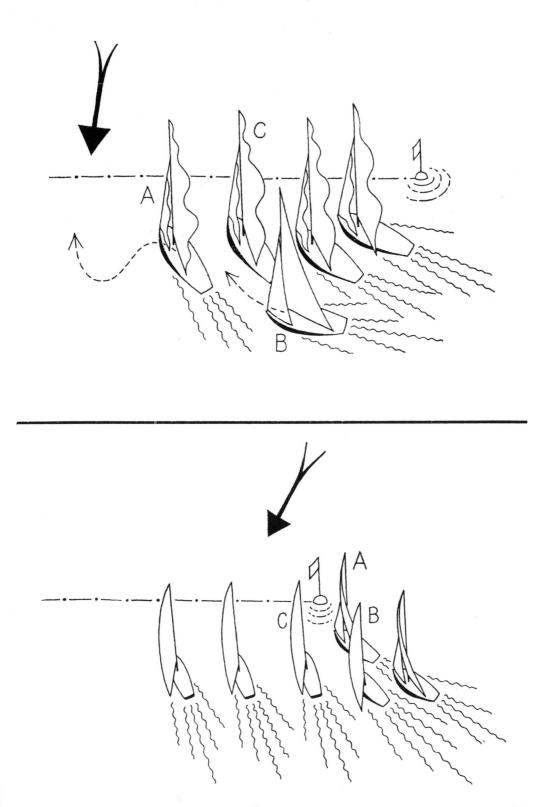

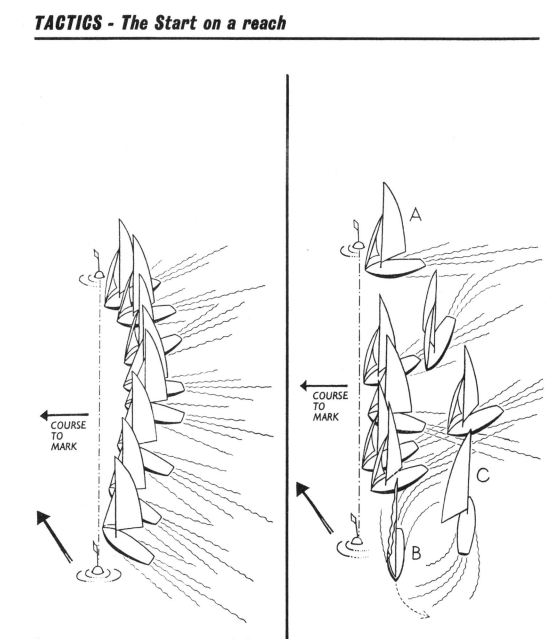

COURSE
TO
MARK

COURSE
TO
MARK

A

C

B

In running starts it is dangerous to start at the leeward end because you are liable to be blanketed by the entire fleet. But if the wind is anywhere forward of the beam it is much the best to start at the leeward end exactly with the gun. This is especially true in light winds because you can luff up towards the next mark, and thus gain speed.

It is only when most of the boats are working up towards the windward mark that it is possible for A to start to leeward in a clear wind. As well as making a good start, A does not risk having to make a circle in the same way as B and C.

The Start on a biased line

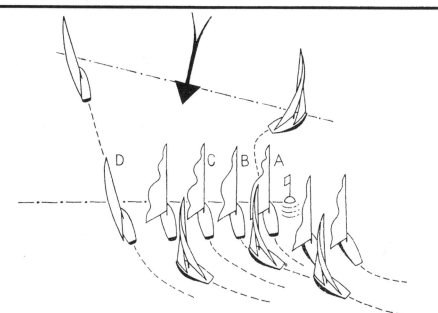

At the start there is a very heavy bias to the starboard end of the line, and so all the boats are crowding there. A has the best starting position but is almost stopped at the gun. Also, B and C have safe leeward position on A.

D starts just to leeward of the main group and with full speed. A must tack as soon as she can because if she carries on she will steadily lose more. If she tacks when she is two boat lengths clear of the line she will be no further ahead than D even though she has taken a very big risk to gain a starting position next to the buoy.

In my experience skippers always underestimate in these conditions and are still 1½ to 2 lengths from the line at the gun. This is usually because the boat nearest the mark finds she can barely lay it and starts pinching which causes the others to pinch also. Thus everyone is slowed down.

Therefore the right tactic is to come from the windward side of the line at the last minute, crossing the line on a reach at full speed, and then steadily harden up without losing speed to start in one of the best positions travelling fast.

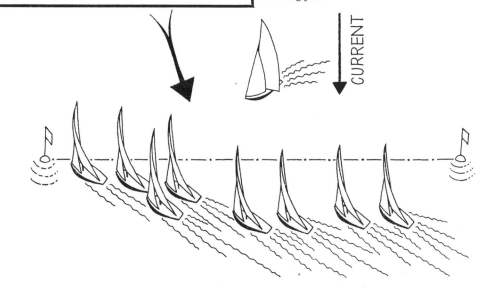

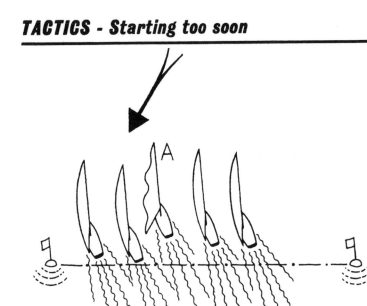

How much better it would have been for A to have realised sooner that she would be over the line early. She would then have gone full speed across, reached along the line and gybed to start again. Here she will lose a great deal whilst she waits for the others to pass before she can go back.

B is early over the line. She must not slow down or try to get back now or she will lose all her rights. She must continue as if she was still racing and call C about because of the starboard tack boat A.

If B does not want to be disqualified she must not slow down until she can do so without affecting any other boat.

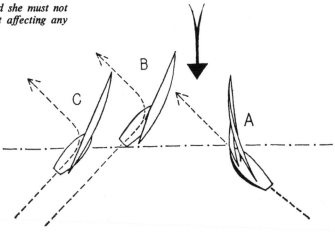

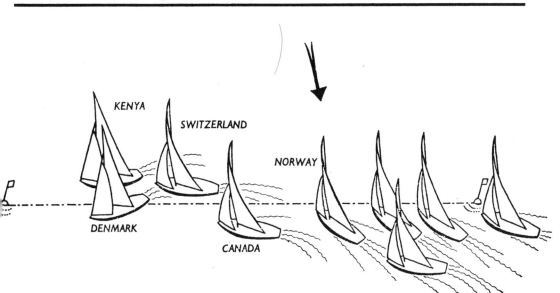

It can be very risky to come from the wrong side of the
starting line. I nearly ran into trouble in the Olympic
Games at Naples when, in one race, I was disqualified
because I was thought to have started too early. I was
over the line together with Kenya and Switzerland but
I bore away then tacked on to port crossing just ahead
of Canada. The committee did not see this because of
the presence of the windward boats, but as Kenya,
Switzerland, Canada and Norway all witnessed in my
favour my place was finally reinstated.

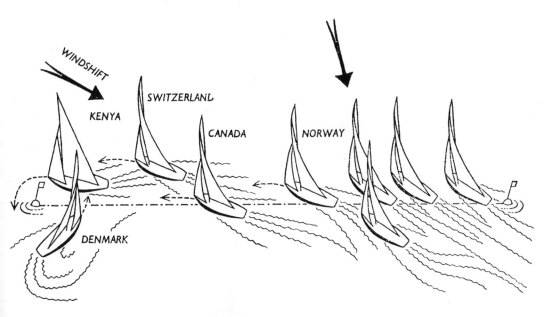

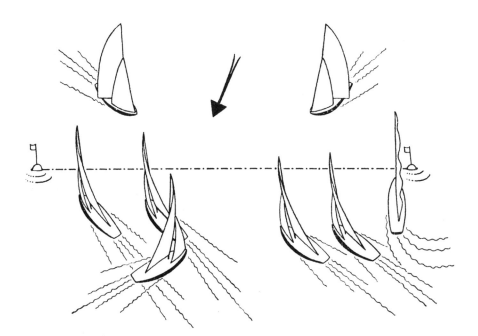

In a shifting wind when the advantage keeps changing from one end of the line to the other, you can start from the other side of the line. This is where you can leave your decision on which end of the line to start to the last minute and until you can find a hole.

The two arrows show the amount that the wind is shifting. The black arrow shows the direction of the wind at the moment. It is correct for the five boats to carry on on the starboard tack. Boat A is on the wrong tack for when the wind is in the direction shown by the black arrow, and should immediately tack back on to starboard.

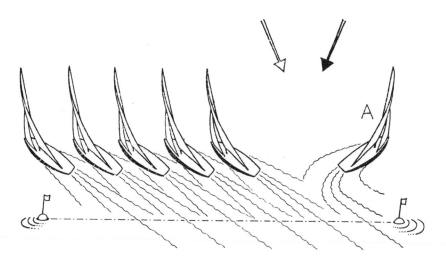

The Windward Leg

As soon as the starting gun is fired and if there is no special consideration regarding the current, you must immediately try to get your wind free and keep clear of all other competitors, in order to go at top speed. An ordinary shifting wind varies up to 20° from side to side, and under special conditions up to 40° or even right round the compass; therefore you must take care to be on the tack which allows you to lay closest to the windward mark. But you must not always sail by the wind but also think of the position of the mark – so that you do not go too far to one side and overstand. It is ridiculous to keep sailing on the most advantageous tack and then find that you have gone too far over to one side and that you will have to bear off on to a reach in order to arrive at the mark.

If you are behind and the leading boats are going the right way to windward, either because they are in a favourable current or because they are on the right tack for the shifting wind, then you have no option but to follow them and hope they will make some errors later.

The basic rule when sailing to windward is always to sail on the tack which will bring you closest to the mark. You must never break away from the others in the hope of picking up a lucky shift when you know for certain that the others are going the right way.

Never forget the overall object of the race and never waste time duelling with one other competitor. Often you see two boats fighting together and forgetting the race as a whole, so that by going the wrong way they are losing several places. What is the point of gaining one place, if you both lose several places?

In a large fleet and especially when there is a very shifty wind try to disregard all the other competitors and only take notice of the wind. It is much better to tack when the wind changes and then bear away half or one boat's length underneath another competitor, than to carry on on the wrong tack. In a big fleet with a shifting wind it is best to try to find a clear area where you can concentrate on getting to the next mark as soon as possible by working the windshifts.

If you have been covered by another competitor, and you cannot get clear by tacking, you must not just try to tack for no other good reason. If at any moment the other boat hits a wave and you have an opportunity to tack quickly, then tack. Even if he then tacks immediately, you will certainly come closer to him.

You are sailing on a rough sea and you want to tack. If you are not certain that you can tack and cross a starboard boat on your weather quarter, make sure that you tack when you are in a smoother patch of sea and whilst your opponent is pitching into a steeper sea.

Very often the sea is smoother on one tack than the other and you will sail much faster on this tack. If two boats are sailing nearly level on the smoother, faster tack, remember that, if you want to tack and try to cross the other boat, you will be travelling much more slowly on the new tack.

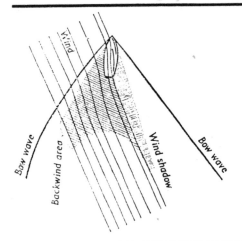

A boat leaves a wind shadow to leeward and most of the air which should have filled this area is deflected aft and to windward so that it acts as a back-wind to any boat that is within its influence. The bow wave can also be difficult to pass and therefore you must take great care to avoid the area of dirty wind when you are trying to break through bow waves. You must take great pains when trying to pass to keep out of the area of dirty wind, the wind shadow, and also outside the bow waves.

A has safe leeward position and B has no chance of passing unless she tacks or alternatively drops back and falls off through the lee. In order to make B drop back faster, A can pull in her sheets and point closer to the wind.

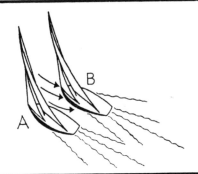

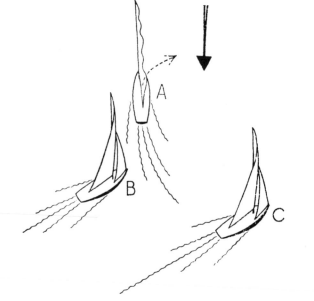

A has made a big mistake in tacking to cover B, because the latter is then forced to tack away again. B and C are now going in different directions and A is not able to keep in touch with B. A should have waited until B had got clear of her wind shadow. Only when a windshift or an advantageous current gives the port tack boat an advantage should A tack to cover B.

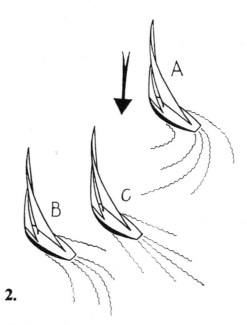

Below:

If you are leading when going to windward you must try to make the boat behind you go in the same direction as you are. If the fleet is splitting up across the course and you are not sure which side holds the advantage, you must try to keep close to the boats that are nearest to you. A has done the right thing here. B cannot pass ahead of C, and must tack under her lee bow. A continues on a little in order not to cover C exactly, and thus force her to tack . . .

2.

Above:

. . . A must tack when she is not exactly covering B and C, and in this way is able to keep in touch with them. If one of them tacks away then A should also tack in order to force the boat to come back on to starboard. This tactic can only be used in fairly constant wind in which it is not important on which tack to be.

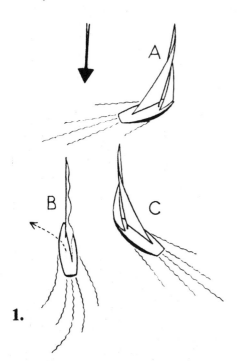

1.

TACTICS - Covering and breaking cover

This manoeuvre can be used if you want to be 100 per cent. certain of keeping your leading position. And also if there is only one competitor within range of you. This manoeuvre needs the wind to be constant and for there to be no current to cause one tack to be better than the other. The worst of this manoeuvre is that you reduce your lead by two boat lengths, assuming that the second dinghy continues on the same tack after rounding the mark. I feel this is not a very good form of tactics because it to some extent spoils the fun for the second boat. In my opinion, it is more amusing to look ahead to see how quickly you can reach the next mark, rather than to sail so safely.

A false tack can be used against a boat which is covering you closely, but wait until you have both done two or three tacks together so that the covering boat is used to having you tacking immediately. If you have the bad luck to fail in your false tack you will not be able to succeed again, because the other boat will then be watching you too closely.

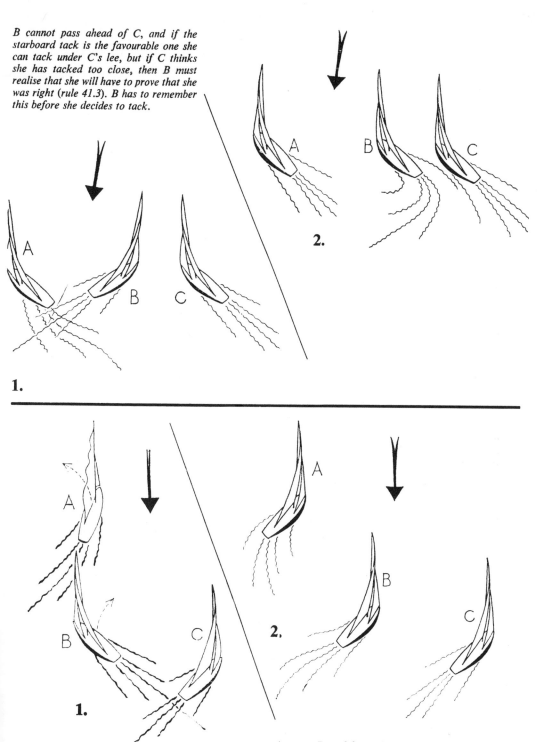

B cannot pass ahead of C, and if the starboard tack is the favourable one she can tack under C's lee, but if C thinks she has tacked too close, then B must realise that she will have to prove that she was right (rule 41.3). B has to remember this before she decides to tack.

A

B

C

1.

2.

A

B

C

A

B

C

1.

2.

A

B

C

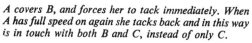

A covers B, and forces her to tack immediately. When A has full speed on again she tacks back and in this way is in touch with both B and C, instead of only C.

259

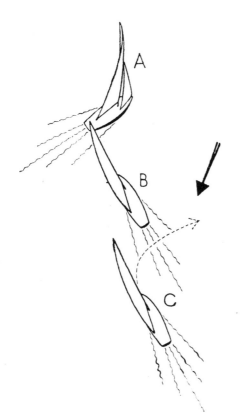

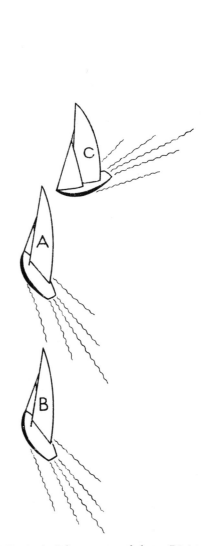

B has covered C, who has to tack in order to get clear.
But it is impossible for B to tack because she will then
find herself under A's lee.

43.2 (b). A asks B for room to tack, but as B is interested
in getting a safe leeward position on A, she must hail
'You tack' in order to get the right to postpone her
own tack.

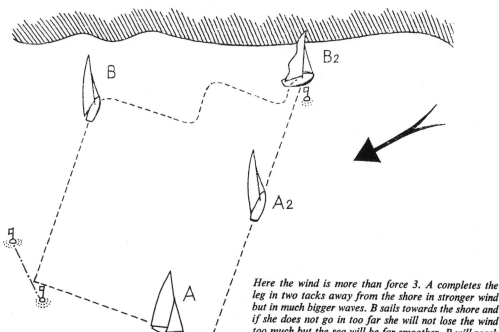

Here the wind is more than force 3. A completes the leg in two tacks away from the shore in stronger wind but in much bigger waves. B sails towards the shore and if she does not go in too far she will not lose the wind too much but the sea will be far smoother. B will reach the mark sooner because A will have travelled further since she has to go up and down bigger waves.

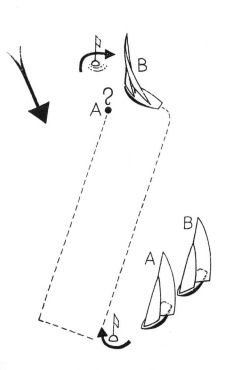

In this situation there is no doubt that B should fall off to leeward slightly and make the smoothest possible rounding of the mark and then tack immediately so that she takes the long leg first.

B must decide on her tactics before she reaches the lee mark because she can see that the next leg is going to be one very long board and one very short one. If she rounds immediately she will have her wind clear the whole way up the long leg and if the wind shifts she will not lose and may gain. There is also a chance that B can catch A when B tacks on to starboard for the mark.

A's tactic is to make as smooth a rounding as possible as soon as she is within the two length's radius. Then she should carry on a few yards and make a smooth tack. If she then sails slightly free she may be able to cover B.

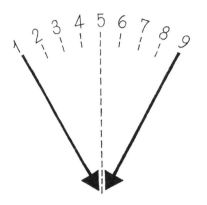

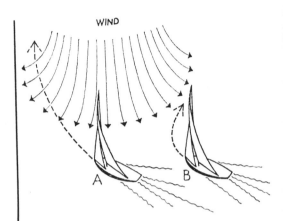

A must continue and B must tack.

A compass can be a great help in detecting wind shifts but if you have no compass you will have to learn how to estimate shifts.

For example, most people might easily be able to feel a shift from direction 1 to direction 9, but suppose that it only shifts from 1 to 5. In other words the regular shifting about a mean suddenly is biased to one side. Most people would estimate that it was shifting from 1 to about 8 and they would therefore tack. But 5 is the mean direction and there was no need to tack since the courses are equally favourable on either tack. Also, if you tack you will lose the distance lost when actually tacking the boat. And even more, whilst you are tacking the wind may shift again, possibly back to 3 for example. In fact you will rapidly become 'wind-shift-groggy'.

Whether you tack when the wind shifts between, say, directions 4 and 6, or perhaps 3 and 7, depends entirely on the characteristics of the boat you are using. You also have to estimate the length of time the shift is going to last. For example, a trapeze dinghy should only tack on the major shifts and the skipper should pay no attention to shifts from 4 to 6.

If the wind is only shifting between extremes of say 4 to 6 then you can start a race at the starboard end of the line and immediately tack on to port. The object is to get yourself clear of the fleet and, once there, you can start working the shifts. If the wind then starts shifting a greater amount, even if it starts by going to direction 1 or 2, you will still almost certainly be leading because you can tack when it moves back to 8 or 9.

If the wind is shifting over a great range at the start then you have to start somewhere not too far from the middle of the line so that you can sail after the gun toward the next big shift.

● WIND SHIFT

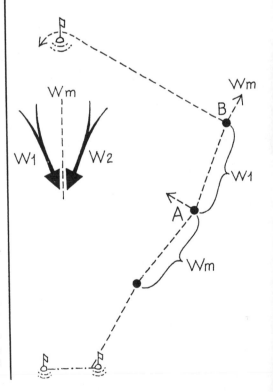

Left:

There is one situation where you would be right to carry on to the lay-line and this is where the wind has been shifting between W1 and W2 but, after the start, it only shifts between the mean direction and W1. In this case you carry on until you are nearly on the lay-line and then tack.

You would normally tack at position A but since the wind goes back at this time to W1 you carry on and when it shifts back to the mean direction at position B you tack.

Remember always that you should never tack unless you gain by tacking, except of course if your only interest is in saving your position or covering another boat.

Above:

Boat No. F126, which seems to be last in the fleet at the moment, is able to take some advantage from the other boats which are ahead of her by being able to see the wind changes before they reach her.

This was a start in the Star Class World Championships in Kiel in 1966. 5070 has made a nearly perfect start at the lee mark. She can now sail faster than all the others by freeing off slightly. She can also point higher if she wants to and will backwind 5077 and force the latter to backwind 5011. She should then be able to draw ahead and will be able to tack quite soon.

4969 has made the best start because she has no one backwinding her and is also free to tack at any time since she does not appear to have anyone on her weather quarter. 14924 has made the worst start. She cannot tack at all and her only chance is to free off and pass well to leeward of 5070 and 5077. If the wind heads later she could gain a great deal.

This British O.K. Dinghy, sailing against the tide, goes as close to the shore as possible where the current is weakest.

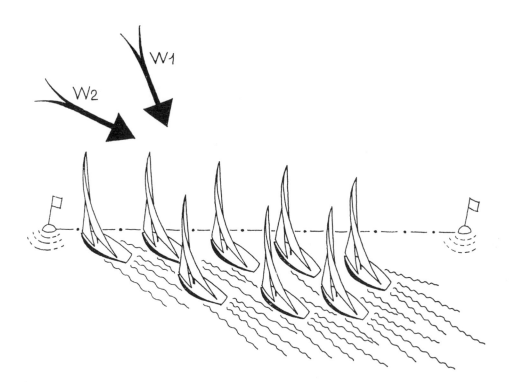

When the mean wind direction favours the port end of the line you must try to start as near as possible to the port buoy. Only one boat can, of course, get the best position right by the buoy on starboard tack but if you are somewhere near and with a clear wind it will not be too bad since, sooner or later, the boats on your weather will tack. You should then wait a little and tack yourself, and you will find yourself with a clear wind and in one of the top positions.

If you start at the other end of the line, even if you have your wind clear, you will have lost a lot of distance immediately.

In this type of start, if you feel that you cannot safely estimate your run-up so that you are exactly at the port buoy at the gun, then always err on the safe side. If you arrive too early you will be in great difficulty. If you realise in time that this is going to happen, then gain speed, gybe without delay and try to find another hole. If there is such confusion that you cannot find a hole then wait on port tack near the line as boat D in the drawing on page 247.

Opposite, top:

It is very important not to try to lay the windward mark from too far away. If there should be a good freeing shift on your approach to the mark you will lose a great amount on boats which had tacked earlier. Here A1 will reach the mark a long way ahead of A2 if the wind frees at the black dot.

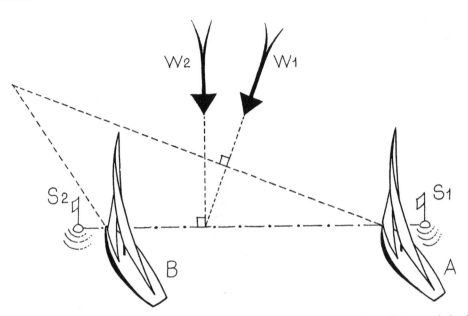

In this case the wind is changing regularly from direction W1 to W2 and back again. At the time of the start the wind is in direction W1 and therefore it will be best to start at the starboard end (S1). A will then be in effect nearer to the windward mark if the wind stays steady.

But there is only one perfect place to start and that is where A is. It is very easy for other boats to lose two or more boat lengths if they also try to start by the buoy but it will be easy for B to make a good start at the other end of the line.

When the wind changes back to direction W2, A will have lost her lead again and B will be exactly level with her. You have to work out whether you will be worse off starting with a clear wind at the lee end of the line and lose say three lengths on the boat making the best start, or at the weather end of the line where you might lose as much as ten lengths in the confusion by the buoy.

You must make up your mind when you know the number of starters and can decide how many are likely to be trying a windward-end start. Then estimate the risks. You also have to consider whether you need a safe finishing position or if you have to go all-out for a win

Opposite, bottom:

Here A2 has gone off to the starboard side of the course again but this time the wind backs to W2 at the black dot. A2 loses again because, whether she carries on or not, A1 can tack and lay the mark. By going off on to the starboard lay-line A2 can only hold her position if the wind remains steady, but A1 has two good chances of gaining on A2.

Therefore if you tack out to the lay-line in a shifty wind you can only stay the same or lose and you will never gain.

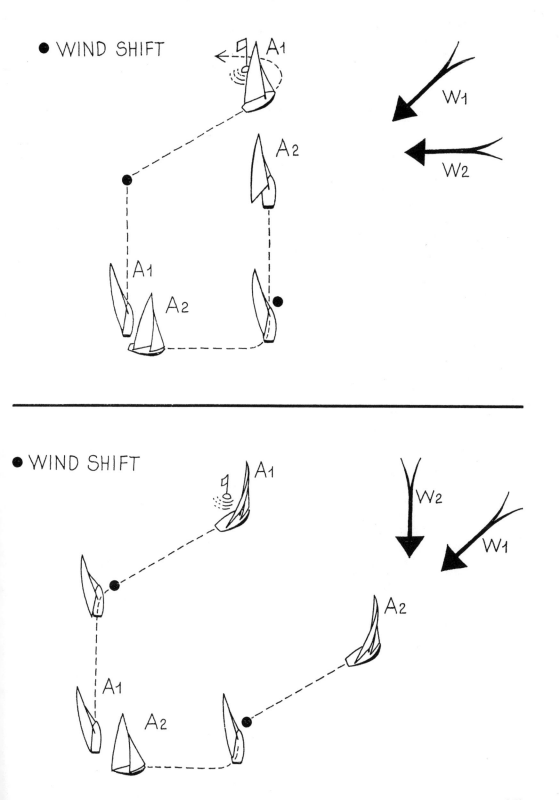

● WIND SHIFT

A_1

W_1

W_2

A_2

A_1

A_2

● WIND SHIFT

A_1

W_2

W_1

A_2

A_1

A_2

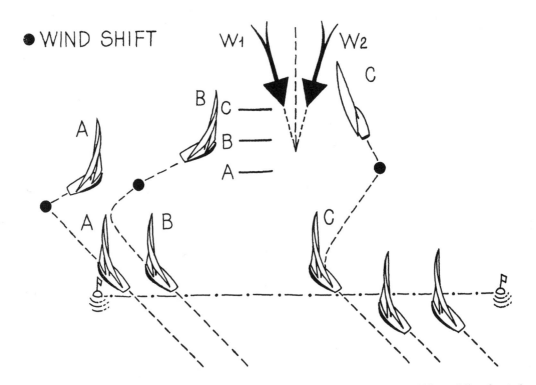

• WIND SHIFT

There is a wind shift from W1 to W2 at the point marked by the black dot. A has taken the worst course possible whilst C has taken the best.

If B had realised that the shift was coming she could have started on port tack if there had been room, but she has tacked as soon as possible when she was sure she could clear starboard tack boats. C does the same but when she realises that the wind is heading her she tacks again and is already 1½ lengths ahead of A.

If the wind and current are the same all over the course then your main aim should be to follow the wind shifts as indicated here. Even though it was more favourable here to start at the port end, the windshift made the starboard end eventually best if you made your tacks at the right moments.

This over-simplified drawing only shows a big shift of wind. Of course there are also small shifts and you have to decide first what is the mean direction and how large a shift is needed to persuade you to tack.

Sailing against a current

In waters where there is a strong tidal stream against you it will be less close inshore and stronger out in the middle of the channel, and you may also find around the time of the turn of the tide that the current may be running in the opposite direction close inshore.

If the current is against you and you can get five to ten yards closer to the shore by raising your centreboard one-third, then it will be an advantage. If the water is very shallow a couple of hundred yards from the shore, then it may even pay to raise the centreboard half way up. If you are able to sail with your centreboard hoist held in your hand it will not matter touching the bottom every now and again.

Sooner or later you must make a decision whether you can yet lay the mark. The leading boat must not risk going out into the tide if there is the least doubt whether she can lay the mark unless she is very far ahead of the next boat astern.

If the boats are going to windward towards a mark which is out in the tidal current, then the difference between them after they have rounded the mark can be four times as much as it was beforehand. If the leading boat has overstood the mark she will normally still round ahead even if she goes out towards it at the same time as the next astern. If the third or fourth boats set out to round the mark then the leading boat must make a decision as to whether she can then lay the mark. If she thinks there is a fair chance that she can lay the mark, she ought to go, but if she is not sure she should wait until she is certain or alternatively until the second boat decides to go.

If the current is so strong that it is impossible to make to windward against it, you must be absolutely sure that you can lay the mark before going out, otherwise you will have to come right back to the shore again.

On some racing courses you will find the current is going in different directions on different parts of the course. You should watch the condition of the sea because if you see a particularly steep chop in one area that will be where the wind is going against the strongest current. When the current is going in the same direction as the wind the sea looks smoothest. This can be a great help if there are no buoys or land marks in sight.

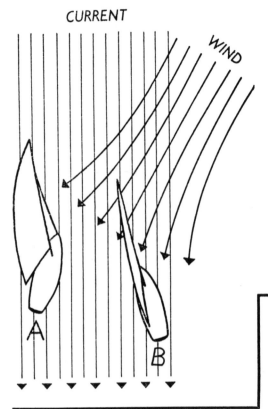

CURRENT

WIND

SAILING IN CURRENT. *In such a situation it is absolutely essential to be sailing on the right tack when going to windward, because the current against the port bow will help you to get to windward as is happening to A. B has a heading wind which means that she cannot point so high and the current is pushing her starboard bow, which takes her away from the wind.*

A

B

A covers B in order to try to force her out into the stronger current but the only chance is for B to bear away through A's lee, so that she can call for water along the shore. When eventually the two boats have to tack because of the shore it will be certain that A will be in the safer position, therefore B must look ahead and try to get up enough speed after the tack so that she can tack back again on to port.

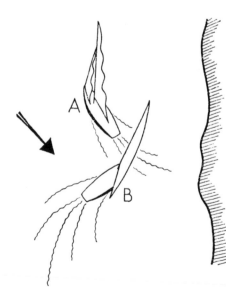

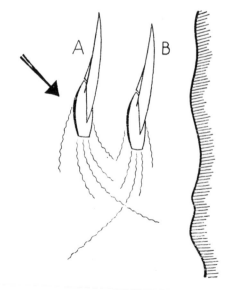

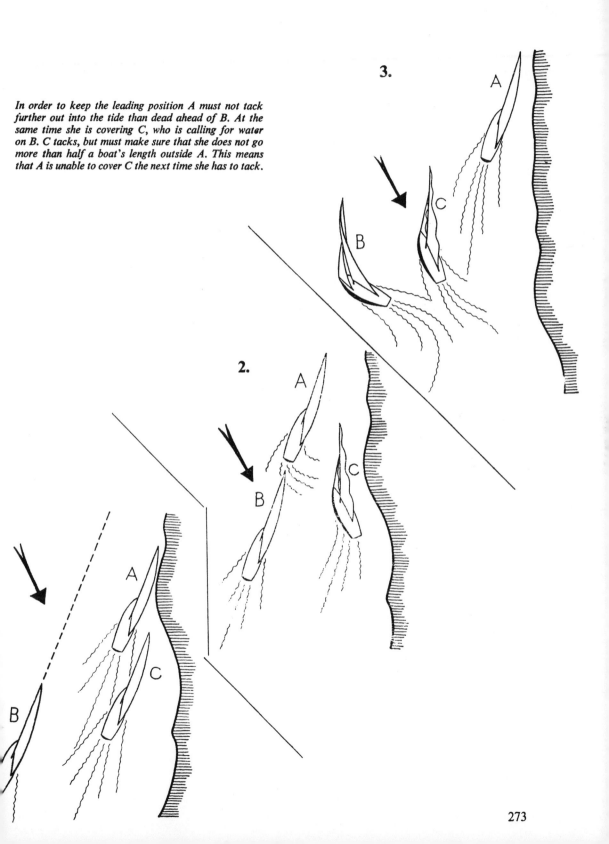

In order to keep the leading position A must not tack further out into the tide than dead ahead of B. At the same time she is covering C, who is calling for water on B. C tacks, but must make sure that she does not go more than half a boat's length outside A. This means that A is unable to cover C the next time she has to tack.

3.

A

C

B

2.

A

C

B

A

C

B

Rounding marks

In starts with between 30 and 200 boats it is very important to start thinking about rounding the mark when you are on the windward beat. If you have to leave the first mark to starboard there is no need to be afraid of using the port side of the course because by overstanding the mark a little you are certain of being able to round it. It often pays to overstand the mark a little, rather than being caught in the starboard tack queue sailing directly for the mark.

It is different when the weather mark has to be rounded to port, for in this case it is essential to keep over on to the starboard side of the course, because, if you have to come into the mark on port tack, you risk not being able to find room to round the mark, owing to the long queue of starboard tack boats approaching the mark. You can easily lose ten, twenty or thirty places through this error because even if you are able to find a hole through which you can pass and then tack you may not be able to do so owing to the cut-up wind caused by so many boats to windward.

In small fleets you will be fairly well spread out at the first mark and therefore you do not have to think too far ahead about the rounding manoeuvre. You can easily lose speed when rounding a mark, but if you do it correctly in light winds you can actually gain speed because as you luff up towards the wind its speed will increase.

The rounding must be made smoothly and the sails must be pulled in gently so that they always present the most effective angle to the wind. It is most important that you do not pull either the mainsail or the jib in too soon since you often see a dinghy stopped dead by this means during the rounding. If you do the manoeuvre correctly you should feel that the dinghy is being pulled round the mark.

The best way of rounding a mark is quite different for different classes of boats, and also depends on how quickly the crew can work the boat. If you have a crew who is working rather slowly in a fast dinghy then you must round the mark more slowly than you otherwise would. A Finn dinghy can round the mark more sharply than can a Flying Dutchman. An O.K. Dinghy can round a mark even more sharply than can a Finn. It is the same for all classes of boat, that a boat which rounds as C does will always lose ground. B is rounding the mark in a normal way, which is quite usual with helmsmen who are not so experienced.

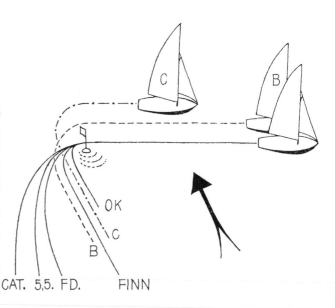

CAT. 5,5. FD.   FINN

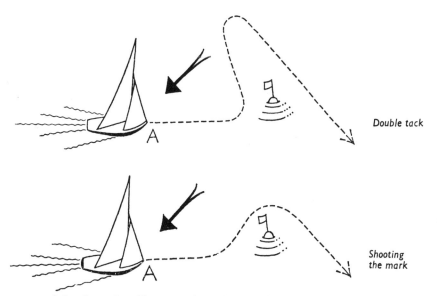

Double tack

Shooting the mark

If you can very nearly lay the mark and have enough speed you can luff head to wind and thus shoot past the mark and then bear away again, and in this way can avoid making a double tack. This manoeuvre is called shooting the mark. In smooth water this manoeuvre is very easy to do if the wind is reasonably steady. In strong winds and rough sea it is risky and you must decide at the last minute whether you are liable to be hit by a big wave or a sudden puff which would stop the boat and prevent you passing the mark. If you are not absolutely sure that you can bring off the manoeuvre it is better to make a double tack because you will then only lose three boat lengths instead of having to retire because you have hit the mark.

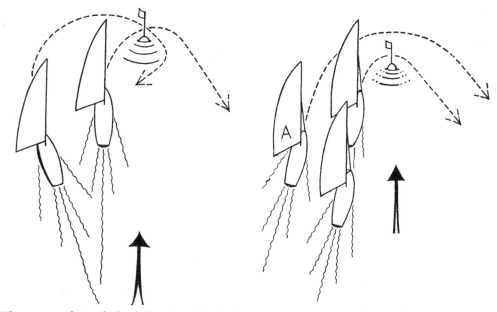

When you are closing the leeward mark and running in company with other boats and you do not round first, then your placing will depend on the direction in which you will be going on the next beat. If you want to tack immediately after rounding then you must drop out to leeward and luff up and round the mark very close so *that you come in behind and as far as possible to windward of the others. If you are rounding at the same time as several other boats and you are the outside boat as A is here, and if the right course is to carry on on the same tack, then you must fall off to leeward so that you get your wind clear of the leading boat.*

275

3.

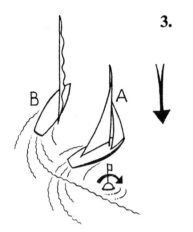

A and B have overstood the mark and it looks as if A will have to give B room to round the mark inside. A now sheets in her sails and slows down, dropping behind B without B noticing this. As soon as A gets her wind clear she pulls in behind B, who then cannot round the mark until A does. (Rule 41.1.)

2.

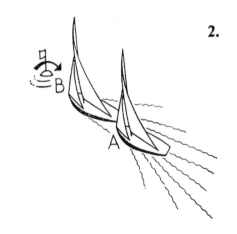

1.

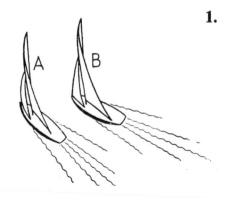

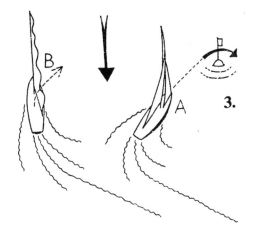

3.

B has safe leeward position on A. The mark has to be left to starboard, and therefore A must keep on until she is sure she can lay the mark. Of course, she loses a little speed by being in safe leeward position, but she saves two tacks by holding on.

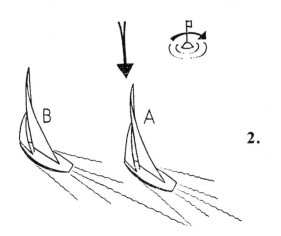

2.

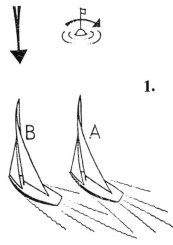

1.

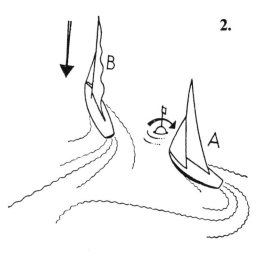

2.

B can lay the mark. If A, coming on starboard tack, passes across B and then tacks to windward of her, then B will go round the mark first. A should therefore tack under B's lee and then fall down three boat lengths to leeward before tacking back on to starboard again. In this way B may not be able to cross A and will be forced to tack.

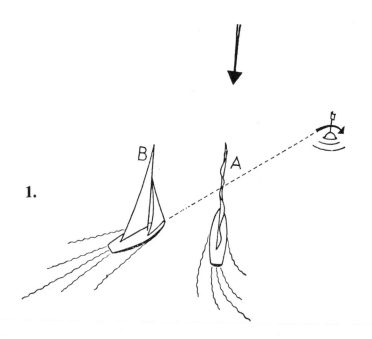

1.

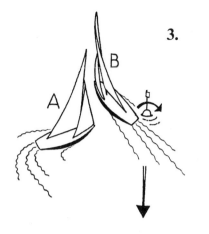

3.

A cannot lay the mark and cannot pass ahead of B, but she has a good chance of preventing B from rounding first.

2.

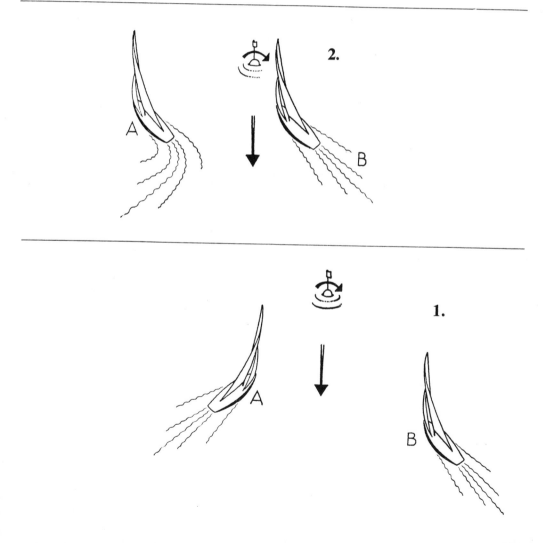

1.

TACTICS - on approaching marks (2 boats)

A is crossing ahead of B on starboard tack, and should tack as soon as she has passed her to prevent B changing on to starboard tack, and thus coming first round the mark. But in picture No. 2, if B tacks on to starboard at the same time as A is tacking on to port, then A will be in the wrong.

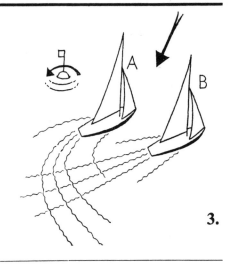

3.

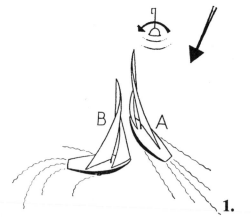

2.

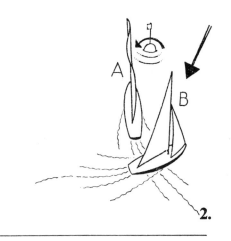

1.

A realises too late that she cannot pass ahead of B. A must not tack but must pass under B's stern. If A tacks she is bound to round the mark behind, but if she passes under B's stern she has a good chance of rounding first.

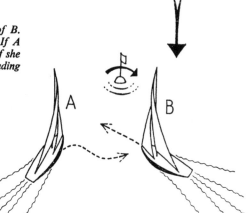

A must never let herself get into the position described above. By slowing down and passing under B's stern she can get round the mark first because B cannot tack until she is clear of A.

1.

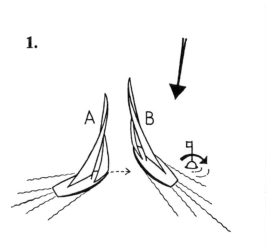

2.

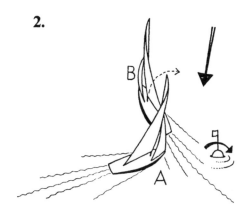

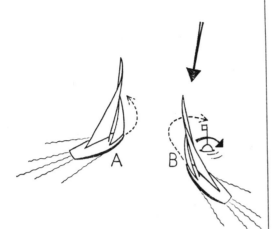

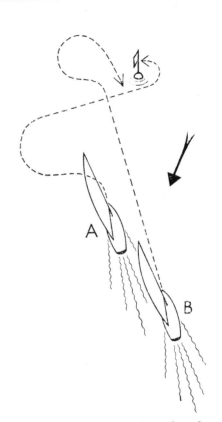

B must hold on until A is tacking and has got the wind on the new tack. A must wait until she has gained speed before tacking again. A will lose up to ten boat lengths by this manoeuvre against B who will only lose one.

This shows A's only chance of rounding the mark in front of B, who can do nothing except to tack immediately until she can lay the mark. By this manoeuvre B will save one tack at the mark, and will probably round ahead of A, as she will be on starboard when coming to the mark.

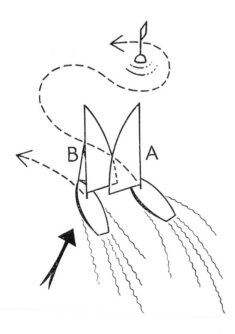

A is on starboard and can in this situation force B to sail the wrong side of the mark and, by this manoeuvre round ahead of B. This is because the definition 'leeward yacht' only applies when both are on the same tack.

Before N15 put himself in this position he ought to have decided whether he wanted to tack immediately after passing the mark or whether he wanted to continue. If he had wanted to tack he should have dropped slightly back and got closer to the mark. But if he had wanted to carry on he ought not to have pulled his sails in so tight but he should have tried to sail free and fast to pass through S52's lee.

283

Opposite page:

(1) In Australia, 12-Meter Dame Pattie takes Gretel nearly head to wind in luffing match. (2) Dame Pattie lays off for mark, Gretel holds high in attempt to take the Dame's wind. (3) As boats near mark, Dame sweeps up across Gretel's bow to get inside for rounding. (4) Both boats drop chutes and sail by the lee, crews holding booms to prevent jibes. (5) Jib still in stops and mark abeam, Dame swings into wind in smart rounding. Gretel fumbles. (6) Ten seconds later, the Dame's jib is sheeted home and she's moving out fast ahead.

Hornet No. 599 has crossed ahead on starboard tack of Hornet No. 564 and she ought to tack immediately to keep her dead to windward, and then she will be able to prevent 564 from tacking, always assuming that the latter cannot lay the mark.

This shows the situation which occurs when boats are gybing round a mark against the tide. The main tactic is to avoid putting yourself into a position where you have to bear off on to a dead run. In such a light wind your speed will then be so slow that you will not be able to gybe or alter course when you want to.

No. 1456 is in the best position and he need not have given room to No. 1326 because of the two lengths rule.

And therefore in the second picture he ought to have gybes a boat's length earlier than this.

In the third picture we can see that all three of them have gybed without having altered course enough to keep their spinnakers full all the time.

Above:

No. 256, unable to cross his opponent on port tack, has just tacked under his lee bow perfectly and will stop him and soon have him safely in his wake, pointing lower.

Below:

After rounding the weather mark boats tend to luff out to weather of those ahead in succession. The third boat is doing right by bearing away firmly onto a direct course for the next mark.

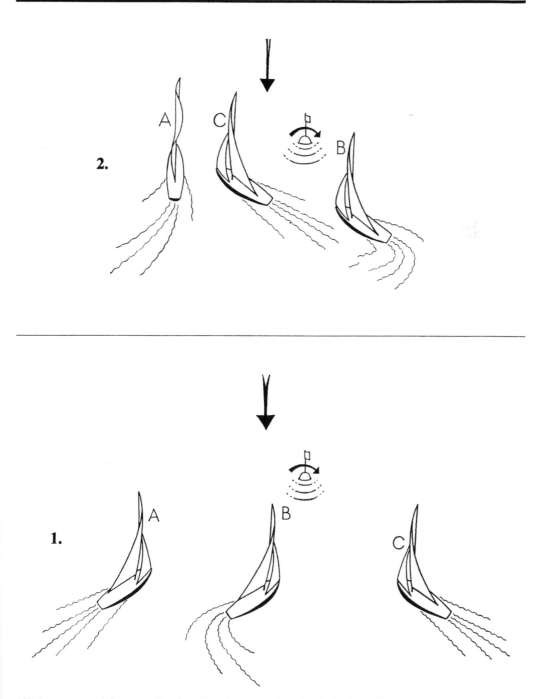

If B is to prevent A from rounding first, then she must tack under the lee bow of A, and then pass under the stern of C, then tacking back on to starboard whilst hoping that C will force A to go about.

TACTICS - on approaching marks (3 boats)

The possibility of B getting round the mark first depends entirely on A. If A tacks to leeward of B, then B can tack as soon as she can lay the mark, allowing C to cross ahead of her. B will then round first and C last. On the other hand, if A elects to pass under the stern of B, and then allows C to cross her, it will be A who will round the mark first.

3.

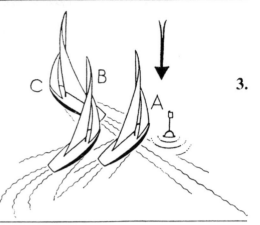

2.

1.

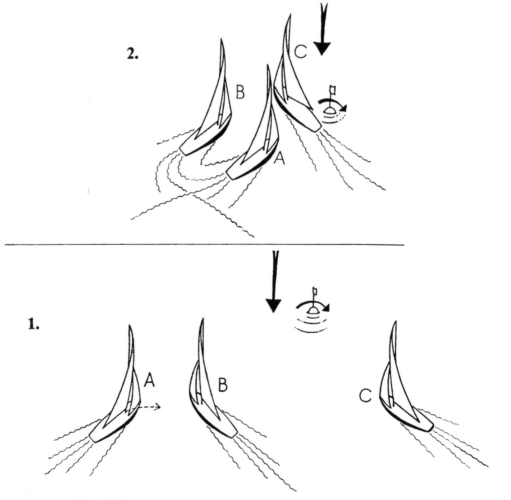

A crosses on starboard tack and ought to continue far enough so that when she tacks on to port she interferes with B's wind to a large enough extent so that B cannot then lay the mark. A should be able to slow B so much that C may be able to close up. A's manoeuvre should only be employed when these three boats are well in the lead or when A is particularly anxious to retain this leading position, because the employment of this tactic will slow all three boats down.

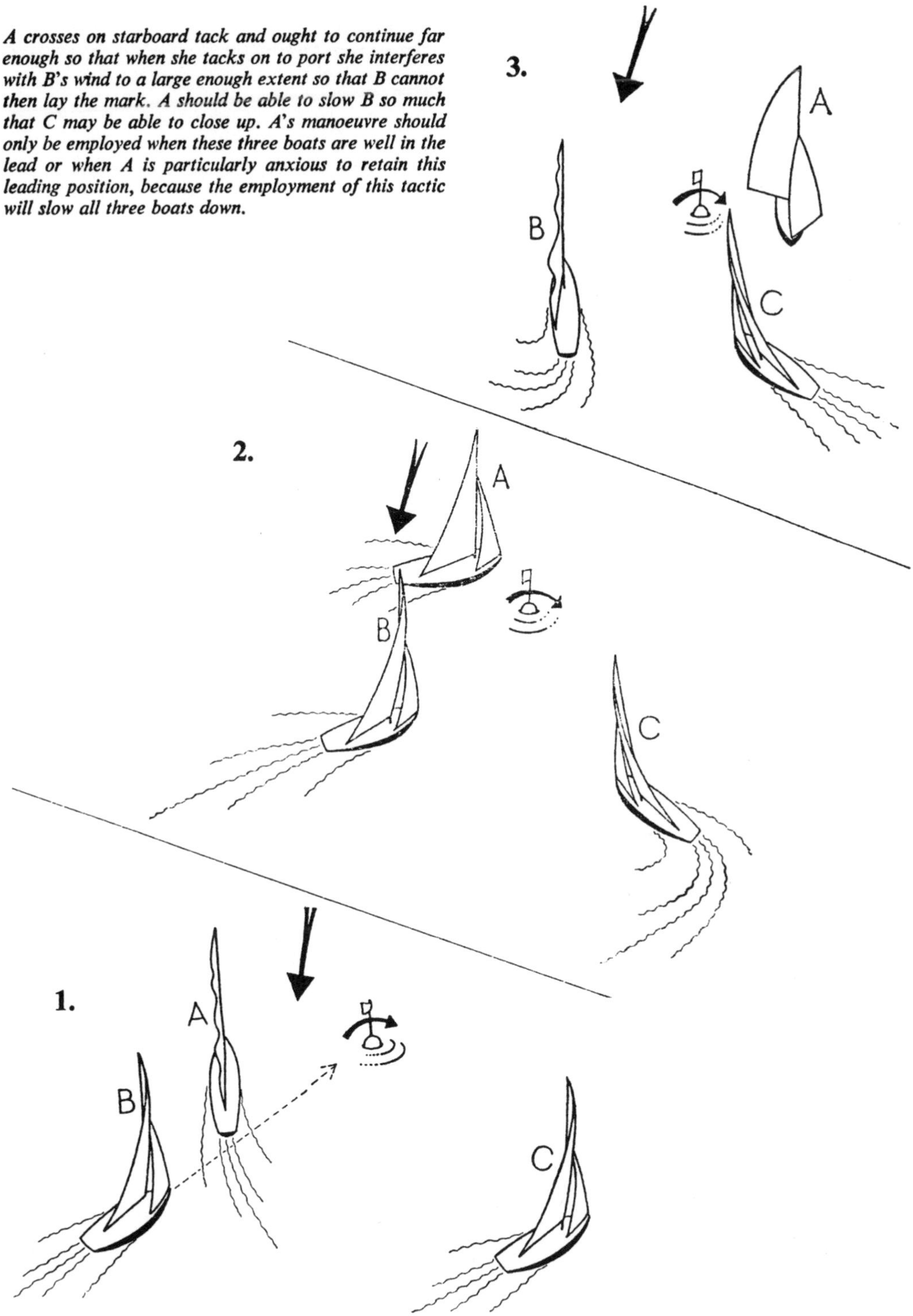

3.

2.

1.

3.

A cannot lay the mark and B and C pass under her stern hoping to catch A when they meet on the next tack. A should therefore tack immediately she has passed C, which will thus prevent B and C from tacking until she does. As soon as A can lay the mark she ought to tack and by this means she should round the mark first.

2.

1.

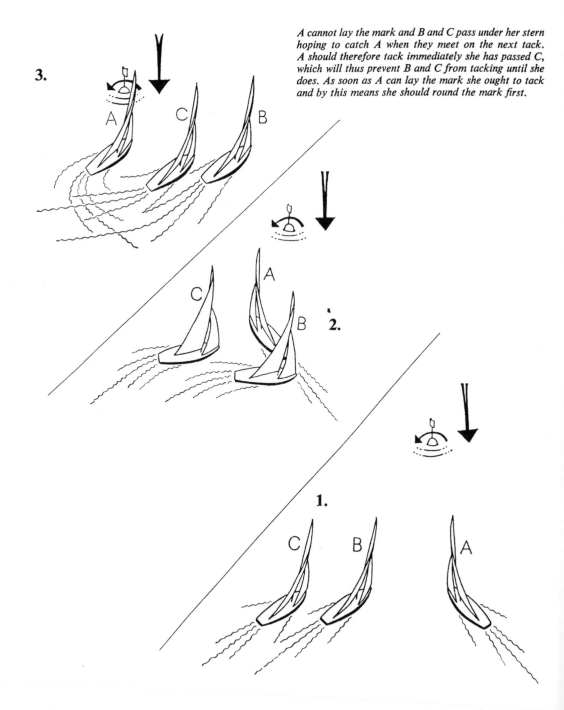

B and C will have to give way to A who is on starboard tack. If B passes under the stern of A, then she must give room for C to do so as well, because A is an obstruction, and in this case B will round the mark last. If, on the other hand, B calls for water on C to give room to tack, then there is a possibility for B to round the mark second.

In the top picture B should tack at this moment, because C is unable to do so because of A. B should then be able to tack back on to starboard and round the mark before C is able to reach it.

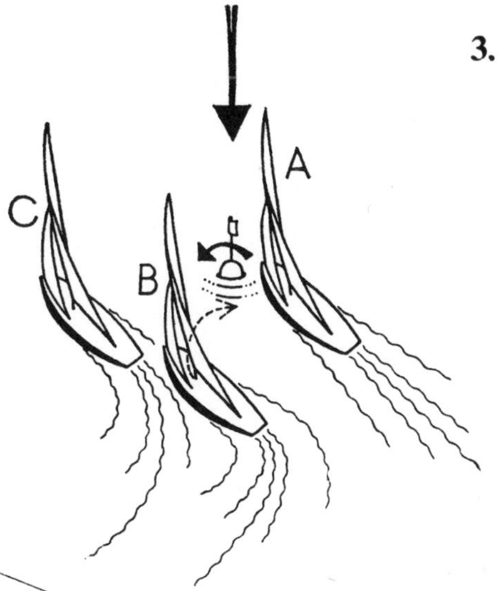

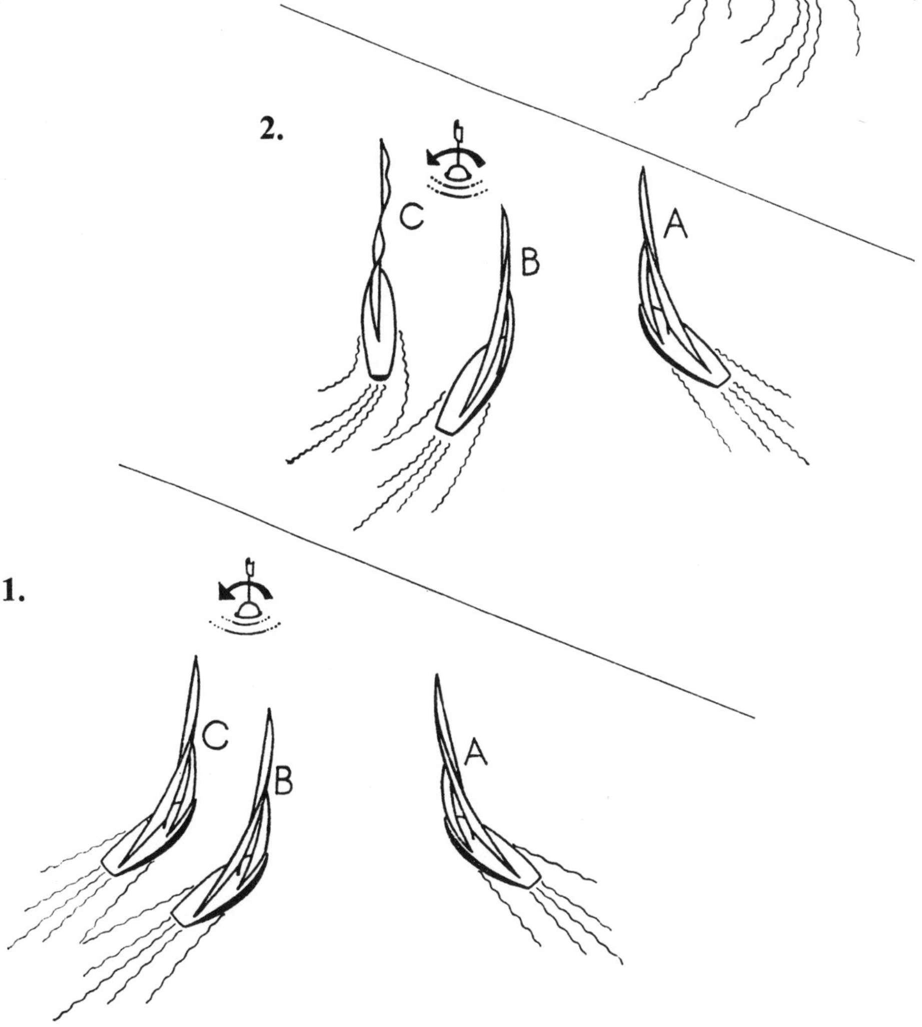

3.

2.

1.

Reaching and Running

Running free is not so interesting tactically as sailing to windward. For example, there is very little one can do on a reach in light wind. If we think from a tactical point of view that all the boats are travelling at the same speed, then in theory there should be no changes of place. However, it frequently happens that two boats sailing close together start to luff out to windward and thus take a longer course, and this gives an opportunity for boats behind to close up to them. If they luff out to windward then they will have to bear away considerably when they get near the mark and their speed will drop and this may allow the boat behind to pass.

When you are sailing on a reach you must try to gain speed by improving the trim of the boat.

If there is enough wind for there to be a possibility of planing you may have a good chance of being able to close up and pass other competitors. If you are just behind another boat, and there is a possibility of being able to plane, you should wait until you are actually planing before luffing out and passing to windward. You will be unable to pass to leeward of the other boats because planing will stop as soon as you get into the blanketing zone. The tactic is that you should not luff and try to pass until you are sure you have enough wind to plane right past the other boat. If planing stops when you are level with the other boat you will immediately get involved in a luffing match and you will both lose a considerable amount of distance.

You must always remember the main object of the race and avoid getting involved in a duel with one or two other boats.

When the wind is freer and coming over the quarter so that there is a possibility of using the spinnaker, and if a large number of boats are pushing each other up to windward, then it is often best to set the spinnaker immediately and bear away to leeward of the main fleet, finally taking the spinnaker down and luffing up to come to the mark. The other boats will be afraid of being passed by those astern and will continue to luff up well to windward of the mark.

If it is not certain that the spinnaker can be carried effectively the leading boat should not hoist it before the second boat does, or he will be in danger of being passed to windward whilst he is engaged in trying to get the spinnaker drawing. With the wind aft you must not sail so far free that the jib is blanketed by the mainsail. It is better to sail a little higher so that you are sure that the jib is drawing one hundred per cent.

If you are in the lead and far enough ahead so that you are not being affected by the blanketing of the boats astern, then you should steer so that you are directly down wind of these boats to ensure you have exactly the same wind as they have.

In the same way, if you are behind the leading boats, and you want to remain in touch with them, you should sail exactly behind them so that you have the same wind as they do.

On the other hand, if you are anxious to gain some distance on the leaders you could go out to one side or the other, so that you have a possibility of picking up a better wind and thus gaining on them.

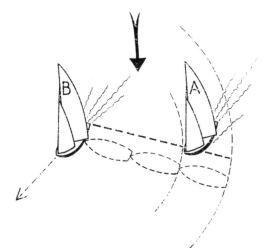

If A is interested in getting luffing rights on B, she must keep within a distance of three boat lengths, so that B has to steer her proper course. At the same time A must take care not to come in closer than two boat lengths, before her mast is ahead of B's helmsman.

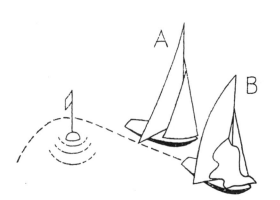

COURSE TO NEXT MARK

You will always lose some distance whilst hoisting the spinnaker and therefore B should not start to do so unless A is also starting or until B is well clear of A.

If B starts hoisting in the situation shown here, A has only to luff in order to run up level with B and take all her wind. Then she can hoist her own spinnaker and will easily pass.

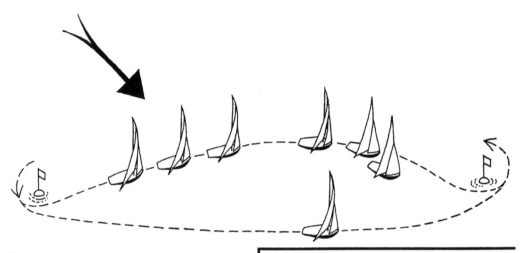

Above:

 You will find that in big fleets on a reach most of the boats will tend to take a more windward course. Therefore if you are not too close to the boat next astern it will be much better to take a more leeward course. This will also be the shortest course and it will also mean that you will be able to luff up and gain speed as you approach the mark. At this period all the windward boats will be travelling at their slowest.

Below:

This is quite a common situation and you should try to sail course 'a.' The current will then lift you up towards the mark and you will have great speed over the part marked X. The actual course that you will be sailing over the ground will be 'b' but if you try to sail this course you will end up by following something like 'c.' You will then travel the part marked Y very slowly indeed since you will be running against the current.

 If the wind is from the direction W2 do not hesitate to free off and put up your spinnaker at the start. You can then lower it half way and luff on to a fast close reach.

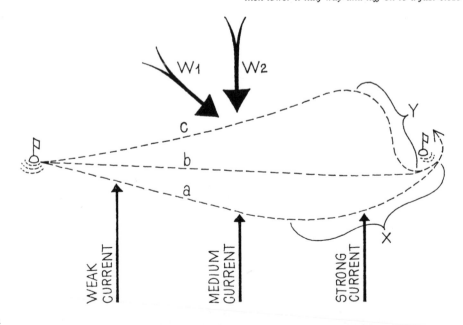

When racing in large fleets it often happens that the leading boats get very far ahead while the tail enders get left a long way behind. Look in the picture at D4, who ought to have tacked long before, but has held on simply to disqualify the Polish Finn PZ, and this is a first-class example of a bad tactic which will lose D4 about fifty yards.

No. 627, who is obviously unsure of himself in this strong wind, should have foreseen this situation coming a long time ago. He should have either gybed earlier and come on to starboard tack, or he should have luffed up and crossed the stern of 106.

When they get near to the finishing line most people make a tack in an attempt to get there first, even though they are not sure that this is doing any good. In this case it looks as though H25 ought to take a chance and tack because she is receiving so much back wind that she is losing ground. On the other hand, if H25 had not been receiving back wind from the leeward boat it would have been wrong for her to have tacked, because she would have been able to point as high as the other. You frequently see people losing a race by tacking at the finishing line unnecessarily.

It does not help to cross the line first if by doing so you disqualify yourself. If N16 had passed under the stern of K37 she would only have lost one place. The picture was taken during the Gold Cup for Finn dinghies in 1959.

K. Hashimoto

Whatever happens in a race, if it is still possible for you to continue you ought never to give up. And if there is a possibility of repairing the damage you must try to decide whether you would lose more by stopping to repair the damage or by continuing with the boat not working at full efficiency.

Trevor Davies

No. 9754's only chance is to sail the windward boat on past the mark. But there is very little hope that she can hold back 7964 because she is so badly rigged and tuned. Look at the slack jib luff, the foot of the mainsail not pulled out enough, and the slack leach of the mainsail in the upper part.

SAFETY

Perfectly safe till help comes!

Life Jackets

I have been working on the problem of life jackets since 1956 and I would like to tell you what testing we have done on them. At that time almost no dinghy or keelboat sailors wore life jackets. The reason was that you could not then buy a life jacket which you could wear and still do active work in a small boat. The type of life jacket which we could buy at that time turned a first-class crew into a clumsy idiot in a boat. This type of life jacket was also very dangerous for a dinghy sailor because he could not move quickly and he could not climb in over the side of a boat because it was too bulky.

The old type of life jacket was only useful for keeping a man's head above the waves and that was all. What we need for sailing in keelboats and in dinghies is a compromise because we cannot use a life jacket which is designed to save an unconscious person since

302

it will be far too bulky at the front and will hinder our movements. We have to compromise because it is better to have a life jacket which will help a conscious person to swim than nothing at all. It is also better to have a life jacket that is so comfortable and easy to put on that you always wear it. A bulky life jacket will save an unconscious person but it will be only pure luck if it is being worn on the day the accident happens.

I would like to tell you of a case which I saw myself. The Danish champion in the Pirat Class was hit on the head by the boom and knocked overboard and he fell in head first and unconscious. He came to the surface and he was wearing a buoyancy waistcoat. After hitting the water the buoyancy in the waistcoat kept him afloat and then he put his head up and obviously did not know where he was. This showed that he must have been unconscious when he hit the water but was revived by the shock of the cold. This example could mean that an unconscious person can often revive when he is immersed in cold water. But if he is not wearing anything to help him swim it may be that he will still drown because he will revive when he is under the water.

I would like to ask everyone who does not now wear a life jacket to try jumping overboard in a big sea with a life line tied to them and wearing their full clothes. Then they can see just how difficult it is to swim and how weak they become so that it is impossible to climb in over the side of a dinghy or a keelboat.

It is best to have a life saving waistcoat which is made to fit your body size exactly. A lot of people do not have the right size life jacket and therefore, when putting it on, do not do it up at the front. This is rather dangerous unless they are wearing it underneath sweaters, which will keep it on.

Try not to fall into the water and have to swim round the bottom in order to reach the centreboard because it can be very difficult climbing over the side when you are heavy with water sodden clothes. Also I must mention that you must take care not to use too bulky a life jacket because it may stop you from getting over the edge of the boat when trying to climb in.

In this picture you will see that the helmsman of this boat is wearing a light buoyancy waistcoat. If he had been wearing a bulky life jacket he would have no chance at all of being able to climb up and over the side. Actually, the mast is almost certainly already in the mud. He ought to have dropped off into the water as soon as it was certain that he would capsize, but he must still hold on to the main sheet so that the boat does not blow away.

This shows the type of life jacket which I designed for children. It can be adjusted quickly for size and worn under or over other clothing.

Even in a light wind you should wear your life jackets. You never know what may happen later.

I decided I would not make my life jacket of the type you had to blow up because I felt that people would only say 'Oh well, I can always blow it up when I am in the water', but by then it is too late! A good friend of mine capsized into cold water during the ski-yachting regatta at Cannes, having been sailing in strong winds. He found that he was so tired that he was unable to blow the life jacket up. Because of his wet clothes he found that he was sinking but his wife who was crewing for him swam to him and blew his life jacket up for him and this saved his life.

Another type of life jacket uses a compressed air bottle which can be arranged so that it can blow up the life jacket for you. This is very easy but I have another example where a man had tied his life jacket round himself so tightly that when he pulled the release for the compressed air bottle the life jacket blew up and nearly strangled him.

To be sure that sailors would wear my life jacket even in light weather I decided to make it look really nice and to be so comfortable that everyone became used to wearing it as part of their normal clothing. The main arguments today about life jackets are always concerning their ability to support the head of an unconscious person above the waves but this type is really of no use to yachtsmen at all. This is not the type of equipment that a small boat sailor needs. Today you can buy many different types of very comfortable jackets and waistcoats and you will find that almost all dinghy sailors now wear one of these types and this proves that the main reason why no one wore anything in the way of buoyancy aids ten years ago was because of the poor design. Therefore the people who insist on full life jackets only and write articles to this effect are really hindering the sport more than they help it.

Safety Equipment

The flotation equipment in a dinghy should be so arranged that when the boat is capsized and lying on its side there is the smallest possible tendency for the mast to sink and the boat to turn upside down. If the flotation is in the form of tanks along the whole side of the boat as in many International Finns, you will find that the hull floats so high that there is a very great tendency for this to happen. Therefore you must adjust the buoyancy in the sides of the boat so that when capsized the hull will sink far enough so that the centreboard is about a foot clear of the water when you are standing on it. If you do this there is quite enough flotation to enable the boat to be righted easily. The remaining water in the hull can easily be bailed out. The best method is to have a double bottom so that almost all the water drains out over the side or through the centreboard case.

Another disadvantage of too much buoy-ancy is that if you get thrown out and separated, the boat will blow away from you faster than you can swim.

You can put as much flotation as you like into the stern and the bow of the boat. Plenty of buoyancy in the bow will be very helpful when you try to start sailing again because it is very important to keep water out of the bow. Too much water here will make the boat dive and then you will capsize again.

If you have no bailers fitted to the boat you must keep on stopping to bail the water out because allowing too much water to collect in the bottom of the boat is one of the easiest ways of capsizing.

Here I am testing the prototype of my Trapez class single-hander. You can see that the buoyancy is just about right. I am trying to sink the sealed hollow mast but it will not go down when I am leaning in this position. Note that the rudder and tiller are held on by an elastic strap.

When you capsize you should try to get on to the centreboard as fast as possible so that there is no possibility of the mast sinking and the boat turning upside down.

If you are not very quick getting on to the centreboard there is a big risk that you may not be able to get the mast unstuck from the mud and may even break it.

If the mast breaks you may half capsize and take in a lot of water, and because the suction bailers will not work you will have to bail by hand. Therefore you must always have a plastic bucket tied on and also a sponge in the boat. Even if you are waiting for help the dinghy ought to be emptied. A waterlogged boat is not very seaworthy but a dinghy which has been bailed dry will float like a cork.

If the dinghy should capsize, hold on tight and try not to get thrown into the water, then climb up on to the side as quickly as possible and stand on the centreboard. In single-handed boats you will find it easiest to climb up by stepping on the mast, but you must make absolutely certain that it is unable to come adrift from the mast step, or it will come out and break up the deck.

If you capsize with the centreboard completely raised, you must as quickly as possible push it down again before you climb up on to the side. When a trapeze dinghy capsizes the crew must never unhook himself and jump into the water, from whence he will be unable to right the boat. He must hang on, then unhook himself and climb out on to the centreboard. Especially in light dinghies you must get out on to the centreboard as quickly as possible, otherwise there will be a risk of the boat turning right upside down, and it will then take a long time to get the boat upright again. Don't be nervous; it is very easy to right a capsized dinghy by standing on the centreboard.

When a dinghy without buoyancy capsizes it is completely waterlogged and it is impossible to bail it dry. You will need help and in a single-handed dinghy you ought to assist the rescue boat by taking the boom out of the mast and also taking the mast out of the dinghy. The mast and boom should be tied together with the sail wrapped round them, and then laid along the deck. When help comes you must throw over your painter, which should always be fastened to the stem, to the rescue boat. You should always stay in the dinghy and steer it, which makes it much easier for you to be rescued. Raise the centreboard when being towed and sit aft to lift the bow.

In two-man boats you must take off the sails and then one man must stay on board to steer, whilst the other can jump aboard the rescue boat.

It is not only bad seamanship to allow a capsized dinghy to be towed upside down or on its side by a rescue boat, but it also puts a very severe strain on the dinghy and will certainly result in more or less damage.

A capsize can happen to the best and most experienced helmsman but not being able to rescue the boat is always bad seamanship.

Above:
You can see in this picture that the helmsman has fitted buoyancy bags to keep his boat afloat after a capsize but he must be sure to make the fastenings and the lashings very strong so that they can carry the whole weight of the boat and also the crew when it is lying on its side in the water. These lashings and fastenings do not look strong enough.

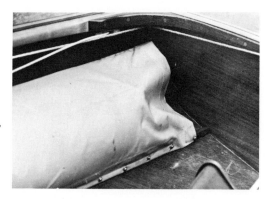

Right:
This is a very secure way of fastening in the buoyancy bags.

Left:
This shows a very good idea for assisting self-rescue in dinghies which have turned upside down or in boats which float so high out of the water that it is difficult to reach the centreboard, such as an O.K. Dinghy. The rope is fixed at one end by passing it through a hole just under the gunwale and clamping it to the inwale. The remainder is clipped into short pieces of split plastic tube screwed under the gunwale. The other end finishes in a good big knot level with the transom. The skipper swims to the stern and grabs hold of the knot and this releases the rope from the clips so that he can throw it over the bottom. He then swims round and grabs hold of it again and pulls the boat upright. One of these ropes is clipped under the gunwale on each side of the boat.

IDEAS

AND THE

FUTURE

TRAPEZ

A new idea I have been developing myself is the sailing and steering of a dinghy from the trapeze. Having now started the Trapez Class which uses such a feature we have found that it is easier to manage than most people thought in advance, and in fact a keen O.K. Dinghy sailor can learn to sail this boat quite quickly. I am sure that this boat will be a fantastically good training boat for all other classes. If you can sail a Trapez you can sail anything.

Below, you can see how easy it is to get out and in, whilst the picture opposite shows the Trapez being used with the high ring position when planing. The skipper should have used the lower ring.

TEMPEST

The Tempest is the newest of the International classes. It was the result of the search for a new two-man keelboat by the I.Y.R.U. and has a very good idea where you can hoist the keel right up until the bulb rests against the bottom of the boat. This makes it very easy to haul the boat out on a slip and to trail it.

The boat has already in its untuned state shown that it is a fantastically good all round performer in any type of weather.

The I.Y.R.U. should, however, have given the class a chance to prove its popularity before granting it International status. The present situation means that sailing organisations are forced to push the class and we shall never know whether the class is growing as a result of its own virtues or because of pressure from the I.Y.R.U. We hope that it will be the first reason so that it will not become like the Flying Dutchman.

On the opposite page is a Tempest being sailed by Keith Musto in the first European Championship at Burnham, England, which he won.
Photo: Trevor Davies

'C' CLASS CATAMARANS

The greatest increases in speed during this century have come from the racing catamarans. The fastest of these are the big International 'C' Class boats which are 25 ft. long maximum and 14 ft. in beam and have a total sail and spar area of 300 sq. ft.

Amazing new developments have appeared in this class and at the present time they have evolved aerofoil masts and special sail shapes and these seem to be very much more important than the very small differences in the best hull shapes. The total weight, however, is also extremely important.

Sailing a 'C' Class catamaran in strong winds is utterly fascinating and gives a feeling which is impossible to explain in words.

On the next two pages you can see how rapidly the development of rigs has been taking place during the past four years. The latest wide mast rig seems to be very much faster than the sloop rig of the same area.

Below:
The third stage. Quest II *from Aus-tralia shows the wide revolving mast on a sloop. There are battens in the jib as well as the mainsail. This was out-standingly better than a simple sloop in spite of the weight.*
Photo: Venn Sturton

Right:
The fourth stage. Lady Helmsman's *una rig with a wide curved mast of nearly half the total rig area proved even better. Some twist had to be allowed to the rig as shown since it was too difficult to sail with the twist absolutely removed.*

COURSES

There was an extremely good starting line which was used in the 1966 Star-boat World Championships in Kiel. This line was formed by the mast on the committee boat at one end and a mark buoy which was also the leeward mark of the course.

Half way between the committee boat and the leeward mark there was another small plastic buoy which was kept exactly on the line by moving the committee boat slightly ahead or astern when necessary. The committee boat was moored to anchors bow and stern in the normal Olympic method so that she could be winched a foot at a time.

The centre mark was not a mark of the course and therefore boats could touch it if they needed to. It was simply a guide to help helmsmen estimate their distance from the line when making their starts.

With this type of line where one can position oneself so accurately it can be laid almost exactly at right angles to the wind instead of giving port bias as is usual.

The result was fantastically successful and all the 83 boats were spread evenly along the line and during the series there was not one single general recall.

I also have a suggestion for laying a course in which we try not to favour the leading boats as usually happens with the normal method. In this way we keep the whole fleet well bunched and boats which have made bad starts have a better chance of gaining places. I also feel that this course could make racing more interesting.

The starting line is formed between a mark, which is usually a buoy, and a staff placed on the stem of a committee boat. The committee boat is preferably low so that it will disturb the wind as little as possible. In big fleets there must also be a guide mark as indicated above in the discussion on the Star World Championship. This mark must be small enough so that you can run over it without damaging anything but it must be easily visible from each end.

The anchor cable of the committee boat must be pulled back under the stem as shown in the sketch.

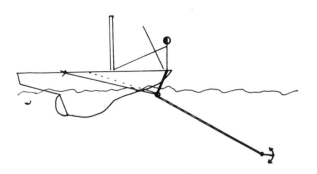

The windward mark and the leeward mark consist of twin markbuoys placed a short distance apart but exactly level with each other with respect to the wind direction. About 10 boats' lengths will be about right.

The first round is a windward/leeward circuit and boats can round either 1a or 1b at their option and then they can round 3a or 3b also at their option.

The second round is a triangle and they will round 1b and 3b since they are nearer to the beam mark.

The last round is a beat and a run again and they can again round either mark of each pair.

Normally the marks are always to starboard for the reasons given under the discussions on Racing Rule 3·2 (page 151), except where local conditions need the opposite direction.

Mark 2 should be a dinghy or rubber boat with a motor so that it can be exactly placed immediately after the start according to the wind conditions. For example, in light weather it can be placed very close to the committee boat, in medium weather further away and in strong winds it can be well out abeam to give the best course for planing.

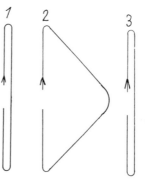

PSYCHOLOGY

You must take great pains to keep clear and calm during racing. Psychological upsets can cause you great trouble and may make you do stupid things which you know you ought not to have done.

If you are racing against another competitor whom you believe to be better than yourself, then you must try to force yourself not to think of this. If he is sailing just a little bit faster you must say to yourself, 'Ah well! This is just happening at this moment; shortly it will be my turn to go faster.' You should concentrate on this. It is quite clear, however, that if he is sailing twice as fast then there is nothing much that you can do. Even if you have heard that this helmsman sails very fast and has won a great many races, you must still never think about it. You must concentrate only on the race which you are in, and you must always think what is the right thing to do and not consider that the other competitor might eventually beat you. I have too often had an easy victory when an opponent has allowed me to pass through an inferiority complex and without giving me battle.

When you enter for a points series it is very important to show your worth during the previous practice races. When you are entering for an important series of races you ought to arrive two days in advance, sail round the course, tune up your boat and mast so that everything is ready for the start. Whilst you are practising and if you are sailing in company with some of the other top class competitors, you must try to sail as fast as you possibly can. This will look impressive to the others and they may finally get a complex about you.

My cleverest and most dangerous opponent, the Belgian Andre Nelis, and I trained together for the Olympic Games in Melbourne,

and I did everything I could to pass him all the time, and I was able to do this quite easily. He was so shaken by this that one day when we were at the Stadium he came and spoke to me saying, 'Paul, I think that you will win your third Gold Medal.' As soon as he said that I realised that he had got an inferiority complex about me and I said to myself, 'Now I know I can win.' I am sure that when a man has an inferiority complex his sailing will immediately suffer.

There is another very important psychological fact in hard racing. You must keep up your spirits and I always say to myself when I am getting to the end of a very long beat and am very sore in the legs through hanging out, 'The others are just as sore as I am and the sooner I reach the mark the shorter time I will have to hang out. I must hold out for as long as I possibly can.' If you are behindhand in the fleet and are very tired you must think that the others are also tired and say to yourself, 'Hold on! Hold on! There is a chance that the others will give up, if they see that I am still holding out.'

If your boat is travelling well you must never give up, however much bad luck you may have during the race. If you are unlucky in the start you must say to yourself, 'I must still do absolutely the right thing, and go the way that I know is fastest.' You must under no circumstances get flustered or take a chance, or make a hundred short tacks in order to try to gain a small amount – never do the opposite of what the leading boats are doing in the hope that you might pick up a little distance. If you are sure the leading boats are going the right way, and by this I am particularly thinking of beating to windward, then all you have to do is to follow them.

Should there come a moment when the

leading boats take a wrong course, then you should go in the direction which you know to be right. By this means in a long race you may be able to get closer and closer to the leading boats and eventually have a chance to pass them.

It is very important to train yourself to recognise the difference between good and bad luck, and also skill and good fortune. If competitors in front of you have been lucky, for instance, with favourable windshifts, you must be very careful not to allow this to influence you in future races. On the other hand, if this happened to you, you must tell yourself that you won by good fortune and do not start the second race saying to yourself, 'I won the previous race and therefore I ought to win this one.' Instead, say to yourself, 'The last race was a washout. I won by luck. Now I must concentrate one hundred per cent. on the new race in order to prove to myself that I am faster than the others.' When going to windward you often see another competitor going off on his own hoping that he can pick up a lucky windshift in order to take the lead – this is pure chance-racing. In 99·9 per cent. of cases he will lose.

On the run it often happens that the bad sailors keep clear of the better sailors, in order not to interfere with them. To the bad sailors I would say they should never do such a thing. You should always do everything you possibly can, and this is the only way to improve.

I think that the best way of enjoying your racing is to concentrate on trying to make as few mistakes as possible and to carry out perfect tactics. Think of your competitors only as being a guide to your own performance. The worst thing that can happen to a yachtsman is that he is racing in a class in which he does not like some of the competitors personally. If this happens then the skipper should try to forget this by concentrating on the tactics. Think only of the next mark and how to get round it in the shortest possible time. When you are racing in a series try to train yourself to be completely calm so that you do not do stupid things like starting half a boat's length too early for example, or tacking too close across another competitor, or taking chances where there is a risk of becoming disqualified. In this way you will always finish in a good place when the series is over.

TRAINING

Balancing the boat when sailing to windward in a strong wind is and always will be the most difficult part for a beginner and especially one who is twenty years old or more. At this age it will take a long time for a man to get used to the hanging technique. I took me about five years before I was able to relax in this position. It is most important to be able to relax so that full concentration can be given to the tactics during the race.

During my first Olympic Regatta I realised that the weakest point of all my competitors was in their hanging- and sitting-out technique, and therefore when I returned home I made myself a practising bench. I thought at that time that I could train myself to be able to sit out with my knees outside the boat, but I had to give up after a year and a half of practice. It was not possible to hold this position for more than six minutes of racing.

At the same time it was so tiring that it upset the sailing and destroyed one's concentration on tactics. Therefore I started to move farther inboard and placed my knees over the middle of the sidedeck. This made it much easier physically to hold the position but a new problem arose as the sharp edges of the deck tended to stop the blood flowing. It helped a great deal to use shin protectors on the legs.

After a year of training I was able to train myself not to need any padding, but now that I am getting older I may have to start using it again. Foam rubber inside the trousers is very comfortable to use as padding.

If you train on a practice bench you must not just hang there. Do some gymnastics, swing the arms up and over the head, and lean forward and back just as if you were in the dinghy. Training on a bench is harder than really sailing.

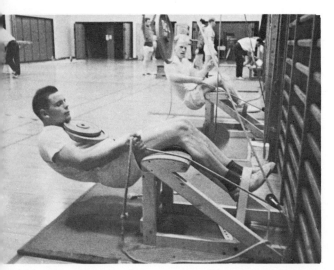

Opposite:
This is the series of exercises we use to train helmsmen during the winter.
1. *Lifting the knees high whilst standing on the same spot.*
2. *Using alternate arms, pull on the rope whilst in the hanging out position. Weight 10 kilos (22 lb.).*
3. *The elbows touch alternately the floor and then the opposite knee.*
4. *Arm exercise done whilst in the normal sitting position. Weight 10 kilos (22 lb.).*
5. *Stand upright with arms reaching up. Then drop to a crouch, hands flat on the floor. Toss the legs out straight behind. Then reverse the sequence.*
6. *Sitting out position held steady and with increasing weights on the chest.*
7. *Same as No. 4.*
8. *Same as No. 2.*

Left:
This is an apparatus that we use for training the muscles used in sitting out. The rope is connected to a weight to make it feel like the mainsheet.

To start with you will get very sore in the leg muscles. Then you should stop for a couple of days until the soreness disappears. Every time the rest periods will get shorter until eventually you will be able to train every day. To start off with you will find it very hard to do this but you must always think ahead that one day it will merely be a routine. You must always keep your speed and fitness and therefore you must keep doing gymnastics outside the season, which will help a great deal.

Here I show the basic physical training that we used for our Olympic team.

Of course physical fitness is only a small part of winning a race, and extreme fitness is only needed in strong wind, and even then it is still only a small fraction of the whole technique. Nevertheless it is an advantage to be fit and many times you can see skippers who are not fit lose a race towards the end.

If you are not in good physical training you may decide not to tack when you ought to do so, because you are tired. You may decide to tack but then fail to carry out the correct sequence of movements and lose many lengths getting going again. You may do something silly, like missing the toestraps, or fall into the bottom of the boat or even go overboard. Probably even worse, your physical tiredness may cause you to become mentally tired and you may work out the tactics wrongly.

A fit man who is not tired can often win a race on the final leg to the finish!

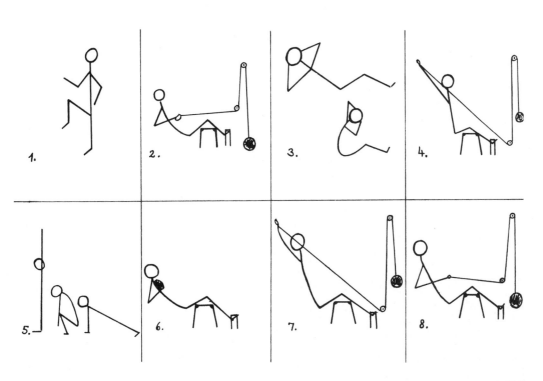

1

2

3

FIBREGLASS DINGHIES

In recent years fibreglass has become the ideal new material for the construction of dinghies because it lends itself to making boats cheaper and also allows them to have a very long life. In addition fibreglass dinghies have the advantage that they remain on the minimum weight because they absorb hardly any water.

1. *The inside of the mould is sprayed with colour pigment.*
2. *On top of this gel coat you put glass-fibre and polyester resin.*
3. *In the event of a collision the tanks may be pierced and fill with water and therefore we fit about 350 lb. of Styrofoam which is enough to keep the dinghy and its crew afloat.*

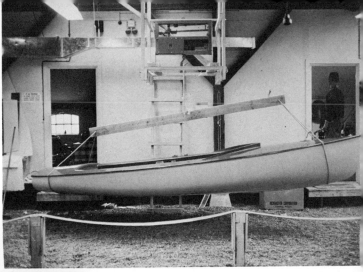

4

5

4. *The finished hull is weighed accurately to check that it is on the minimum weight of 105 kilos.*
5. *This shows a glass fibre Finn with girders glued to the inside of the skin on the floor to keep the bottom stiff.*
6. *The completed boat is strong and light and needs very little maintenance.*

6

CONTROLS

After the boat has been built it is necessary to have it carefully measured to ensure that it conforms to the building rules. You will certainly find that there are many occasions, such as World, European or National championships, when your boat will be submitted to measurement checks or even complete remeasurement. It is stupid to go to one of these regattas when you know something is wrong. It is also stupid not to make absolutely sure that at all times the boat is right.

The sort of things that can easily change are the weight and the length of the leach on the sail. If you have any alterations made anywhere, check afterwards that these have not altered the measurement certificate.

Nowadays the racing is so keen and close that all competitors must be certain that all the boats are legal. That is why it is all the time more necessary to have tighter rules.

A good thing about the new Tempest Class is that they have tried to design it from the start to have as little measuring as possible. This is the first time that this has been attempted with an international class.

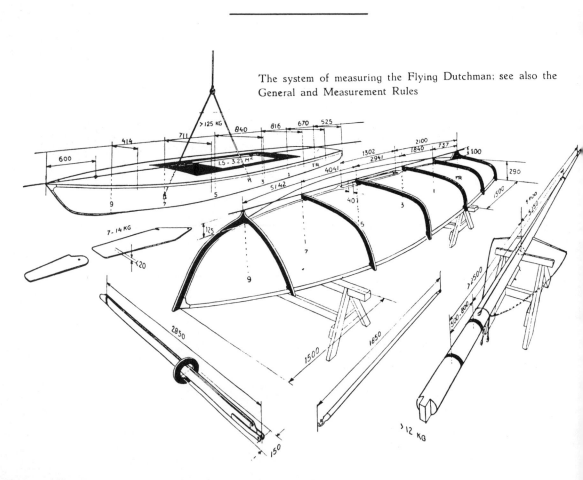

The system of measuring the Flying Dutchman; see also the General and Measurement Rules

These pictures from Japan show:

Top left:
A Dragon being weighed by a mobile crane carrying a man sitting on the weighing machine.

Top right:
Measurement of a Finn sheerguard height with callipers.

Upper centre right:
Height of deck camber, using a base line.

Lower centre right:
Width of cockpit measurement.

Bottom right:
Sail window area.

Bottom left:
A spinnaker being measured on a special large table.

ENOSHIMA, *Sagami Bay, Japan.*

This must be the finest yacht harbour in the world. Built especially for the Olympic Games at a cost estimated at £2½ million, is has every possible facility, and on the right is a key to some of its main features.

The harbour is built on the inshore side of the small, high island of Eno and the entrance faces landwards and is thus sheltered. In the right background to the east were the courses for the large keelboats. The other courses were to the south and south-west.

Key: 1 and 2, Two 300 foot wide concrete slips for Finns (left) and Flying Dutchmen (right). 3, Three floating piers for Stars and Dragons. 4, 5·5 metres moored stern to quay. 5, Spectator and patrol boats. 6, Committee ships. 7, Sail measuring and repair lofts and stores. 8, Gear stores. 9, Measuring tank. 10, Clubhouse and restaurants. Also to be seen are the two tower cranes at the edge of the concrete apron between the piers; one of the mobile cranes and the keelboat cradles on the vast tarmac forecourt which is 300 yards long. So long, in fact, that bicycles were provided for officials.

Whatever happens . . .

always enjoy your racing!

SCORING

Before the start of a series you must always study the sailing instructions so that you understand completely the scoring system.

I would like to suggest that all clubs holding races for international classes use the standard Olympic scoring system given below. Of course, this is designed for a seven-race series with one discard, whereas many international regattas are held over a weekend of two or three days and there can only be from three to six races in all. Nevertheless, the system works quite well if one race is discarded when there are five or more races. For four or less races, all should count.

Do not be upset if the scoring system for your series is different from the standard. Just study the rules very carefully and work out your strategy accordingly.

Remember that to be successful in yacht racing you must take everything into consideration.

OLYMPIC SCORING SYSTEM

There shall be seven races for each class, of which the best six for each yacht shall be counted for her total points.

Any yacht which starts within the meaning of the rules and does not finish, including any yacht which commits a breach of the rules but retires within reasonable time, shall score the points for a last place finish, that is to say for the finishing place equal to the number of yachts starting in the race. Any yacht which commits a breach of the rules but fails to retire within reasonable time, or is disqualified pursuant to the provisions of International Racing Rules 72 and 73, shall score points for a last place finish plus 10 per cent. of the number of yachts starting in the race, fractions being raised to the next higher whole number. Any yacht which does not start shall score the points for the finishing place equal to the number of competitors. A competitor is an entrant who starts in any race of the series.

Each yacht finishing shall score points in each race as follows:

First place	..	..	..	.. 0
Second place	..	..	..	.. 3
Third place	..	..	..	.. 5·7
Fourth place	..	..	..	.. 8
Fifth place	..	..	..	.. 10
Sixth place	..	..	..	.. 11·7

Seventh place and thereafter   place plus 6
Lowest total score wins.

When the international jury decides that a yacht is entitled to the relief granted by Rule 12, Yacht Unduly Prejudiced, an equitable arrangement may be deemed to be the awarding to the yacht whose finishing position has been materially prejudiced of points for that race equal to the average points, to the nearest tenth of a point, of her best five races.

In the event of a tie on total points between two or more yachts the tie shall be broken in favour of the yacht or yachts with the most first places, and if any such yachts remain tied the most second places and so on, if necessary for the six races which count for total points If this method fails to resolve the tie, the tie shall stand as the final placings of the series.

APPENDIX A
CONVERSION TABLE: INCHES TO METRIC (approximate)

inches	mm.	inches	mm.	inches	mm.	inches	mm.
$\frac{1}{8}$	3	$3\frac{1}{8}$	79	$6\frac{1}{8}$	156	$9\frac{1}{8}$	232
$\frac{1}{4}$	6	$3\frac{1}{4}$	83	$6\frac{1}{4}$	159	$9\frac{1}{4}$	235
$\frac{3}{8}$	9	$3\frac{3}{8}$	86	$6\frac{3}{8}$	162	$9\frac{3}{8}$	238
$\frac{1}{2}$	12	$3\frac{1}{2}$	89	$6\frac{1}{2}$	165	$9\frac{1}{2}$	241
$\frac{5}{8}$	16	$3\frac{5}{8}$	92	$6\frac{5}{8}$	168	$9\frac{5}{8}$	345
$\frac{3}{4}$	19	$3\frac{3}{4}$	95	$6\frac{3}{4}$	171	$9\frac{3}{4}$	248
$\frac{7}{8}$	22	$3\frac{7}{8}$	98	$6\frac{7}{8}$	175	$9\frac{7}{8}$	251
1	25	4	102	7	178	10	254
$1\frac{1}{8}$	29	$4\frac{1}{8}$	105	$7\frac{1}{8}$	181	$10\frac{1}{8}$	257
$1\frac{1}{4}$	32	$4\frac{1}{4}$	108	$7\frac{1}{4}$	184	$10\frac{1}{4}$	260
$1\frac{3}{8}$	35	$4\frac{3}{8}$	111	$7\frac{3}{8}$	187	$10\frac{3}{8}$	264
$1\frac{1}{2}$	38	$4\frac{1}{2}$	114	$7\frac{1}{2}$	190	$10\frac{1}{2}$	267
$1\frac{5}{8}$	41	$4\frac{5}{8}$	118	$7\frac{5}{8}$	194	$10\frac{5}{8}$	270
$1\frac{3}{4}$	44	$4\frac{3}{4}$	121	$7\frac{3}{4}$	197	$10\frac{3}{4}$	273
$1\frac{7}{8}$	48	$4\frac{7}{8}$	124	$7\frac{7}{8}$	200	$10\frac{7}{8}$	276
2	51	5	127	8	203	11	279
$2\frac{1}{8}$	54	$5\frac{1}{8}$	130	$8\frac{1}{8}$	206	$11\frac{1}{8}$	283
$2\frac{1}{4}$	57	$5\frac{1}{4}$	133	$8\frac{1}{4}$	210	$11\frac{1}{4}$	286
$2\frac{3}{8}$	60	$5\frac{3}{8}$	137	$8\frac{3}{8}$	213	$11\frac{3}{4}$	289
$2\frac{1}{2}$	64	$5\frac{1}{2}$	140	$8\frac{1}{2}$	216	$11\frac{1}{2}$	292
$2\frac{5}{8}$	67	$5\frac{5}{8}$	143	$8\frac{5}{8}$	219	$11\frac{5}{8}$	295
$2\frac{3}{4}$	70	$5\frac{3}{4}$	146	$8\frac{3}{4}$	222	$11\frac{3}{4}$	299
$2\frac{7}{8}$	73	$5\frac{7}{8}$	149	$8\frac{7}{8}$	225	$11\frac{7}{8}$	302
3	76	6	152	9	229	12	305

APPENDIX B
CONVERSION TABLE: FEET AND INCHES TO METRIC

ft. in.	mm.	ft. in.	mm.	ft. in.	mm.	ft. in.	mm.
1 1	330	2 10	863	4 7	1,397	10 0	3,048
1 2	356	2 11	889	4 8	1,422	11 0	3,353
1 3	381	3 0	914	4 9	1,448	12 0	3,658
1 4	406	3 1	940	4 10	1,473	13 0	3,963
1 5	432	3 2	965	4 11	1,498	14 0	4,267
1 6	457	3 3	991	5 0	1,524	15 0	4,572
1 7	482	3 4	1,016	5 1	1,549	16 0	4,877
1 8	508	3 5	1,041	5 2	1,575	17 0	5,182
1 9	533	3 6	1,067	5 3	1,600	18 0	5,486
1 10	559	3 7	1,092	5 4	1,625	19 0	5,792
1 11	584	3 8	1,117	5 5	1,651	20 0	6,096
2 0	609	3 9	1,143	5 6	1,676	21 0	6,401
2 1	635	3 10	1,168	5 7	1,702	22 0	6,706
2 2	660	3 11	1,194	5 8	1,727	23 0	7,011
2 3	686	4 0	1,219	5 9	1,752	24 0	7,316
2 4	711	4 1	1,244	5 10	1,778	25 0	7,621
2 5	736	4 2	1,270	5 11	1,803	26 0	7,926
2 6	762	4 3	1,295	6 0	1,829	27 0	8,231
2 7	787	4 4	1,321	7 0	2,134	28 0	8,535
2 8	813	4 5	1,346	8 0	2,439	29 0	8,840
2 9	838	4 6	1,371	9 0	2,744	30 0	9,145

1 kilogram = 2·2 pounds

1 litre = 1·76 pints

1 litre = ·22 gallons

1 square metre = 1·196 square yards

1 cubic metre = 35·31 cubic feet

1 metre = 1·094 yards

1 kilometre = ·62 mile

1 pound = ·454 kilograms = 454 grams

1 gallon = 4·55 litres

1 square yard = ·84 square metre

1 cubic foot = ·028 cubic metre

1 yard = ·914 metre

1 mile = 1·61 kilometres

APPENDIX C
CONVERSION TABLE: METRIC TO FEET AND INCHES (approximate)

mm.	inches	mm.	inches	mm.	inches	mm.	ft. in.
1	$\frac{1}{25}$	115	$4\frac{9}{16}$	265	$10\frac{7}{16}$	2,750	9 $0\frac{5}{8}$
2	$\frac{1}{12}$	120	$4\frac{3}{4}$	270	$10\frac{5}{8}$	3,000	9 $10\frac{1}{4}$
3	$\frac{1}{8}$	125	$4\frac{15}{16}$	275	$10\frac{13}{16}$	3,250	10 $7\frac{15}{16}$
4	$\frac{1}{6}$	130	$5\frac{1}{8}$	280	11	3,500	11 $5\frac{13}{16}$
5	$\frac{1}{5}$	135	$5\frac{5}{16}$	285	$11\frac{1}{4}$	3,750	12 $3\frac{11}{16}$
6	$\frac{1}{4}$	140	$5\frac{1}{2}$	290	$11\frac{7}{16}$	4,000	13 $1\frac{1}{2}$
7	$\frac{5}{16}-$	145	$5\frac{11}{16}$	295	$11\frac{5}{8}$	4,250	13 $11\frac{3}{8}$
8	$\frac{5}{16}+$	150	$5\frac{7}{8}$	300	$11\frac{13}{16}$	4,500	14 $9\frac{3}{8}$
9	$\frac{3}{8}$	155	$6\frac{1}{8}$			4,750	15 $7\frac{1}{16}$
10	$\frac{3}{8}+$	160	$6\frac{5}{16}$			5,000	16 $4\frac{7}{8}$
15	$\frac{5}{8}$	165	$6\frac{1}{2}$	mm.	ft. in.	5,250	17 $2\frac{3}{4}$
20	$\frac{13}{16}$	170	$6\frac{11}{16}$	400	1 $3\frac{3}{4}$	5,500	18 $0\frac{9}{16}$
25	1	175	$6\frac{7}{8}$	500	1 $7\frac{11}{16}$	5,750	18 $10\frac{3}{8}$
30	$1\frac{3}{16}$	180	$7\frac{1}{16}$	600	1 $11\frac{5}{8}$	6,000	19 $8\frac{1}{4}$
35	$1\frac{3}{8}$	185	$7\frac{1}{4}$	700	2 $3\frac{9}{16}$	6,250	20 $6\frac{1}{8}$
40	$1\frac{9}{16}$	190	$7\frac{1}{2}$	800	2 $7\frac{1}{2}$	6,500	21 $3\frac{7}{8}$
45	$1\frac{3}{4}$	195	$7\frac{11}{16}$	900	2 $11\frac{7}{16}$	6,750	22 $1\frac{3}{4}$
50	$2\frac{1}{16}$	200	$7\frac{7}{8}$	1,000	3 $3\frac{3}{8}$	7,000	22 $11\frac{5}{8}$
55	$2\frac{3}{16}$	205	$8\frac{1}{16}$	1,100	3 $7\frac{5}{16}$	7,250	23 $9\frac{1}{2}$
60	$2\frac{3}{8}$	210	$8\frac{1}{4}$	1,200	3 $11\frac{1}{4}$	7,500	24 $7\frac{5}{16}$
65	$2\frac{9}{16}$	215	$8\frac{7}{16}$	1,300	4 $3\frac{3}{8}$	7,750	25 $5\frac{3}{16}$
70	$2\frac{3}{4}$	220	$8\frac{11}{16}$	1,400	4 $7\frac{1}{8}$	8,000	26 3
75	3	225	$8\frac{7}{8}$	1,500	4 $11\frac{1}{16}$	8,250	27 $0\frac{7}{8}$
80	$3\frac{1}{8}$	230	$9\frac{1}{16}$	1,600	5 3	8,500	27 $10\frac{11}{16}$
85	$3\frac{3}{8}$	235	$9\frac{1}{4}$	1.700	5 $6\frac{15}{16}$	8,750	28 $8\frac{1}{2}$
90	$3\frac{9}{16}$	240	$9\frac{7}{16}$	1,800	5 $10\frac{7}{8}$	9,000	29 $6\frac{3}{8}$
95	$3\frac{3}{4}$	245	$9\frac{5}{8}$	1,900	6 $2\frac{13}{16}$	9,250	30 $4\frac{1}{4}$
100	$3\frac{15}{16}$	250	$9\frac{13}{16}$	2,000	6 $6\frac{3}{4}$	9,500	31 $2\frac{1}{8}$
105	$4\frac{1}{8}$	255	$10\frac{1}{16}$	2,250	7 $4\frac{5}{8}$	9,750	31 $11\frac{7}{8}$
110	$4\frac{5}{16}$	260	$10\frac{1}{4}$	2,500	8 $2\frac{7}{16}$	10,000	32 $9\frac{3}{4}$

APPENDIX D

CONVERSION TABLE: SQUARE FEET TO SQUARE METRES

1 sq. ft. = ·092903 sq. m.

sq. ft.	sq. m.	sq. ft.	sq. m.	sq. ft.	sq. m.	sq. ft.	sq. m.
2	·186	80	7·44	230	21·4	380	35·3
3	·279	90	8·37	240	22·3	390	36·3
4	·372	100	9·29	250	23·3	400	37·2
5	·465	110	10·2	260	24·2	410	38·1
6	·558	120	11·2	270	25·1	420	39·1
7	·651	130	12·1	280	26·0	430	40·0
8	·744	140	13·0	290	27·0	440	40·9
9	·837	150	13·9	300	27·9	450	41·8
10	·929	160	14·9	310	28·8	460	42·8
20	1·86	170	15·8	320	29·8	470	43·7
30	2·79	180	16·7	330	30·7	480	44·6
40	3·72	190	17·7	340	31·6	490	45·6
50	4·65	200	18·6	350	32·5	500	46·5
60	5·58	210	19·5	360	33·5	1,000	92·9
70	6·51	220	20·5	370	34·4		

APPENDIX E

CONVERSION TABLE: SQUARE METRES TO SQUARE FEET

1 sq. m. = 10·7639 sq. ft.

sq. m.	sq. ft.	sq. m.	sq. ft.	sq. m.	sq. ft.	sq. m.	sq. ft.
·25	2·69	4·25	45·7	8·25	88·8	18·0	193·7
·5	5·38	4·5	48·4	8·5	91·5	19·0	204·5
·75	8·07	4·75	51·1	8·75	94·2	20·0	215·2
1·0	10·76	5·0	53·8	9·0	96·8	21·0	226·0
1·25	13·45	5·25	56·5	9·25	99·5	22·0	237·0
1·5	16·14	5·5	59·2	9·5	102·1	23·0	247·5
1·75	18·84	5·75	61·8	9·75	104·8	24·0	258·0
2·0	21·5	6·0	64·6	10·0	107·6	25·0	269·0
2·25	24·2	6·25	67·3	11·0	118·4	26·0	280·0
2·5	26·9	6·5	69·9	12·0	129·1	27·0	291·0
2·75	29·6	6·75	72·7	13·0	139·8	28·0	301·0
3·0	32·3	7·0	75·3	14·0	150·7	29·0	312·0
3·25	35·0	7·25	78·0	15·0	161·4	30·0	323·0
3·5	37·7	7·5	80·7	16·0	172·1	50·0	538·0
3·75	40·4	7·75	83·4	17·0	183·0	100·0	1,076
4·0	43·1	8·0	86·1